USER ERROR

resisting computer culture

Ellen Rose

Between the Lines
Toronto, Canada

User Error

First published in Canada in 2003 by
Between the Lines
720 Bathurst Street, Suite #404
Toronto, Ontario M5S 2R4
1-800-718-7201
www.btlbooks.com

National Library of Canada Cataloguing in Publication

Rose, Ellen, 1959–
User error : resisting computer culture / by Ellen Rose.

Includes bibliographical references and index.
ISBN 1-896357-79-2

1. Computers and civilization. 2. Human-computer interaction. I. Title.

HM851.R668 2003 303.48'34 C2003-904200-6

Cover and text design by Jennifer Tiberio
Printed in Canada

Between the Lines gratefully acknowledges assistance for its publishing activities from the Canada Council for the Arts, the Ontario Arts Council, the Government of Ontario through the Ontario Book Publishers Tax Credit program and through the Ontario Book Initiative, and the Government of Canada through the Book Publishing Industry Development Program.

Second printing January 2004

For Tony

Contents

List of Illustrations

Acknowledgements

Writing a book may seem, to the writer, a very solitary pursuit, but the reality is that such work is made possible by the generous support of family members, friends, and colleagues.

I cannot overstate my gratitude for the unwavering encouragement provided by my husband, Tony Tremblay, not only during the writing of this book but through all our years together. I know of no one else who has Tony's strength of purpose and of mind; he gives me, by his example and his confidence in me, the inspiration to achieve my own personal bests.

Special thanks are also due to those whose friendship helps me to persevere in the generally thankless task of technology critique: in particular, to Henry Johnson, whose thoughtful correspondence has meant more to me than I can say, and to Heather Menzies, who offers, in her writings on the social effects of global digital networks, the eloquent, prolific model to which I aspire.

Finally, many thanks to my father, Richard Rose, who has always been my biggest fan and who has never doubted my ability to succeed at whatever I undertook.

User error: Replace user and strike any key.

— programmers' gag from the days of DOS

In a society that is perpetually bombarded with new technologies, it is important to reflect on what it means, in terms of the larger social order, to be a user of technology.

— Robert Johnson

Introduction

Do You Compute?

In the early 1980s, I became a computer user. In those days, one could choose to become a computer user, just as one's personal values, talents, or inclinations might lead one to become a gourmet cook, a downhill skier, a marathon runner, a poet. In fact, my decision to become a computer user was entirely anomalous, for, while I knew people who were cooks, skiers, runners, and poets, I did not know anyone who was a *user*. Not that I thought of myself in those terms: I was simply someone who happened to own an Apple II Plus, with which I wrote essays and played the occasional game.

All that, of course, would soon change. Not only would my Apple II Plus, with its 48K of RAM, soon become obsolete, but, as I became a relatively skilled computer user and obtained employment within the computing industry, I would meet many people who, like me, were enamoured of the possibilities of this intriguing device. During the late 1980s and the 1990s, that fascination spread like wildfire, until the technolust that once was confined to an eccentric niche seemed to consume all of society. (A society in which, let it be noted, use of a non-word such as *technolust* was perfectly acceptable, since it was becoming increasingly de rigueur to prefix nouns with "techno-," "cyber-," or a just plain "e-" to denote the way in which various social realities were being radically transformed by the so-called cyber-revolution.)

Today, becoming a computer user seems to be less a matter of choice than something that society requires of us. Offices have been retooled to accommodate data processing technologies and computer networks; stores have automated their inventory and sales systems; government departments have put many of their services on-line; and just about every other social institution, from hospitals and factories to banks and libraries, has become computerized. The people who work, or wish to work, in these places are now expected to be competent users of the new technologies, and it is considered vitally important that our schools provide young people with access to computers so that they, too, may develop the skills necessary to become productive, contributing members of society. And we have all begun to think of ourselves in new terms: as *users*.

What does it mean to be a computer user? The term is problematic, to say the least. The popular discourse surrounding technology—the rhetoric of information-highway-obsessed politicians, bottom-line-oriented businesspeople, hyperbolic journalists, and self-interested data merchants—may lead us to believe that there is a certain cachet to being a user, but the word itself inevitably conjures up meanings that have more to do with degradation, ignorance, and powerlessness than social standing and personal empowerment. For one thing, *using* is disassociated, by definition, from *knowing*, since the former term itself connotes a distinctly parasitic relationship with technology in which the user taps into and exploits a technology that has been created by more knowledgeable individuals, while contributing nothing in return. As users of that which someone else has made and handed down to us, we devolve into unenlightened dabblers, interacting with a technology over which we have little control and no responsibility—certainly less control and responsibility than might be attributed to, say, computer *operators*.

And then there is the troublesome fact that *user* denotes both a drug addict and a person who operates a computer—a linguistic conundrum which has given pause to a number of individuals who are inclined to reflect on the social and personal implications of rampant computerization. In Clifford Stoll's view, the same word is applied to both types of people because, like drugs, "[c]omputers teach us to withdraw, to retreat into the warm comfort of their false reality."[1] Sherry Turkle puts a rather more positive spin on the association of *user* with both computers and drugs, regarding the association as stemming from the computer's "holding power" and its ability to become the object of a profound attachment that Turkle prefers to regard as infatuation, even a form of love, rather than a form of addiction.[2]

In fact, the opposing perspectives offered by Stoll and Turkle represent the two most prevalent modes of thought about computer use. Computer use is considered as either dehumanizing or potentially life-enhancing, depending, of course, upon whether one regards digital technology as an out-of-control steamroller that heedlessly flattens those who refuse to submit to its imperatives or as a powerful tool offering exciting new outlets and opportunities for human creativity and self-actualization.

However, the two perspectives share one important similarity: they are both couched in what Bonnie Nardi and Vicki O'Day call "the rhetoric of inevitability"[3]—a language which represents technological change as unstoppable and unavoidable. Thus, technocelebrants repeatedly emphasize that the marvels of which they speak are not science fiction but imminent realities. As Nicholas Negroponte, the director of MIT's Media Lab, proclaims, when it comes to the wonders of being digital, "My optimism is not fueled by an anticipated invention or discovery. . . . We are not waiting on any invention. It is here. It is now."[4] Similarly, in *The Skin of Culture*, Derrick de Kerckhove continually refers to accomplishments that are happening or that we will see soon, "before the end of the decade";[5] Bill Gates asserts in *The Road Ahead* (the title itself speaks to the inevitability of the magnificent journey into the future which he foresees) that "[w]ithin twenty years virtually everything I've talked about in this book will be broadly available";[6] and Ray Kurzweil peppers *The Age of Spiritual Machines* (subtitled *When*—not if—*Computers Exceed Human Intelligence*) with confident predictions about the "inexorable emergence" of machine intelligence, while smugly conceding that his previous forecasts "turned out to be overly pessimistic by one year. Hopefully," he writes, "my predictions in this book will be more accurate."[7]

And if the confidence with which the predictions are made does not convince us as to the inevitability of technological progress, it is further drummed into our minds through the technoprophets' hypnotic repetition of the word *will*, as in the following passage, in which Gates discusses "the impact of the new technology" with the kind of assurance normally reserved for reference to past events:

> It will enhance leisure time and enrich culture by expanding the distribution of information. It will help relieve pressures on urban areas by enabling people to work from home or remote-site offices. It will help relieve pressure on natural resources because increasing numbers of products will be able to take the form of bits rather than manufactured goods. It will give us more control over our lives . . . . Citizens of the information society will enjoy new opportunities for productivity, learning, and entertainment. Countries that move boldly and in concert with each other will enjoy economic rewards. Whole new markets will emerge, and a myriad new opportunities for employment will be created.[8]

Kurzweil goes Gates one better: by offering his prophecies in the present tense, he divorces them entirely from the realm of speculation. For example, of the year 2019, Kurzweil writes:

> Computers are now largely invisible. They are embedded everywhere—in walls, tables, chairs, desks, clothing, jewelry, and bodies.
>
> People routinely use three-dimensional displays built into their glasses, or contact lenses. These "direct eye" displays create highly realistic, virtual visual environments overlaying the "real" environment.[9]

The critical voices that oppose this kind of techno-utopianism wisely suggest that we take the time to reflect on technological developments which the hypesters would have us believe carry no negative implications or political freight. Neil Postman, Theodore Roszak, Jacques Ellul, and others ask us to consider what is gained, and what is lost, when we allow our lives to become increasingly computerized. I have a great respect for these social critics, but I am also troubled by the fact that, welcome and necessary as such critical perspectives are, their effectiveness as a counterbalance to the hype is tempered by the fact that they are often based on a similar conviction that technology is an unstoppable dynamo which changes everything willy-nilly. As Raymond Williams puts it, the techno-utopians' sense of "technology as inevitable or unstoppable . . . is powerfully assisted by a mode of cultural pessimism, among quite different and even apparently opposed people."[10] John Seely Brown and Paul Duguid concur that pessimistic critiques tend, as much as the utopian visions, to exclude broader social responses by "unintentionally disarming [society] with a pervasive sense of inescapable gloom."[11]

Of the social critics, Ellul, in particular, is best known for his dire visions of a society at the mercy of a technological juggernaut. In *The Technological Society, The Technological System,* and *The Technological Bluff,* Ellul elaborates on his thesis that our technologies have merged into an autonomous ensemble of interrelated devices and methods that envelops us and shapes our habits of mind. As a result, the qualities we come to value are increasingly those—such as efficiency, rationality, and standardization—that promote the further enlargement of the technological system. "Technology," writes Ellul, "is no longer, as in the past, one factor among others in a society which produces a civilization. . . . It has, on the contrary, become not only the determining fact but also the 'enveloping element,' inside which our society develops."[12] Ultimately, we become less users than used, with no choice but to serve the system in which we are trapped. "The human being who uses technology today," Ellul contends, "is by that very fact the human being who serves it."[13] It may seem, for instance, that we consciously decide to use computers, but the reality, according to Ellul, is that we are simply unable to resist the force and momentum of the vast system from which there is no escape:

> Naturally, we can say that it is man himself who decides. But technological growth has manufactured an ideology for him, a morality, and a mystique, which rigorously and exclusively impel his choices toward this growth. Anything is better than not utilizing what is technologically possible.[14]

Thus, caught in the frenzied forward rush of the system, our values become its values: we grow convinced that whatever fosters technical progress is good, while whatever or whoever hobbles it is bad. The upshot is that we not only use computers, we increasingly *demand* the right to use them. As parents, we insist that schools provide our children with the basic computer skills that we assume they will need in order to survive; as adult learners, we flock to the universities that promote themselves as cutting-edge, high-tech institutions; as voters, we rally around those political candidates who speak the loudest about the need to invest tax dollars in the development of the information highway; and as consumers, we spend more and more of our own money on the latest hardware and software innovations. And the more money, energy, and planning that our society invests in computerization, the more difficult it becomes to make—or even to contemplate—any other choice.

I find Ellul's perspective on technological developments more compelling and convincing than the superficial utopian tales could ever be. While the technoprophets busily weave an ideological web, Ellul reveals, in terms almost as irresistible as the technological dynamo he describes, the ways in which that web ensnares us. However, despite their fundamental differences, both versions of reality—the glowing picture of happy computer users benefiting in untold ways from the forward thrust of technology and the darker image of an enslaved population, blind to the ways in which their lives and even the possibilities that they can imagine are determined by an all-encompassing technological system—depict technological development as inevitable. And since the technology is viewed as the determining force, it becomes, in both cases, the focus of discussion, at the expense of direct explorations of users and use. Thus, most considerations of the increasingly ubiquitous computer user continue to arise incidentally from a much more sustained dialogue about a technology which, whether it is viewed in positive or negative terms, is regarded as a powerful, inexorable force that plays a primary role in determining both the social conditions in which it is used and the nature of the computer user.

The Social Construction of the User

My purpose in this book is to shift the focus of this discussion from an autonomous technology to the computer user. In so doing, I offer a view of technology as *produced by* the very social order that the optimists and pessimists would have us believe it produces. In other words, I contend that every technology—whether the sewing machine, the bicycle, or the computer—is socially negotiated rather than imposed, and furthermore that *use* is part of that process of social negotiation whereby we determine what a technology will mean within the bounds of the society from which it emerges. Consider the telephone: its inventors had every expectation that it would function primarily as a means of one-way information transfer to a dispersed audience, but its users transformed it into a pervasive means of person-to-person communication. Today, ironically, with the prevalence of voice mail and recorded messages, users are participating in the telephone's transformation back to an increasingly one-way form of communication. My point is that, as users, we do not simply interact with a received technology over which we have no control. Rather, we each bear some responsibility for its manifestations and repercussions within our lives.

Concomitant with this understanding of technology as socially produced is a view of the user as a *social construction* rather than as an inevitable human by-product of technological progress. To assert that the identity of the computer user is a social construction is not, of course, to deny that each person who uses a computer is a unique individual. Nevertheless, it is simplistic to regard one's identity as something that arises spontaneously or as a result of individual purpose and volition. Post-structural thinkers such as Jacques Lacan and Michel Foucault make a persuasive case for a view of subjectivity as emerging through participation within a social network, a network of language and power which "categorizes the individual, marks him by his own individuality, attaches him to his own identity"—in short, which "makes individuals subjects."[15] This social network does not act upon us in the manner of a determining technology; rather, since each of us is a part of the network, it involves us in a process of self-determination. Insofar as we agree to participate within society, we accept the subject positions that are conferred upon us: Spouse. Friend. Parent. Employee. And, increasingly, User.

Of course, when we sit down in front of a computer, we believe that we do so as individuals, each with a unique set of needs, abilities, styles, and interests. Indeed, the notion of a "personal" computer, a device that can be customized in ways that accord with each user's unique desires and requirements, draws upon and feeds back into the tradition of individualism, the humanist view that the rational individual's consciousness is the source of all meaning and truth. Part of the computer's mystique lies in its ability to make users feel personally recognized and valued as unique entities: the computer "knows" intimate details about us, "remembers" when we last "met" (logged in), responds to our inquiries and personal requirements; perhaps it even addresses us by name or with a happy smile. But in the chapters that follow, I will suggest that the moment we sit down in front of a computer, we become enmeshed in a social network of assumptions and ideologies that constructs us not as autonomous and diverse entities existing within diverse social contexts but as a single entity: the User. Throughout this book, I use the capitalized term *User* to designate this conceptual, socially constructed identity—this amorphous being without gender, form, place, time, knowledge, voice, or power—while the uncapitalized *user* refers to actual, embodied individuals. In other words, the user is produced by nature while the User is a subject position which is produced by society.

Why should it matter to us as individual users, each engaging with digital devices in different ways and to different ends, that the devices themselves are premised on the existence of a homogenous User? We should care, quite simply, because, in using the artifacts of computing culture, we accept certain rules, limits, and ways of being that benefit the digital elites who create and market these artifacts but that are not always in our best interests. We accept, in particular, a social order that increasingly requires computer use as a condition of existence while at the same time denying us the opportunity to have input into the human ends that hardware and software will serve.

Consider that, while many individuals choose to become involved in public inquiries into the social consequences of planned highway constructions, few would even contemplate the possibility of participating in the discussion about where the information highway will go and what form it will take. In fact, as one commentator observes, "public debates on these developments that affect everyone are absent. Issues of who we are in relation to technology seem to be played out only on TV in a genre of pop movies."[16] Our failure to speak up is not a reflection of our absolute satisfaction with the design and implementation of the technologies we are increasingly compelled to use; rather, it has a great deal to do with the fact that we have accepted, without even realizing it, the socially constructed identity of the fundamentally voiceless, unknowledgeable User. We have become convinced that we are unable to contribute anything meaningful to a conversation that will have a profound affect upon our lives and the lives of our children.

By way of answering, from a more personal perspective, the question of why it should matter to us, let me describe how I came to realize that computer use necessarily involves accepting the socially constructed identity of User. The realization did not come to me as a sudden revelation, but dawned on me over a period of many years, during which I worked in the burgeoning information technology industry of the 1980s and 1990s. As a technical writer, instructional designer, and eventually manager of software development projects, I was in a unique position to achieve this understanding, for all of my roles placed me in a fuzzy boundary land between software developers and end users. Although technically a member of the development team, I also served as the user representative, as the sole user liaison, and, often, as the user surrogate within the software production facility.

Over the years, I became keenly aware not only of the boundary itself, but also of the ways in which my own efforts paradoxically functioned to maintain the distinction and resulting power imbalance between users and developers. For example, the organizational framework in which I worked often required me to do my job without having the opportunity to meet with actual end users. Hence, the disavowal of human diversity and the emergence of the disempowered, generic User had as much to do with my efforts to represent users' interests as it did with other developers' tendency to disregard them. But the users themselves also participated in the construction of the homogenous, voiceless User by accepting without question a technology into which they had only nominal input. Together, we all constructed and maintained a power structure, which, though it benefited some and disenfranchised others, was somehow accepted by all parties as natural and inevitable.

Gradually, it occurred to me that I was participating in the construction not only of digital artifacts but of a technological social order which powerfully structured how individuals could be and could interact within that social order. With this understanding came a new goal: to help users reclaim some of their volition and responsibility in a computing culture that increasingly requires that we become users and at the same time deprives us, in that role, of the power of self-determination. Hence, this book.

A User's Guide to This Book

Chapter 1 establishes the groundwork for this discussion of the User by exploring the mythology of computer use. Computers may be viewed as relentlessly logical devices, unrelated to the realm of fairy tale and myth. In fact, that aura of rationality is merely an element of the mythology that we have constructed in order to explain to ourselves what it means to enter into a relationship with these complex, fundamentally unknowable, and seemingly autonomous products of our own imagination and ingenuity. The mythology of computer use has become so foundational to modern culture that it is unrealistic to contemplate engaging in the kind of resistance organized by the Luddites in the early nineteenth century. Since there is no longer a traditional mode of life to which, having smashed all machines, we could revert, it is vital that we now discover other, more appropriate ways of responding to technological developments.

Chapter 2 traces the origins of the User as a social concept. An examination of the history of computing reveals that the User is not a natural social category. Rather, the User's emergence as a monolithic, unknowing entity has much to do with the efforts of those involved in the burgeoning world of computers to determine who would and would not have access to computer power. This includes, of course, users themselves, but perhaps more surprisingly, it also implicates the hacker counterculture which arose during the 1960s and 1970s, and which was ostensibly dedicated to the project of making computer power available to everyone.

The struggle for computer power certainly did not cease with the emergence of the personal computer. The next four chapters, therefore, offer explorations of a variety of specific discourses and transactions that continue to play significant roles in the social construction of the User. In chapter 3, I delve into the culture of software production. Software development is based on the fundamental premise of User idiocy, and this understanding of the User is hardwired into the software code, where it manifests itself in the guise of a "user-friendliness" which further minimizes users' power and knowledge.

Chapter 4 examines the relationship between the computer consumer and the User. Since advertisements, ceaseless upgrades, and the Internet keep us in a constant state of hyped-up desire and concomitant fear of social obsolescence, it is less meaningful to distinguish between these two subject positions than to acknowledge their amalgamation in the single identity of the emergent, socially produced User-consumer.

The emphasis in chapter 5 is on user manuals and the stories that they tell about the User. Tracing the development of user documentation from the early 1980s on, I suggest that, while software and hardware manuals are offered as a means of bridging the gap between those who know and those who do not know, most manuals have tended to maintain the existing hierarchy of computer knowledge by telling a story that fails to consider the social contexts of computer use and that therefore constructs the User as a one-dimensional entity, characterized solely by a lack of technical knowledge.

In chapter 6, I explore research on the condition variously known as computer anxiety, technostress, and computer phobia. Although scholarly research which yields rotated factor analyses of computer phobia items and taxonomies of technostress may seem to bear little connection to the assumptions and attitudes held by the mass of humanity, the fact is that purportedly objective and distanced researchers are also social agents whose research functions to perpetuate a popular view of the fearful computer User as someone who is "sick" and in need of treatment.

The youthful User is the subject of chapter 7. In particular, this chapter examines the popular belief that children have a natural affinity for digital devices. Many books and advertisements celebrate the computer-friendly youngster as the next step in the evolution of childhood (indeed, of humanity as a whole), but to what extent is this a figment intended to disarm adult resistance? And to what extent do children today—well-versed as they are in the mythology of computer use—engage with technology in rote, compulsive ways that merely prepare them to grow from youthful users to adults who are inclined to regard computer artifacts as natural rather than as constructed and who are therefore ready to mindlessly assume the identity of User?

Finally, in the Conclusion, I extend the historical discussion offered in chapter 2 by taking a brief look forward, specifically at three commonly forecasted futures: artificial intelligence, ubiquitous computing, and transhumanism. Each forecasted future emerges from a view of technological development as inevitable rather than socially negotiated, as well as from specific though generally unstated assumptions about the mindlessness and even expendability of the human User. In response to these hyped forecasts, I offer the quiet hope that individual users will begin to assert some control over what the future will bring and who they will become through what I call *responsible action*.

What is responsible action? Let me first establish what it is *not*: responsible action is something quite different from the critical reflection that many social critics call for, and which they emphasize is contingent on somehow (they rarely tell us how) achieving a distance from technology. Jacques Ellul, for instance, insists that "[w]e have to locate ourselves on the outside in order to look at the phenomenon" of an all-encompassing technology.[17] Neil Postman also reiterates the importance of maintaining "an epistemological and psychic distance from any technology, so that it always appears somewhat strange, never inevitable, never natural."[18] And, in *Cracking the Gender Code*, Melanie Stewart Millar agrees that "[w]e simply need to step back" because as long as we remain caught up in the speed and novelty of digital discourse, "critical understanding of what is going on *is* impossible."[19]

While I believe absolutely in the importance of contemplating the ways in which computers and other technologies impact on our lives, I also recognize that not everyone has the luxury of indulging in moments of quiet, distanced contemplation. In fact, for most computer users, the computer itself seems to preclude the possibility of deep reflection by keeping us constantly occupied and by demanding our intense involvement. Whether we are using computers for work or pleasure, the machine somehow compels us to input data ever faster, to churn out ever more documents and spreadsheets, to spend ever more time dealing with and contributing to a serious e-mail glut, to participate in on-line chatrooms and multi-user domains (MUDS) more and more compulsively, and to play video games ceaselessly for hours, sometimes days, on end. With the proliferation of small devices, such as laptops, personal digital assistants (PDAS), and cellphones that we are increasingly required to carry with us at all times, it becomes even more difficult to remove ourselves from the ceaseless din and distraction. As we run to keep up with the frenetic pace of our cybersociety, opportunities for quiet reflection become rarer and rarer; however, at the same time, opportunities for responsible action increase.

Of course, in distinguishing action from reflection, I am not by any means suggesting that one precludes the other, or that computer users should act thoughtlessly. Indeed, I have qualified the word "action" with "responsible" precisely in order to imply the importance of considering the social contexts and meanings of one's actions. However, I do mean to suggest that responsible action is something quite different from the sustained reflection on technology advocated by many social critics because that kind of distanced contemplation in a rarefied, technology-free atmosphere represents, for most computer users, an unachievable ideal. Whereas critical reflection seems to depend upon the individual's ability and willingness to achieve a requisite distance by refraining from technology use, responsible action goes hand-in-hand with use. It means choosing to become an active member of the technological community, making conscious decisions about computer use rather than conceding all decision-making power to an "autonomous" technology and the massive corporate interests which vie to control it.

Acting responsibly does not mean resisting computer use—that is, after all, not always an option—but finding small ways, in the midst of use, to promote human rather than technological ends. Ellul, to be fair, lived a commitment to responsible action through his involvement in numerous grassroots, community-based initiatives. And while the importance of such activities is not a central theme of his books on technology, he does exhort his readers to find ways of transcending technological ends: "Each man must make this effort in every area of life, in his profession and in his social, religious, and family relationships."[20]

It remains for me to add three points of clarification. First, I recognize that, in undertaking an exploration of the ways in which individual users are socially constructed as a single, generic entity, I run the risk of perpetuating that characterization. That is certainly not my intention. It goes without saying that we do not all use computers in the same ways, for the same reasons, and in the same social contexts.

Thus, what it means for me—a woman who for many years held a fairly high level position in New Brunswick's information technology industry—to be a computer user is quite different from what it might mean for another woman working for minimum wage in one of the province's call centres.

Indeed, one of the reasons I undertook this study in the first place is because I regard the homogenizing tendency of software, user documentation, and other artifacts of computer culture not only as dehumanizing but also as depoliticizing, in that it removes from the realm of debate the relationships of power inherent in very different subject positions. The social construction of a homogenous User smoothes over, for example, the differences between managers who use computers to keep tabs on employee productivity and clerks who eke out a minimum wage by laboriously entering data into the machines day after day. Writers such as Shoshana Zuboff and Heather Menzies[21] have done a fine job of articulating the very different meanings that such diverse modes of computer use have for individual users. While not wishing to replicate their work, I draw attention to it here and elsewhere as a means of ensuring that I do not lose sight of the diversity that characterizes both users and their modes of computer use. In this regard, I should add that my tendency to frame this discussion in terms of what "we" experience as users stems not from an assumption that all readers will share my perspectives and experiences but from a wish to create an informal tone that will open this vital conversation to a wide readership.

Second, I want to make it very clear that my intention in embarking on this exploration of the social construction of the computer User is not to lay blame at the feet of software developers, hackers, writers of user documentation, advertisers, researchers, and others who play a role in that construction. After all, I have been there myself—have, at least, spent many years writing user manuals and participating in the development of software—and I know that no one who undertakes this kind of work does so with the express intention of diminishing the computer user's power and autonomy. The fact that the User has devolved into an undifferentiated, disempowered entity has nothing to do with the ill will of individuals, but a great deal to do with organizational imperatives for efficiency and profit, which preclude the possibility of gaining a deep appreciation for the needs and lives of individual end users. Indeed, we will see that, where steps are being taken to alter ingrained attitudes about the User and to acknowledge the diversity and contributions of end users, such actions are not being initiated by users themselves but, in particular, by software developers and technical writers. Ascribing blame would therefore be inaccurate; what is more, it would contravene an important theme of this book: the notion that each computer user is a fully participant social agent who must accept responsibility for the ways in which the User is constructed within social and discursive networks. This book represents, in part, a call to all users to recognize the ways in which they are called into being when they engage with the new technologies and to reassert their own responsibility and power in this process.

Third, I am well aware that, as I pursue my thesis, I make the same kinds of generalizations about other social groups that I deplore when it comes to discourse about computer users. For instance, in the very process of contending, in chapter 2, that hackers played a pivotal role in the emergence of the homogenous User, I construct the hacker as an undifferentiated entity: Hacker. That is, of course, a false representation. As Bruce Sterling observes in *The Hacker Crackdown,* hackers "come in a variety of odd subcultures, with a variety of languages, motives and values."[22] My tendency to lump all hackers—or software developers, or computer-anxiety researchers, or documentation writers—into a single homogenous group is not a deliberate strategy of retaliation but simply a consequence of a gaze too intently focused on computer users to be diverted by attention to heterogeneity among impinging groups. The only excuse for my single-mindedness is indeed also my rationale for this entire book: the relative absence, in the discourse of computation, of cultural studies which deal in a sustained, comprehensive, and direct way with the increasingly ubiquitous figure of the computer user.

1

"We Like to Be Smart": The Mythology of Computer Use

In an episode of the TV series *Star Trek: The Next Generation,* the crew of the Starship *Enterprise* encounters the Pakleds (see fig. 1), a race so apparently—well, stupid—that, as android Commander Data observes, "How they ever mastered the rudiments of space travel is a genuine curiosity." A curiosity, that is, until the dim-witted Pakleds kidnap Chief Engineer Geordi and demand that he and the *Enterprise* provide them with advanced technology—or, as the Pakleds put it, the "computer things" necessary to "make our ship go." It seems that the Pakleds are technology thieves who roam the galaxy collecting, through devious means, the high-tech devices that provide them with the sense of power and intelligence that they crave. Thus, contemplating the new weapon systems that they have acquired from the *Enterprise,* the Pakleds are able to insist, in idiot voices: "We are smart."

PARAMOUNT

FIGURE 1: *The Pakled race: "We like to be smart."*

Rewind to the first decade of the twenty-first century, when, watching *Star Trek* reruns, we cannot help but share the *Enterprise* crew's feeling of amused superiority as we regard the pathetic Pakleds, who "like to be smart" yet so clearly are not. We snicker knowingly when Geordi responds to the Pakleds' initial plea for help with their "broken" spaceship by joking, "Let me guess, their rubber band broke, right?" It's certainly hard not to feel superior to this simple-minded, technologically underdeveloped race. Humans, after all, do not have to steal machines: we have the wit and wisdom to invent and construct our own technologies.

Nevertheless, in the Pakleds' attempt to achieve social relevance and self-esteem through possession and control of advanced technologies, there is more than a kernel of truth about the human situation today. Consider the word *smart*, which is currently undergoing some extremely significant but largely unexamined changes in meaning. Increasingly, the word is used to designate not the quality of wit and cleverness that makes human beings uniquely flexible and adaptable, but simply a connection to computers. Thus, just as computerized houses, offices, and classrooms are now deemed *smart*, so people who use high technology are assumed to be more quick-witted and discerning than the "dinosaurs" who are unable to adapt to the demands of a changing world. In other words, like the Pakleds, we view so-called intelligent devices as somehow conferring smarts upon those who possess and use them.

As a result, millions of North Americans respond to the lure of the "smart machine," not by stealing technology but by flocking to computer stores, where they each spend hundreds or even thousands of dollars for the privilege of possessing their own piece of high technology. This is no mere indulgence; computers have so far transcended the status of luxury items that many people go into debt to own one and thus, presumably, to achieve the cybersmarts that are widely touted as the key to personal and social prosperity. (I have heard of more than one welfare mother who somehow diverted scarce dollars from food and money in order to rent or purchase a computer, so that her children would not be disadvantaged—permanently relegated to the status of "have-nots" or "technopeasants"—because of their lack of computer access and skills.) Indeed, given the computer's apparently limitless utility, survival in our society increasingly seems to depend upon one's ability to use this high-tech tool for accomplishing such day-to-day tasks as writing documents, collecting and charting data, and preparing and delivering presentations—not to mention finding employment, paying bills, and buying birthday gifts.

However, it is important to understand that, unlike a hammer or a shovel, this so-called tool possesses no innate utility. Rather, the computer's instrumental value is for the most part socially prescribed. In Langdon Winner's terms, the computer is a solution that, lacking any innate utility, must go "frantically in search of a problem."[1] Think back to the 1980s, when those who manufactured the new machines also attempted to manufacture a need for them by promoting computers as, among other things, elaborate recipe files. Although many homes built at the time actually included a computer desk in the kitchen, this particular marketing strategy soon fizzled, as it became painfully clear that the time-honoured method of collecting and storing recipes, on random scraps of paper and index cards, was still preferable to the rigorously ordered database.

However, although the computer turned out to be a kitchen appliance that most cooks could do without, it has become the tool of choice for many other tasks. When it comes to producing documents at work, for example, we now have little choice but to use a computer and word-processing software—not because the previous system of handwritten and typed documents was inadequate, but because the "solution" itself has created standards—such as printed output and electronic file sharing—to which we are all compelled to adapt. My own reliance on the word-processing functions of the computer has created a dependency which I might rationalize in terms of its utility were it not for the fact that I am continually running up against tasks that the computer vastly complicates. (Recently, for example, I spent hours scanning images and pasting them into an on-line document when the same end might have been accomplished in minutes using scissors and glue.) In short, ownership of the machine, as Sherry Turkle puts it in *The Second Self*, has very little to do with the computer's instrumental value; rather, it is "a way of asserting status, a way of saying that this is someone who has not been left behind."[2]

Our longing to acquire technological smarts, and to thus ward off the threat of social obsolescence, also explains the phenomenal popularity of technical training. Several months ago, I ran into an acquaintance, a recent graduate from a Bachelor of Arts program, who proudly announced that she had enrolled in an intensive one-year Information Technology Professional Program offered by my university. The purpose of this course is to give university graduates the skills they need to become valuable members of society—something, it is suggested, that the mere acquisition of a liberal arts degree cannot provide. (As one advertisement for the program puts it, "Your B.A. or college diploma mean something to us. Now add these certifications, and they'll mean something on the job market.") And this is just one of hundreds, if not thousands, of computer-training initiatives being marketed, in similar terms, across North America.

The widespread appeal of such training programs goes beyond their ability to help participants develop skills or sell themselves in a competitive job market. True, the advertisements for such programs would have us believe that to become a computer user is to become above all *useful*, to be rendered a productive member of society through the acquisition of valuable technical skills. However, the power of these claims is undermined by the enduring evidence, all around us, of the transitory nature of employment in the information technology sector: it's hard not to notice that high-tech fortunes rise and fall like stock prices, and computer skills become obsolete as quickly and regularly as computer hardware and software. For example, one recent article on work in the high-tech sector describes the reality that lies behind "the bad-news headlines": a reality that includes corporate takeovers, sweatshops, bad bosses, foreign owners, layoffs, and job-hopping.[3] Another newspaper article, entitled "Tech Workers Fend for Themselves," offers "snapshots of four people who were recently handed their pinkslips" and refers to the phenomenon of the "pink-slip party, an increasingly common gathering for unemployed tech workers."[4] And, in *Whose Brave New World?* Heather Menzies cites a survey which revealed that many of the adults using the Toronto food bank during the mid-1990s actually had computer skills[5]—a situation which we can be sure has not improved in recent years, given the widely reported toppling of billion-dollar high-tech corporations. In their frantic struggles to survive, companies such as Worldcom have not only perpetrated massive accounting frauds but have sent thousands of tech workers to the unemployment lines.

Moreover, even those who are fortunate enough to obtain relatively stable computer-based employment are just as likely to be disenfranchised as empowered by the experience—trapped in what Menzies calls McJobs, routinized positions in which human skill, intuition, and responsibility are increasingly transferred to computer systems:

> People then find themselves working directly for computer systems, as extensions of their operating software, with no opportunity for advancement or involvement past the silicon curtain descending inside the operating system. This is the essence of the McJob and the new cybernetics of labour: the system software controls and defines the work to be done; people are reduced to being functionaries of the

> system. . . . Many jobs that previously involved a good deal of talent, intelligence, and commitment—for instance, in hospitals, stores, insurance and law offices, and factories—have been turned into McJobs. As the context for their work is digitized, people are being systematically stripped of their capacity for human involvement and judgement.[6]

But despite the readily apparent insecurities and inadequacies of high-tech employment, the training institutions continue to flourish. Why? Because the real appeal of high-tech training lies deeper, within our Pakled depths, where the utilitarian varnish of high-tech discourse gives way to tacit allusions to the liberal humanist myth of individualism: the notion that we are all self-directing, independent unities rather than members of a social network that plays a significant role in shaping the actions and decisions which we believe to be entirely self-determined. Thus, based on her discussions with computer users, Turkle concludes that people approach the computer not simply in order to tap into its enormous number-crunching and symbol-manipulating powers, but in order to achieve a sort of intimacy with a device that functions as a potent avatar of human aspirations to achieve status and a sense of self-worth. Turkle found that, for the personal-computer users with whom she spoke, "the computer is important not just for what it does but for how it makes you feel. It is described as a machine that lets you see yourself differently, as in control, as 'smart enough to do science,' as more fully participant in the future."[7] Similarly, in *The Trouble with Computers*, Thomas Landauer contends that the appeal of computers has less to do with efficiency and productivity—in fact, Landauer marshals reams of evidence to show that computers rarely do improve the efficiency of information work—than with "reasons of deeper psychology." In particular, he cites the desire to be competent and "effectance," which he defines as "the sheer pleasure of doing something that makes the world change in interesting ways."[8] In short, we use computers because, as the Pakleds put it, "we like power" and "we like to be smart."

This conclusion is corroborated by an interrogation of the advertisements for technical-training programs, which typically promise not to provide merely skills, nor even employment, but something more ephemeral: the means whereby students can achieve, through their intimacy with the machine, personal metamorphoses into confident, empowered individuals. As one ad for the Information Technology Institute suggests, it is all about "transforming" graduates into e-learning professionals, while Atlantic Canada's CompuCollege promises to "help you reach the top." Often, these advertisements depict students in smart-looking business suits leaning over a computer, apparently engaged in deep conversation about the machine's inner workings, which, thanks to the high-tech training they are receiving, are no longer mysterious and opaque. The message is that the moment students enrol in the course and begin working with the computers, their social success will be sanctioned—irrespective of what they actually learn and of the employment opportunities which are or are not available upon completion of the training.

Other training institutes, such as HomeEd, cleverly capitalize on our deep-rooted Pakled desires by offering not only instruction but also a new computer, which is included in the cost of the course. HomeEd's television advertisement shows a happy trainee sitting engrossed before a computer that has been set up on her living-room coffee table, transforming both the prosaic living room (which is traditionally dominated by another sort of screen) and, by extension, the new user herself. True, the computer has not been stolen; but the new computer user is driven to take the computer training because of a tacit and largely unexamined Pakled belief that access to digital technology will empower her, and move her from the margins to the centre of society. That computer on her coffee table is a talisman against social obsolescence: it offers concrete assurance that she will not be excluded or left behind by a society that is rocketing into a digital future. Now, like the Pakleds, she and other students in the program can confidently assert, "We are a force now. We will have respect, power."

In short, beyond the transitory quest for employment, each individual who enrols in a course on Web Page Development or Introduction to Computers or Network Management does so with at least some Pakled hopes that the new proximity to digital devices will make him or her "smart"—that is, will provide cachet in an information society. The computer is thus rendered a sort of digital mirror in which the user's reflection, conflated with the (often personalized) iconography of the screen, becomes a shrine to an empowered, completed selfhood. And like Narcissus gazing at his own image in the clear pool, we love what we see.

The purpose of this chapter is to take a closer look at the assumptions—or, as I will suggest, the *mythology*—underlying the widespread belief that it is possible to achieve social relevance, personal empowerment, and a sense of individual self-worth by becoming a computer user. Subsequent chapters will disrupt that mythology by examining the social network in which computer users participate and which constructs the User in ways that often contradict the rhetoric of empowerment—or to put it bluntly, which constructs the User as not very smart.

A Tale of Two Screens

We are accustomed to watching the screen. For over fifty years, North Americans have been mesmerized by the zany antics of *I Love Lucy* and *Seinfeld*, the compelling sagas of the daytime soaps, the high-powered drama of shows such as *Dallas* and *ER*. And, having grown up in front of the TV, we are not inclined to view the events enacted upon that screen as either requiring or provoking deep thought. Even those shows that challenge us to match our wits against game-show contestants are offered as pure entertainment. And like the shows themselves, the endless commercials invite a visceral rather than an intellectual response.

But, although most of us spend what represents years of our lives in front of the television, we are at the same time dimly if not keenly aware that TV viewing breeds a sort of mental drift. After all, we refer to it disparagingly as "the boob tube" and "the idiot box"—epithets which make it clear that we are smart enough to recognize that the television is dumbing us down. Though we continue to watch, we sense, as Harlan Ellison puts it in *The Glass Teat*, that allowing oneself to be lulled by "pretty pictures of idiot shows" will "burn out your brains."[9]

Here, then, is one technology that perhaps even the dim-witted Pakleds would gladly do without. Indeed, while simply owning a home computer confers a certain degree of status and clout, television ownership tends to signify something quite different in our society. Today, asserting a distance from the TV by claiming that you don't watch it or, better yet, do not even own a set, is the moral equivalent of claiming intellectual superiority, of saying "I am smart." In *Why Viewers Watch*, Jib Fowles calls this highbrow attitude to television "TV Priggery," and adds that, "[a]s much as Prigs may publicly belittle television viewers, it appears to be the case that privately they watch as much video fantasy as anyone else."[10]

Our society's mindless acquiescence to the dictates of TV land is beautifully parodied by the television show *The Simpsons*. From the opening credits on, it is clear that television is the focal point of both the show and the Simpson household: the credits roll against a sequence in which the various Simpson family members are shown rushing home from school, work, and grocery shopping to their places on the couch in front of the TV. Indeed, the show's self-referentiality—a television show about the puerility of television culture—made it a real novelty when it first arrived on the scene in 1989. Witness, for example, Homer, the family patriarch, who is, to put it mildly, not the sharpest knife in the drawer. Homer can often be found sitting in underwear and T-shirt in front of the tube, drinking Duff beer and belching loudly while baby Maggie crawls unnoticed out the front door. The Simpsons are the ultimate TV family: their inanities are constructed both by and for the tube.

The Simpsons has been hailed by some critics as "intelligent" television, a TV show that not only entertains but actually comments on the human condition and, more particularly, on the inherent shortcomings of North American TV culture. Watching the foibles and failings of Homer, Marge, Bart, Lisa, and all the other inhabitants of Springfield, we are compelled to see ourselves reflected on the screen. But refreshing as the self-referentiality of *The Simpsons* may be, it is clear after over ten years of broadcasting that the insightful social commentary is and has always been a ploy, offered in order to keep an increasingly jaded and TV-saturated public glued to the screen with material that allows us to feel "smart," even as we continue to watch.

"Intelligent television" remains, in short, a contradiction in terms. The images and sounds emerging from the TV screen are simply not meant to be contemplated deeply. As Neil Postman observes in his aptly named book on television culture, *Amusing Ourselves to Death*, "what a good television show always aims to achieve" is "applause, not reflection."[11] It is, adds Postman, in the nature of the medium to suppress ideas, which do not play well on the TV screen, and to provide instead continually shifting images, which are meant to keep viewers entertained and gratified even as they preclude the possibility for deep thought.

Now, of course, we have a new screen that is competing for space and time with the television. Statistics suggest that, for the first time in years, television viewership is actually declining, while computer use is on the rise. But although it is, to some extent, replacing the television, and although it looks very much the same as the familiar "boob tube," the computer screen is, in fact, quite a different social phenomenon. Rather than flickering with transitory images, this screen offers us "data"; and rather than dumbing us down, it is widely seen as possessing an "intelligence" of its own and as conferring "smarts" upon those who spend time before it. Paul Levinson's description of the fundamental difference between the ways in which human beings interact with the two screens represents the common wisdom on the subject:

> In contrast [to television viewers], users of computer screens are interacting with the computer—they are participants in what is happening on the screen, since they are often its very creators—rather than passive observers. They sit up, faces alert, a few inches from the screen, and constantly control what they see via keyboard or mouse, in sharp distinction to "couch potatoes" who only trouble to change the channel by remote control during commercials or between programs.[12]

Users, Levinson further enthuses, are "interactively connected, absorbed, and focused in the work or play they are doing via the computer screen."[13]

Given this commonly accepted distinction between the two screens, the parent who experiences pangs of guilt when little Johnny or Susie sits for hours with eyes glued to the screen of the "electric babysitter," can actually feel well-content to see Johnny or Susie sitting in a similar posture of engrossed contemplation before the computer screen. The former image connotes mindless passivity, while the latter image often accompanies articles on the subject of computer-based instruction, and is offered as an emblem of the kind of keen intellectual involvement with which we receive the material displayed on the computer screen.

In short, what we see in these two juxtaposed images—virtually identical and yet completely different in terms of what they are meant to represent—is the distinction between being a viewer and being a user. While television viewing is widely perceived as a waste of time, an activity—though it would hardly seem to merit the term—that transforms the individual into a mindless couch potato, using a computer is seen as an extremely worthwhile use of time that is deeply associated with personal growth, self-fulfillment, and, above all, empowerment. This dichotomy may become less meaningful if and when promises regarding the advent of interactive television—which merges computing, the Internet, and traditional broadcasting media—achieve fruition. Will we *view* or *use* digital TV? In the meantime, it behooves us to consider the fundamental split between the screen that dumbs us down and the screen that confers smarts, so that we may better understand the cultural significance of a convergence between the two.

The Mythology of Computer Use

In *The Cult of Information,* Theodore Roszak offers a sustained critique of this popular view of the computer as conferring smarts. He argues that the belief that we can, as individuals, enhance our personal power through the use of computers is so deeply entrenched within our technological mindset that it has become the folklore of our time, and thus, like all folklore, remains largely unacknowledged and unexamined. According to Roszak, the potency of this belief is such that everyone who approaches a computer does so with a single hope, a single vision, which is the unspoken mythology of our times.

> The vision is this: one sits before a brightly lit screen, stroking keys, watching remarkable things flash by on the screen at the speed of light. Words, pictures, images appear out of nowhere. Like a child, one begins to believe in magic all over again. And because one is making the magic happen, an intoxicating sense of power comes with the act. One has the culture of the entire planet there at one's fingertips! All the databases, libraries, archives, movies, art museums, bulletin boards, telephones and fax machines in the world are in this one box.[14]

This heady vision, Roszak emphasizes, has very little to do with the reality of computer use. Rather, it is a "fairy tale," a story of the magical capabilities of digital devices that is assiduously packaged and sold by hardware and software manufacturers, government agencies, universities, and others with a vested interest in marketing the potentials and pleasures of computer use—and, ultimately, in defining who the computer User is. Consider, for instance, the slogans used, respectively, in the advertising campaigns of Microsoft and Rogers Digital Cable: "Where do you want to go today?" and "Where will it take you?" Both slogans conjure up a powerful device that can, like the magic carpets in stories of old, whisk users to faraway worlds. This theme is expanded in the Hewlett-Packard slogan "Everything is possible," as well as in the television ad for the Windows XP operating system, which depicts users in flight, being physically and effortlessly transported to the places to which their computer connects them. Today, these ads suggest, it requires not a magic carpet but a computer, and not a special incantation but dollars spent on the right software and network services, to be transported to the magical realm beyond the screen.

Roszak is not alone in suggesting that the popular discourse of computer use is nothing more than a fairy tale. Jacques Ellul has written widely on the subject of propaganda as it functions to sustain a technological mindset through the "prolonged and hypnotic repetition of the same complex of ideas, the same images," to the extent that, in Ellul's view, our actions and decisions are governed less by free will than by "reflex and myth."[15] Ellul observes that, in hyped prophecies of the amazing advances that new technologies are bringing about, "[e]verything happens as in a dream world. The great wizard discovers a new technology, his magic wand touches reality, and presto! Everything is transformed."[16] Ursula Franklin concurs that new technologies "have entered the public sphere in a cloud of hope, imagination, and anticipation"—hopes that are, in many cases, fictional.[17] And polymath Lewis Mumford wrote a two-part tome dedicated to the cause of helping us overcome "the myth of the machine," of disassociating ourselves from a mythology whose "premises are now so thoroughly institutionalized that most of our contemporaries continue to act upon them without even a quiver of doubt."[18]

Yet to speak of a mythology of computer use may seem, to say the least, a contradiction in terms. Computers, after all, are the products and emblems of enlightened scientific thought. Their mere existence on desks around the world offers indisputable evidence of the power and prevalence of human rationality and logic. Computers embody that rationalism and, what is more, support it through a continual supply of information and numerical data. The supremely rational world of computation would seem to bear no relation to fairy tales and myths, which emerge from the murky realms of human desire and fear, and represent attempts to explain, in comprehensible terms, phenomena that elude human understanding. The classic mythologies were the means by which the Greeks and Romans attempted to humanize the unknowable natural world, which was both bountiful and harsh, familiar and terrifying. But now that we have technologies that allow us to probe the stars, and even to study subatomic structures that cannot actually be seen, there would seem to be very little in the world that remains unexplored, unquantified, and unexplained. Having become computerized, human beings would seem to have no further need to mythologize.

However, despite the carapace of high reason, numerical data, and scientific objectivity with which we buttress ourselves from the unfathomable, the fact is that we continue to mythologize, and the subject of modern myth is the very means by which we have gained ascendancy over nature: our machines. These machines are, for some users, sources of enormous personal and social power, and therefore many of the stories that we tell about computers are indeed as glowing and hopeful as the faces that sit in engrossed contemplation before the screen. But the fact that these enormously powerful technologies are our own creations, the fact that they offer the potential to liberate us from the whims and perils of the natural world even as they also threaten to deprive us of the very autonomy and creativity from which they have sprung, renders the stories we tell about the mythical relationships and boundaries between human and machine extremely nuanced and complicated. Mumford sums up this paradox in *Technics and Civilization*:

> One is confronted, then, by the fact that the machine is ambivalent. It is both an instrument of liberation and one of repression. It has economized human energy and it has misdirected it. It has created a wide framework of order and it has produced muddle and chaos. It has nobly served human purposes and it has distorted and denied them.[19]

Thus, modern myths continue to negotiate the inexplicable metamorphoses of objects of beauty and desire into objects of fear, and vice versa.

Human beings need myths in order to survive in a perplexing and often frightening world. As George Lakoff and Mark Johnson observe in *The Metaphors We Live By*, "[M]yths provide ways of comprehending experience; they give order to our lives. . . .All cultures have myths, and people cannot function without myth."[20] Necessary as they may be, however, myths are also hegemonic insofar as they become so embedded in our culture as to disappear entirely from sight. Lewis Mumford, Jacques Ellul, Ursula Franklin, Neil Postman, Langdon

Winner, David Noble, and other individuals who write critically about the social implications of technology therefore devote themselves to exposing as mythology the ideas and values that lie behind the peculiar attraction of digital artifacts.

Many of these thinkers avoid using the word *technology* entirely because they wish to disassociate themselves from its primary emphasis on concrete artifacts, particularly the electronic devices (televisions, computers, microwave ovens, and so forth) developed during recent years. Thus, Ellul's *technique* and Mumford's *technics* encompass much more than just hardware: the terms are used to describe the discourses, ideas, desires, and cultural forces—that is, the *mythology*—that play as important a role as the things themselves in shaping the use and impact of a technological device. Just as Greek mythology was what made a statue of, say, Apollo, an object of worship, so it is the mythology of computer use, far more than any intrinsic capabilities of the computer, that gives digital artifacts their power and appeal, and makes them seem indispensable. It is therefore to an examination of the elements (or "deities") of which this heady vision is comprised that I now turn.

The Technopantheon

The Major Deities

Technology. Technology is the vast and mighty deity that rules supreme in our (post)modern world. True, it did not create the universe, but the mythology of computer use suggests that Technology is now rapidly reshaping society according to its own imperatives: the mandates of logic and efficiency. Hence, one often hears expressions such as "You're either part of the steamroller or part of the road," "Adapt or you're toast," and (the advertising slogan for Apple's Power Mac) "Some eat, some get eaten"—all testaments to the necessity of surrendering personal responsibility and choice and bowing down before the relentless advancement of Technology.

Technology, however, is a deity of *things*, not ideas. In its unrelenting quest to produce more and better things—faster computers, "smarter" appliances, smaller cellphones with more functions—Technology deliberately eschews involvement with ideas and discourses, with the social world from which it springs and in which it exists, and purports to be absolutely neutral. Thus, we often hear it said of the computer, which is popularly viewed as both the supreme manifestation and symbol of Technology, that it is "just a tool," like a socket wrench or a pitchfork. Of course, unlike most tools, which are highly adapted to specific purposes, the computer can be used to accomplish a myriad of different tasks more efficiently—hence, its enormous power, and its ability to "empower" the individual user. But since the computer is really "just a tool," using a computer is believed to have the same social and political significance as using a food processor or a lawn mower—that is, none at all.

This aura of neutrality is a key element of the mythology surrounding Technology. It creates the assumption that computer use is absolutely non-political, a neutral encounter with a neutral artifact that has nothing to do with social forces and everything to do with a natural desire to interact with an object that has the power to enhance the quality of our lives. Hence, the current tendency to market computer hardware and software as "solutions," a usage which tends to depoliticize computers and computer programs by suggesting that they are created only in order to fulfill pre-existing personal or business needs. Hence, too, the words of Paul Tsaparis, president and CEO of Hewlett-Packard (Canada), who is quoted in a *Maclean's* advertising supplement on "The Digital Revolution 2001" as saying that new devices such as Internet-ready cellphones and wireless-enabled pocket computers will become as important to us as electricity and running water "because, increasingly, we will rely on them to simplify our lives."[21] Like most self-interested promoters of digital systems, Tsaparis invokes the neutrality of Technology by depicting such developments as inevitable and progressive while diverting attention from the social processes by which such devices will come to be regarded as necessities.

Technology's presumed neutrality is a function, then, of its utter usefulness. But if we scrutinize the aura of matter-of-fact practicality and utility that underlies the mythology of Technology, what we discover is a conundrum along the lines of the chicken and the egg: which came first, the problem or the solution? Common sense would dictate that problems come before solutions, but in the case of digital devices, a consideration of ends is often subverted to a celebration of technical means. We begin, says Postman, "with the question of how we should proceed rather than with the question of why."[22]

Thus, the computer has become a means which must now go in search of appropriate ends, a solution in search of a problem. Which is precisely why, as Craig Brad points out in *Technostress*, many new computer owners find that what to do with the new, so-called solution becomes a bit of a problem in itself: "Computer store managers have reported in surveys that first-time buyers have returned to the store after a few days to ask for ideas on how to use their new acquisitions."[23] Indeed, what Brad neglects to mention is that many of these new users are doubtless persuaded, during that second visit, to fork over additional dollars in order to make their machines more "usable" through the addition of invaluable accessories such as scanners, joysticks, colour printers, and modems. The same phenomenon occurs on a larger scale when school administrators decide to prove themselves forward-thinking by investing thousands of dollars on new computers, whose use—not always readily apparent to teachers and students, let alone to the administrators themselves—must subsequently be mandated. And it occurs on a national scale when governments spend billions of dollars establishing on-ramps to the information superhighway, and are then compelled to invest more billions to prop up the languishing infrastructure in order to justify the initial expenditure. Technology, it would seem, is a duplicitous deity: though it purports to fulfill existing needs, its true role is to create new ones.

Time and again, then, the deity of Technology is represented, in books and articles, as a social necessity, a neutral force, a *thing* to be worshipped for its absolute utility and ability to improve our lives. That, however, is merely the potent mythology surrounding a deity which is continually invoked by individuals and interest groups who seek to use Technology to assert and extend power and control. If Technology has become naturalized and integrated into virtually every facet of society, it is not because it is so very useful, but because as users we are persuaded by Technology's handmaidens (see Technoprophets, below) to assimilate its requirement for endless information, and its proclivity to reduce all human processes to the remorseless logic of zeroes and ones—so that, more and more, the things that we consider to be problems in the first place, and the solutions that we deem appropriate, are related to the capabilities of the computer. Nevertheless, the deity of Technology continually denies its own provenance in human attempts to assert power, knowledge, and control in the age of information, and purports instead to be an entirely neutral tool whose use is as apolitical and value-free as using a shovel to dig a hole.

Progress. Harvard Professor Jacob Bigelow is generally credited with bringing the word *technology* into popular parlance with the 1829 publication of his book *Elements of Technology*. Some thirty-six years later, in an address to commemorate the founding of the Massachusetts Institute of Technology, Bigelow was quite clear about the relationship between Technology and Progress. Technology, he said, "has done more than any science to enlarge the boundaries of profitable knowledge, to extend the dominion of mankind over nature, to economize and utilize both labor and time, and thus to add indefinitely to the effective and available length of human existence." In short, Technology, in Bigelow's view "has had a leading sway in promoting the progress and happiness of our race."[24]

Progress and Technology are indeed, in the pantheon of techno-gods, Siamese twins, sharing many of the same vital organs. Progress impels Technology: without the driving spirit of Progress, we might never have advanced, as a society, beyond the horse and buggy, nor is it likely that the so-called industrial and digital revolutions would ever have taken place. At the same time, Technology gives rise to the creed of Progress: technological developments breed a faith in the power of such innovations to bring humanity ever closer to achieving the good life here on earth. And that hope is the essence of Progress.

Twins though they may be, Technology and Progress differ in one important respect: while Technology has a concrete reality, Progress remains an ephemeral idea. An idea, moreover, which, as John Bury cautions in *The Idea of Progress*, is based on two unproven and unprovable assumptions: first, that society is moving in a direction that is indeed desirable for all people and, second, that there are no barriers or limits to human knowledge of the world, nor to human moral, social, and physical perfectibility. Given that a belief in Progress requires one to make a leap of faith beyond these unproven assumptions, Bury concludes that "the Progress of humanity belongs to the same order of ideas as Providence or personal immortality. It is true or it is false, and like them it cannot be proved either true or false. Belief in it is an act of faith."[25]

Bury also notes the close relationship between Progress and Evolution. The emergence of the latter as a theory of biological development in the mid-nineteenth century gave scientific credibility to the idea of Progress: if social life obeyed the same laws of change as biological forms then, to the Victorian mind, the progress of humanity could be established as "a necessary fact."[26] The link between Progress and Evolution, between technological and human development, remains firmly fixed up to the current day. We are inclined to believe that as tools and machines develop (or evolve, as in "generations" of software), so too do people, who are thereby enabled to create even more powerful machines, and so on. Thus, as Mumford observes, the tendency in textbooks, encyclopedias, and other records of early culture has been to describe human development in terms of epochs of tool use, suggesting that our ancestors evolved to a higher state than other animals primarily if not exclusively because of their ability to make and use tools.[27] For example, the Stone Age is so named because primitive people of that period made most of their implements out of stone, while in the Bronze and Iron Ages, more advanced tools and weapons were associated with developments in human brain capacities.

While modern-day anthropologists may be less inclined to perpetuate the simplistic link between Progress and Evolution, it nevertheless remains firmly entrenched in our popular mythology. According to one commentator, "the identification between biological, technological, and social evolution . . . dominates public discourse on technological achievement and technological change, and thus shapes our attitudes and practices in relation to the Web."[28] Witness the fact that we refer to our own time as the Computer Age, suggesting that our most defining characteristic, as a people, is our ability to create and use digital devices. Indeed, in *Being Digital*, Nicholas Negroponte contends that the state of being digital "is almost genetic in its nature, in that each generation will become more digital than the preceding one."[29] Many movies, such as *Robocop* and *The Terminator*, extend this myth by depicting subsequent stages in human evolution which involve the creation of "cyborg" beings who are half human and half machine.

Both Progress and Evolution speak of an unbroken movement towards an inevitable future. (The Future is a minor deity, described below.) Evolution conjures an unbroken line of development, from the protoplasm gathered in some fortuitous crevice of the earth to *Homo sapiens*. Progress is similarly viewed as an inexorable development from a primitive state to higher civilization—a development that, with the growing power of Technology, seems to have taken on a life of its own. Our belief in Progress therefore leads us to view contemporary technologies as both inevitable and perfect. As the computer multiplies around us, "we confidently assume that it represents the best history had to offer" and, says David Noble, "we accept it as inevitable, a fact of life—beyond the realm not only of politics but even of thought and discussion."[30]

But a careful look at many familiar technologies reveals that they are neither inevitable nor representative of the heights of technical perfection. Consider the VHS standard of video-recording, which not so long ago triumphed over the technically superior Beta format, just as Microsoft's Windows operating system won out over the easier-to-use Macintosh. The success of these designs had little to do with their superiority and everything to do with corporate strategies to disarm and marginalize the competition. "[I]t's a dirty little secret in high tech," writes Paulina Borsook, "that superior marketing and inferior technology will beat out superior technology and inferior marketing every time."[31] Thus, although, as technology users, we believe ourselves to be liberated individuals, empowered by our proximity to powerful devices, we are also pawns in a much larger power struggle—a struggle which is smoothed over and forgotten as we accept our technologies as inevitable and use them accordingly.

According to Bury, the ultimate effect of the synthesis of Progress and Evolution was "to raise the doctrine of Progress to the rank of a commonplace truth in popular estimation, an axiom to which political rhetoric might effectively appeal."[32] It is hard for us to understand now, when the myth of Progress has indeed become commonplace, that there was a time when people resisted technological change and innovation, which they did not view as leading inevitably to improvements in the human condition. Postman points out in *Building a Bridge to the Eighteenth Century* that, even in the era of its birth, the creed of Progress was disputed by many thinkers who "criticized and doubted it, initiating powerful arguments about its limitations and pitfalls."[33] Rousseau, Shelley, Wordsworth, Keats, Byron, and Blake were among those Enlightenment thinkers who understood that, despite the utopian rhetoric, Progress was a two-faced god which did not necessarily lead inevitably to improvements in the human condition—at least, not for everyone. In fact, in their time Progress was already translating into a reality of belching smokestacks, poverty, and enforced rote labour. We may conceive of our lot as being vastly improved (through the beneficence of Progress, of course), but it is also the case that many people today are compelled to use computers in the same "dehumanizing, dispiriting, downgrading-the-quality-of-work-and-life-and-privacy ways"[34] in which industrial-era factory workers used their machines.

Some of the dissenting voices of the Enlightenment are still heard today. For the most part, however, their power is largely dispersed upon the flimsy pages of Norton anthologies. It was the collective voice of the scientists and industrialists who held out the irresistible lure of technological Progress as the means to the future achievement of the good life—those who, moreover, stood to benefit most when the public swallowed this lure—that was heard across the land; and it is their message that has persisted and become entrenched today as mythology: a truth propagated in books, articles, and media reports, which remains largely outside the realm of critical debate.

Revolution. Akin to Progress and yet seemingly at odds with the notion of Evolution is the deity of Revolution, which is also frequently invoked in the discourse of information technology. Numerous articles and advertisements suggest that the advent of digital devices represents a revolutionary development, that is, a total break with the past. These texts celebrate computer technology in the language of radical transformation, as articulated in refrains such as "revolution in full swing," "the new millennium," "cultural realignment," "social transformation," "radically changing the way we live," and, of course, "paradigm shift." Thus, in *The Road Ahead,* Microsoft mogul Bill Gates suggests that, having survived one revolution—that is, the rapid advent of the personal computer into homes and offices—we now "stand at the brink of another revolution" in which "all the computers will join together to communicate with us and for us."[35] In fact, Gates's entire book is a paean to revolutionary change, of what *will* come to pass in the near future (with dollar signs tacitly affixed). And, since the book is written almost entirely in the future tense, the word "will" functions as a refrain: as readers, we too are meant to look forward eagerly—to be thrilled by the act of "squinting into the future and catching that first revealing hint of revolutionary possibilities"[36]—while entirely neglecting the historical origins and social meanings of the technologies upon which Gates has built his vast empire.

The deity of Revolution is a key element of the mythology of computer use. As Rob Kling observes, "The discourse about computerization advanced in many professional magazines and the mass media is saturated with talk about 'revolution,'"[37] most of it based upon the unquestioned assumption that computerization will lead to widespread social change. Indeed, the mystique of computer use no doubt owes a great deal to this sense of being part of an unprecedented phenomenon, a digital "explosion" that has the power to transform society as a whole as well as its constituents into something hitherto unknown. As users, we stand on the leading (or bleeding) edge, heralding the arrival of the brave new world that will emerge from the computer revolution. The utopian promises proliferate: hand-in-hand with the notion of radical social upheaval goes what Winner describes as "the almost religious conviction that a widespread adoption of computers and communications systems along with easy access to electronic information will automatically produce a better world for human living."[38]

But, as Mumford's treatises on technology amply demonstrate, there is really no such thing as a revolution. Even so-called revolutionary movements arise from past events and should be seen not as breaks with the past but as outgrowths of it. "Whatever future we see," agrees Postman, "is only—can only be—a projection of the past."[39] Thus, the so-called industrial revolution did not just happen; rather, it was the cumulative result of ideas, values, assumptions, and purposes that evolved over the centuries—a lengthy process of "ideological and social preparation" which it is Mumford's purpose, in *Technics and Civilization*, to detail:

> Before the new industrial processes could take hold on a great scale, a reorientation of wishes, habits, ideas, goals was necessary. . . . Not merely must one explain the existence of the new mechanical instruments: one must explain the culture that was ready to use them and profit by them so extensively.[40]

The same is true of what we call the computer revolution. Powerful it may be, but the computer was not a breakthrough development that changed everything. Rather, the advent of computer technology was made possible by centuries of thought and innovation, during which people began gradually to accept the ideas that rationalism was the only valid way of knowing, that technological change constituted progress, and that progress was the key to human happiness. The notion that the computer empowers and liberates its users is merely the latest manifestation of a potent mythology that has been many hundreds of years in the making, and which does not benefit humanity in general so much as the technological elites, like Gates, who perpetuate it.

In the end, it would seem that the deity of Revolution is misnamed, for the computer revolution is discursively represented as a massive, inevitable, and non-violent restructuring of society by technology—not by human beings motivated by conflicting agendas. The messy power struggles and negotiations that attend most social revolutions are disavowed in popular texts that evoke the deity of Revolution to describe, in celebratory tones, the forthcoming social change that we must not resist, and in which we can only participate as hopeful computer users.

The Minor Deities

Reason and Science. The parents of Progress, and strongly affiliated with Technology, Reason and Science emerged as minor deities during that period of intellectual flowering known as the Enlightenment. As the eighteenth century dawned, social trends and circumstances were culminating in what would eventually become a widespread celebration of rationalism, a way of thinking about the world that called into question the authority of religious faith, superstition, folklore, and other non-rational ways of knowing. As rationalism flourished, so too did scientific thought and innovation. And along with inventions ranging from small pox inoculations to steam engines came the fervent conviction that Reason and Science had the power to transform the conditions of human life and to eliminate sickness and toil and want. The mythos of Progress was born.

Today, the tyranny of these deities is such that ways of understanding and talking about the world which are not sanctioned by Reason and Science tend to be dismissed as irrelevant. Our society tends to downgrade personal experience while glorifying scientific method and abstract knowledge. As Ursula Franklin puts it, "Today scientific constructs have become *the* model of describing reality rather than one of the ways of describing life around us."[41] In *Technopoly*, Postman concurs that we are now inclined to "believe that without numbers [we] cannot acquire or express authentic knowledge." This is why, he adds, "it is possible to say almost anything without contradiction provided you begin your utterance with the words 'A study has shown...' or 'Scientists now tell us that...'"[42] The preeminence of scientific, logical ways of knowing has become, in recent years, the focus of much feminist critique of technology, which points out that Science and Reason are *masculine* deities,[43] which have functioned over the years to devalue subjectivity, emotion, intuition and other modes of understanding the world that are deemed to be more characteristically feminine.

As number crunchers and processors of logical code, computers represent the epitome of the rational, scientific mindset. They "process information," which is to say that they reduce the richness of the human world to something that can be represented in terms of a concatenation of zeros and ones. In the realm of education, for example, Reason and Science as embodied by the computer determine not only what we can know but also what kinds of knowledge we consider worthwhile and "true." Since emotion, imagination, and ritual cannot be reduced to the computer's terms, they tend to be excluded as unimportant and beneath consideration while "drill and kill" programs on basic math skills proliferate.

Ultimately, most computer use can be viewed as an attempt to ally oneself with these two minor, albeit very powerful deities, for in this day and age, anyone who refuses to use computers runs the risk of being deemed irrational and irrelevant.

The Future. As suggested in the above discussion of the deity of Revolution, technological development goes hand-in-hand with, in Mumford's words, "an unconcealed hostility to the past,"[44] a tendency to dismiss as irrelevant the events and ideas from which modern scientific and technological developments emerge. In the legendary words of Henry Ford, a technocrat who is best known for inventing the Model-T and pioneering mass-production techniques, "History is bunk." Mumford further asserts that this "failure to recognize the importance of cosmic and organic history largely accounts for the imperious demands of our age, with its promise of instant solutions and instant transformations."[45] Today, the past sinks into oblivion, but the Future is always with us.

Digital elites and technoprophets (see below) look eagerly towards the Future, and, by virtue of their intimacy with this deity, speak about what *will* happen with an authority once reserved only for descriptions of past events. Thus, Bill Gates's eager gaze into the future in *The Road Ahead* becomes the theme of a recent television advertisement for his corporation, which asserts, "At Microsoft, we see the world not as it is, but as it might someday become." Despite the unexpected modesty of that "might," Gates, like all digital elites, has a clear vision of what that future should be, and he will do whatever he can to ensure that his visions are realized. Indeed, many of his predictions will be realized simply because, as Max Dublin suggests in *Futurehype*, the tyranny of prophecy is such that it compels us to succumb to the prophet's self-interested prescription of how the world ought to be—and thus to make it so.[46] As Borsook puts it in her exposé of the high-tech mindset, "If you think good thoughts about the future, it will be a good future! Clap your hands if you believe in faeries!"[47]

Once frightening and obscure, the Future has thus become an eminently knowable and desirable deity—at least for those who are wise enough to prepare for it by becoming skilled computer users. For all others, it remains a frightening and obscure prospect.

Other Figures of Myth

Technoprophets. Technoprophets such as Bill Gates, Nicholas Negroponte, and Ray Kurzweil are those demigods who perpetuate the mythology of computer use by telling glowing stories about the major deities: Technology, Progress, and Revolution. Technoprophets suffer from a tunnel vision that prevents them from considering the social contexts and consequences of the technological developments they so eagerly foresee, although many nevertheless confidently offer technological innovation as the key to social change.

The stories told by technoprophets are related in extremely utopian language but, cloaked as the stories are by the mantle of Reason and Science, they are widely accepted as both neutral and authoritative. Of course, most technoprophets have allied themselves completely with the imperatives of Technology, and therefore have a great deal to gain from popular acceptance of the myths they perpetuate. Thus, according to Max Dublin, modern prophecy couches self-interest within a manipulative language that, in fact, compels its listeners to abandon all disbelief, to suspend their common sense, and to act out of fear in ways that will ultimately support the interests of the technoprophets rather than those of the users themselves.[48]

Technicians. This group includes programmers, hackers, and other technical experts who are responsible for maintaining the computer and creating additional hardware and software innovations and enhancements. (Many technoprophets started out as technicians.) These individuals live according to the imperatives of Technology, and are reputed to be so single-minded and devoted to its service that they tend to neglect all other social functions and interactions. Thus, technicians—also known as "chip heads"—are commonly represented as beings who live in darkness and work unceasingly through the night, sustained only by pizza and Coke. Hackneyed as this representation may be, it reflects a deep-rooted sense that the interests and perspectives of those responsible for creating and maintaining computer hardware and software are fundamentally at odds with those who use it.

Though not deities, Technicians possess an almost godlike power, since they create the digital world that users enter. And when things go wrong, when hard drives crash and files become corrupted, our frantic supplications go out not to a deity but to the Technician down the hall.

Telling Tales

A mythology is not simply made up of a pantheon of deities but also, more importantly, of stories about the ways in which those forces affect human life. Such stories surround us, and we absorb them, often without even consciously recognizing them for what they are. Films such as *The Matrix*, *The Terminator*, and *Lawnmower Man* are part of this mythology, as are television shows such as *Star Trek* and all its sequels. Purportedly objective history-book accounts of the lone geniuses who devote their lives to the invention of new technologies belong within this mythology, as do the advertisements for technical training institutes that I referred to earlier in this chapter. Consider the way each of those advertisements appropriates the mythology of computer use to tell a story about acceptable human responses to and interactions with Technology. The ads represent computer use as an empowering encounter with a force that is ultimately apolitical, inevitable, and inherently progressive. And they represent computer users as autonomous individuals who turn to Technology in order to achieve the good life rather than, say, in order to conform to larger social imperatives.

In this way, like all of the diverse stories that comprise the mythology of computer use, the technical training ads implicitly deny that the conditions from which computers emerge and in which they are used are produced through human decision-making and social relations of privilege and oppression. The stories present the computer, as Franklin writes, within "an atmosphere of harmless domesticity"; yet, adds Franklin, a look behind "all that pink fluff" reveals that the purported benefits of Technology are not diffused equally throughout society. Indeed, for many users, "promises of liberation through technology can become a ticket to enslavement."[49] This is precisely the theme of *In the Age of the Smart Machine*, in which Shoshana Zuboff describes the process whereby workplace automation leads, as a result of management decisions and priorities, to a deskilling so demoralizing that, as one interviewee put it, the computer operator becomes a "nonperson,"[50] a User undifferentiated, even to herself, from the mass of other similarly enslaved workers.

Why are such inequalities and struggles for power disavowed in the mythology of computer use? Because that mythology comes to us largely via those who have been, over the years, empowered to speak on the subject of technology: the technocrats who have become authorities by virtue of their technological success and marketplace dominance. It is, in short, those who celebrate and profit from technological developments who tell the stories about it, while those upon whose backs they profit (those whom we would call the users of technology, though the larger social perspective suggests that they might more accurately be deemed *used*) remain for the most part unheard.

Consider, in this context, a very commonly referred to story in the mythology of computer use: the tale of the Luddites. We are all familiar with the bare bones of the tale of these infamous workers in the early nineteenth-century fabric and garment industry. In brief, the Luddite rebellion began in 1811, when the managers of a hosiery factory in Nottingham, England, introduced new machines into the factory, which outraged workers subsequently destroyed. Yet, of course, the destruction was senseless, for we all know that in the end the machines prevailed. All of the elements of the technopantheon are present in this story: Technology, insisting itself in the form of efficient new factory machines; Progress, the force to which the future-minded factory managers bowed; and Revolution, for the Luddite rebellion took place in the heyday of the Industrial Revolution—although it could certainly be argued that the real revolution in this story is not the change effected by the new machines but the grassroots uprising of the angry workers.

Today, technoprophets are fond of using the word *Luddite* as an epithet for those who refuse to worship at the altar of Technology, and whose opposition is senseless and futile. In fact, the term has such mythical resonance that merely referring to someone as a Luddite effectively dismisses their arguments as naïve and irrelevant. But even (or perhaps especially) those who use the term Luddite derogatorily know very little about the extent of the rebellion and the circumstances that compelled the Luddites to take such drastic action. For this is a prime example of a story that has, as Noble points out in *Progress without People*, been skewed by the technocratic perspective.

Noble suggests that, far from being senseless, the Luddite rebellion was the result of the factory workers' keen political awareness of the social meaning and implications of the new technology. Keep in mind that the rebellion occurred at a time of severe economic depression, a time when the labourers' wages barely covered basic needs. Workers were already beginning to organize in order to oppose the low wages, deskilling, and rampant unemployment. So when the factory managers introduced new stocking frames that made it possible for one poorly paid, unskilled labourer to do the work of several skilled workers, the workers immediately recognized that this move on the part of the managers was not motivated by economics—in fact, much of the substandard machine-made product was not marketable and was left to rot in warehouses—but by politics. The workers understood, as Noble puts it, that the machines had been introduced by management as "part of the effort to undo them."[51]

In response, the workers organized. They vocally opposed the introduction of machinery, they demanded social policies on technology, they proposed legislative measures that would ensure equity for labourers, and they attacked the homes of factory owners.[52] And, yes, they smashed machines. The agitation spread to other workers in the garment and fabric industry, and then the following year it spread to other areas of England. Thousands of stocking frames and gig mills and spinning jennies and steam-powered looms were destroyed. But the uprising was short-lived. It came to an end when the English government mobilized twelve thousand soldiers, who rounded up the leaders of the movement for execution, imprisonment, and deportation.

The tale told about this episode in history comes down to us not from the Luddites themselves but from those who sought in the first place to disempower and deskill the workers by compelling them to use machines. It has, therefore, evolved into a story about futile resistance to an autonomous technological dynamo, a story which has over the years rendered pathetic the Luddites' courageous efforts to reclaim power. Consequently, the word *Luddite*, as it is now used, doesn't call to mind the political and social struggles from which technologies emerge but rather adds fuel to the myth of technological progress. In the end, as the waves of history close over all the complexities of the struggle, the real meaning of the Luddite uprising has become lost; and, construed as it has been by those who brought in the machines in the first place, it now takes its place in modern myth as evidence that technology is destiny, and that to ally oneself with technology is the smart thing to do.

However much I believe that the Luddites merit our respect more than our scorn, I must reluctantly agree with the technocrats (albeit for rather different reasons) that we should not, today, look to those up-in-arms factory workers for an appropriate model for responding to technology—any more than we should look to the mindless, unquestioning Pakleds. Certainly, if the Pakleds may be said to represent one extreme on the continuum of technology use, then the Luddites represent the other. And yet there is a significant similarity between the two extremes: in both cases, technology sits uneasily upon the existing social order. The Pakleds' ill-gotten technical capabilities greatly exceeded their intellectual capacities to integrate that new technology into their lives, while the Luddites violently resisted the inroads technology was making into their traditional ways of life.

Unlike both the Pakleds and the Luddites, we live in a time and place in which technology and its mythologies are already well-integrated into the social order. Indeed, technology, for better or worse, has become the very basis of our social order—there is no longer a well-established world of tradition to which we could, having smashed all of our machines, revert. (Jacques Ellul puts it in these terms: "'Detechnicization' is impossible. The scope of the system is such that we cannot hope to go back. If we attempted a detechnicization, we would be like primitive forest-dwellers setting fire to their native environment.")[53] And since survival in this world precludes both ignorance of and resistance to the use of digital devices, neither the Pakled nor the Luddite extreme is appropriate.

It is one of the purposes of this book to suggest that, today, the better mode of response to technology lies somewhere in between these two extremes, in what I call responsible action. As I suggested in the Introduction, *responsible* implies an acknowledgement of the fact that computer use takes place within social contexts in which we are all involved and implicated, such that it is not the technologies but the people who use them who determine the ends to which they are put. *Action* implies choice, and in particular making wise decisions, based on human considerations, about when and how to use digital devices. As I now embark on an interrogation of the ways in which the computer user is socially constructed in networks of power and privilege, I situate myself in this realm of responsible action, where there is neither a mindless acceptance nor a smashing of machines, but a sustained consideration of the discourses and practices that surround them—discourses and practices which may, as we will see, seriously impinge upon our ability as users to choose to act in ways which enlarge human rather than technological possibilities.

2

The Ultimate Hack: A Sociology and History of the Computer User

The New Hacker's Dictionary offers a number of clear distinctions between a hacker and a user. For instance, while a user prefers "to learn only the minimum necessary" about computer use, a hacker "enjoys exploring the details of programmable systems and how to stretch their capabilities." While a user does "real work" with the computer, the hacker sees computing as an end in itself rather than as a means to balancing a budget or writing a letter. And while users simply report or, more often, work around bugs, hackers gleefully submerge themselves in a program's messy internal workings and *make things work.*[1] As Theodore Roszak frames the distinction in *The Cult of Information,* hackers don't simply *use* a computer but "take intellectual control of it."[2] In *Life on the Screen,* Sherry Turkle articulates the difference in similar terms: "A user is involved in the machine in a hands-on way, but is not interested in the technology except as it enables an application. Hackers are the antithesis of users. They are passionately involved in mastery of the machine itself."[3]

Technically, of course, hackers are also computer users. However, in their own lexicon there is a very clear difference between *using,* which involves merely seeking to accomplish well-defined, utilitarian ends (sending an e-mail message to a colleague, finding a recipe for paella, or calculating how many years it will take to pay off the mortgage), and *hacking,* which involves immersing oneself in the guts of the machine. It is a matter of degrees of intimacy with the machine, and above all, it is a matter of power.

This perspective is not unique to hackers; indeed, even novice computer users appear to be tacitly aware of the relationship between power and levels of computer knowledge. Several years ago, I instructed a group of unemployed adults on the basics of computer use, including how to use tools such as word processors and presentation software packages. Since they regarded an ability to use these tools as the key to employment, most of the students were extremely motivated and worked diligently, but there was one member of the group who, though he caught on very quickly, continually expressed a desire for lessons in machine language—that is, the language which most closely resembles binary machine code. It became clear, when I questioned him about this interest, that he didn't know exactly what machine language was. But he did know, intuitively, that although an ability to use PowerPoint and Microsoft Word might increase his job possibilities, there was another sense in which the software tools he was learning to use diminished his power by limiting and structuring his interactions with the computer, and he chafed at the distance those programs imposed between him and the inner workings of the machine. He didn't want to be a mere user; he wanted to be (and later did indeed become) a *hacker*, someone with the ability to interact with the machine on its own terms.

What we are talking about here is a hierarchy of computer knowledge—a hierarchy which, it is important to note, bears absolutely no relationship to organizational pecking orders. Indeed, as Turkle points out, hackers have no respect for organizational hierarchy and "no respect for power other than the power that someone could exert over the computer."[4] An individual computer user might very well be a manager or a director whose standing within an organization is very high; but the User as an entity necessarily represents—by virtue of a presumed epistemological, if not physical, distance from the computer—the lowest rung in the hierarchy of computer knowledge. (In fact, until recently, most company presidents and CEOs could be counted on to have little or no computing experience, since they considered spending time at the keyboard to be beneath them.) But it is the individual with absolutely no corporate status, the individual whose days are devoted to pure grunt labour at the level of the machine, who exists at the top of the hierarchy of computer knowledge.

This absolute lack of correlation between organizational status and computer power is made quite explicit in a set of humorous job descriptions, apparently developed by a programmer. At the top of the facetious corporate hierarchy is the Data Processing Manager who "[l]eaps tall buildings in a single bound, is more powerful than a locomotive, is faster than a speeding bullet, walks on water, gives policy to God." Moving down the corporate ladder, we find the Assistant Data Processing Manager who "talks to God," the Senior Systems Analyst who "talks with God if a special request is approved," and so on, right on down to the lowest element in the organizational hierarchy, the Programmer—who *is* God.[5] Similarly, programmer Ellen Ullman describes her encounters with "Frank," another programmer who, having advanced within the organization to the status of end-user representative, "hated me" because "I was closer to the machine." Ullman adds, "In the regular world, the term 'higher' may be better, but, in programming, higher is worse. High is bad."[6]

Closeness to the machine (and concomitant distance from the User) is precisely what makes hackers *hackers*. All hackers are programmers, but not all programmers are hackers. Programmers who find themselves being promoted to positions such as Senior Systems Analyst and End-User Representative and Data Processing Manager are moving too far from the machine, and too close to the User, to be hackers. Having had their powers co-opted by the real world of e-business and its imperatives—having been, as Bruce Sterling puts it in *The Hacker Crackdown*, "corralled" into offices and "forced to follow rulebooks and wear suits and ties"[7]—they must now be concerned with deadlines and system specifications and end-user needs rather than with the beauty of the code and the compulsion to push the limits of what can be achieved with a computer. It is that compulsion, to the exclusion of every other consideration, that constitutes the essence of the hack. (Part of Bill Gates's genius has been to recognize the importance of preserving the hacking mentality, this closeness to the machine, by making it possible for Microsoft's programmers to advance in terms of salary and benefits while not being required to move into management positions. In this way, "a reclusive guru . . . could be no less esteemed and rewarded than a senior vice president.")[8]

Today, we accept this clear and inviolable distinction between the User and the hacker as common sense. Indeed, it seems only natural, in a world where an ability to use computers is so highly valued, that we distinguish between those whose degree of intimacy with the computer's inner workings is such that it enables them to define the terms and conditions under which others will interact with the machine, and those who, no matter how competent, simply use the computer to accomplish mundane, well-defined tasks. But an examination of the history of computing—a history that is fraught with conflict, though the power struggles are framed within the depoliticized mythology of Technology and Progress—suggests that there is nothing natural about this division. Rather, the User as a social category emerged from attempts by those involved in the burgeoning world of computers, notably, the hackers themselves, to determine who would have access to computer power and, ultimately, who the computer User would be.

The Data Priests: Users as Technicians

Imagine, if you will, a large room dominated by a hulking monstrosity of a machine. The machine is 100 feet long. It contains over 17,000 vacuum tubes, 70,000 resistors, and 6,000 switches, and it weighs 30 tons. The machine breaks down constantly: every few hours a vacuum tube burns out and has to be replaced. A well-trained team of engineers and technicians is in constant attendance, ministering to the machine's unceasing needs. The year is 1946, and the machine is called ENIAC, short for Electronic Numerical Integrator and Computer.

Like most computer research at the time, ENIAC was a military initiative. Though the Second World War was over, the Cold War had only begun, and military dominance continued, as it had throughout the war, to be associated with technical prowess. ENIAC's enormous computing power (though lumbering by contemporary standards, it could perform calculations two thousand times faster than any machine that had come before it) would be used for such ends as calculating the trajectory of shells and accelerating atomic bomb research. Thus, the computer, as well as the calculations it was used to perform, was absolutely top secret. Only a select group of minions with high-level security clearances was allowed to enter the room and minister to ENIAC's needs. Outside the room, conversations about the colossal machine were guarded, secretive, and code-like. (Indeed, the name ENIAC, first in a long line of computer acronyms, can itself be seen as a tacit attempt to make computer discourse as opaque and code-like as possible, and thus largely inaccessible to the average person.) And since the public had absolutely no contact with the computer, and no knowledge of its inner workings, articles in magazines and newspapers tended to use the speculative and fabulistic vocabulary of science fiction ("electronic brain" and "robot") to describe ENIAC and its impressive capabilities.[9]

There was another reason for the reluctance to allow non-technical people access to the new machine: its very fragility and complexity. Massive as these machines were, they were highly susceptible to environmental factors such as humidity, heat, and dust. Moreover, changing a program was a delicate and time-consuming process that involved rearranging the wiring on what looked like an early telephone switchboard. This was a "tedious and frustrating labor of many hours," writes Wade Rowland in *The Spirit of the Web*. "It was made even more frustrating by cleaning staff who would occasionally accidentally knock one of the plugs out of the board and to avoid discovery stick it back into a hole at random."[10] Is it any wonder that those who lacked the esoteric knowledge required to keep ENIAC functioning were not allowed anywhere near the machine?

The computer, then, began life in a backroom, where it was attended by an elite cadre of data priests in white coats who zealously guarded the machine from the eyes and hands of the uninitiated. Using the computer's power meant punching programs on cards, bringing them to a computer centre, and then waiting hours or days, perhaps much longer if higher-priority projects came along, for the batch to be processed by a qualified technician.[11] As Daniel Burstein and David Kline cogently observe, the "original architectures and uses" of ENIAC and its descendants actually "represented the zenith of industrial organization,"[12] in the sense that they involved a centralization of power in a single air-conditioned room, the formation of a clear organizational hierarchy based on levels of access to the machine, and a tendency to equate sheer size with mechanical power. Thus, the massive machines with their mysteriously flashing lights were perceived in the same terms as, a century earlier, progress-hungry industrialists would have viewed the huge steam locomotives: as symbols of the boundless power and forward thrust of technology.

However, while the diverse social applications of steam power were readily apparent from the beginning, there was, during the early years of electronic computing, no sense that ENIAC and its immediate descendants would ever move beyond the cloistered inner sanctums of those air-conditioned backrooms. The accepted view of the experts, those who held power and controlled access, was that the world at large had no need for the computing power those machines represented. Hence, the dire miscalculation of IBM chairman Thomas Watson, who, in 1943, predicted that there was a world market for no more than five computers. Watson's prediction may seem ridiculous now (especially given the current proclivity to hyped prognostication about the directions in which computing is headed), but in the days of ENIAC, it made perfect sense to assume that only large nations and massive corporations would need or be able to afford those hulking beasts. Moreover, since the computer was a military initiative, it was perceived in militaristic terms, as an instrument of social control, a weapon, whose use must therefore be severely limited.

And so the computer was created by an elite group of technicians for use by other technicians within that privileged caste. The word *computer*—which, before the advent of machines such as ENIAC, referred to a person who performed mathematical calculations—had been appropriated to signify the machines themselves, but there was as yet no real need for a specific word with which to refer to the human operators. For if those who built and programmed the mammoth machines of the 1940s conceived of a "user" (neither the word nor the associated concept had yet entered computer parlance) it was simply as Self, someone in their own image—that is, as an "intellectual worker," a technical person whose skills were commensurate with their own.[13] No one else was allowed near the machines.

With the end of the Second World War, however, some of the more entrepreneurial-minded experts began increasingly to contemplate the possibility of marketing computer power to a wider audience via smaller mainframe computers. Such moves were bitterly contested by many of the pioneers of computer development and challenged by others who wished to stake their own claims on the new computing frontier. There followed a "morass of litigation,"[14] bitter conflicts over patent rights and court cases that dragged on for years.

But in the meantime, amidst the spate of legal wrangling, the computer was indeed slowly finding its way out of the carefully guarded backrooms. In the 1950s, IBM launched its Model 650 computer, which, writes Wade Rowland, "rented for $3,000 a month and was tended by a priesthood of clean-shaven, close-cropped, white-shirted, black-shoed IBM service personnel."[15] The Model 650 was an unexpected success. True, computers were still large, intimidating, expensive machines whose use was still dominated by military-industrial principles of hierarchical structure, order, and control. But with the advent of the Model 650 and other mainframes, and the resulting move towards a distribution of computing power, the batch-processing model of use, which put all the power in the hands of a few centralized technical experts, was being eroded for the first time.

The Hacker Counterculture: Users as Anyone

By the 1960s, mainframe computers had moved out into the universities, where they continued for the most part to reside in back rooms. In *Electronic Life*, Michael Crichton recalls:

> In 1963, when I did my college thesis on a computer, I had no direct access to the machine; I never even saw it. I punched my little stack of punch cards, and turned them over to the priests. Some weeks later, I was given a pile of green striped printout. What happened in the interval was a complete mystery; the whole process felt like consulting the oracle at Delphi.[16]

Still, perhaps because of the limited access and the mystery surrounding them, the machines captured the attention and imagination of many engineering students. Anxious for access to the machines, these students, mostly young men, were instrumental in creating a new model for computer use: dumb terminals, which allowed individuals to have direct access, for limited periods of time, to terminals connected to a central machine. For the small cadre of engineers, mathematicians, and scientists accustomed to being the sole purveyors of computer power, this loss of centralized control meant that, for the first time, there was a possibility that the computer user was not necessarily someone who could be counted on to have one's own technical abilities and values, but could very possibly be an unknown and unwanted Other.

As the universities began also to purchase minicomputers, machines which were even smaller and less expensive than mainframes, the students began to take advantage of the increased opportunities for access and to spend more and more of their time—often at night, when the machines were available—sitting in front of the computer. In 1976, this "hacker" culture was immortalized by Joseph Weizenbaum in *Computer Power and Human Reason*. "Wherever computer centers have been established," wrote Weizenbaum, "bright young men of disheveled appearance, often with sunken glowing eyes, can be seen sitting at computer consoles." And, Weizenbaum continued,

> [w]hen not so transfixed, they often sit at tables strewn with computer printouts over which they pore like possessed students of a cabalistic text. They work until they nearly drop, twenty, thirty hours

> at a time. Their food, if they arrange it, is brought to them: coffee, Cokes, sandwiches. If possible, they sleep on cots near the computer. But only for a few hours—then back to the console or the printouts. Their rumpled clothes, their unwashed and unshaven faces, and their uncombed hair all testify that they are oblivious to their bodies and to the world in which they move. They exist, at least when so engaged, only through and for the computers.[17]

In his seminal work on hackers, Steven Levy refers to these young men as "heroes of the computer revolution," and depicts them as leaders of a counterculture which arose during the 1960s and 1970s. Hackers, says Levy, were united by a desire to liberate computer power from the exclusive control of the data priests, and by "a philosophy of sharing, openness, decentralization, and getting your hands on machines at any cost—to improve the machines, and to improve the world."[18]

Levy's book includes what he calls the hacker ethic, a body of tacitly agreed upon precepts which stipulated, among other things, that access to computers should be unlimited and total and that all information should be free.[19] *The New Hacker's Dictionary* frames these principles in the following terms: "information-sharing is a powerful positive good" and "it is an ethical duty of hackers to share their expertise by writing free software and facilitating access to information and to computing resources wherever possible."[20] According to Levy, the hacker ethic is also based on the fundamental beliefs that it is necessary to "[m]istrust authority—promote decentralization," that "[c]omputers can change your life for the better," and that "[h]ackers should be judged by their hacking, not by bogus criteria such as degrees, age, race, or position."[21] The hackers, it seems, brought to the world of computing not only a new libertarian attitude towards computer power but also the idea that access to the computer could empower anyone (if we are willing to accept Weizenbaum's portrait of the obsessed hacker as an emblem of empowerment).

Thus, even as the hippies engaged in drug-induced love-ins, another youth culture was also opposing established hierarchies and power structures in its own way, by working to erode the autocracy of the data priests. Tracing the expansion of the domain of computer users "from a priesthood in the 1950s, to an elite in the 1960s, to a subculture in the 1970s," Howard Rheingold contends that this change was driven not by the motivations and forces that had hitherto spurred computer research and development—that is, the quest for military might and the profit motive—but by the "teenagers in garages" and "young entrepreneurs" who wanted "to make a tool for changing the world."[22] Similarly, in *Being Digital*, Negroponte describes the formation of MIT's Media Lab as a quest to liberate computing power from the hold of an autocratic computing establishment:

> We came together in the early 1980s as a counterculture to the establishment of computer science, which at the time was still preoccupied with programming languages, operating systems, network protocols, and system architectures. The common bond was not a discipline, but a belief that computers would dramatically alter and affect the quality of life through their ubiquity, not just in science, but in every aspect of living.[23]

It was, then, largely thanks to the activism of the hacker counterculture that, during the 1970s and early 1980s, the contemporary notion of the computer user first emerged.[24] For the first time, computer users were understood to include not only the specially trained technical elite who built, maintained, and programmed the machines but also anyone who was driven to manipulate the world inside the computer. This broad conception of the computer user could conceivably include housewives, senior citizens, schoolchildren: in fact, *anyone*, anyone at all.

Of course, there are problems with the idealized retellings of Levy, Rheingold, and Negroponte. Perhaps the hackers of the 1960s, 1970s, and 1980s were not driven by the quest for military might, but, as Douglas Thomas observes, the history of hacking "is not as simple as it sometimes appears."[25] There is certainly reason to suspect that the hacker dictum that "information should be free" arose less from a desire to make technology available to everyone than it did from a wish to increase the hackers' own power. I have suggested that hackers came into being as a social category through the creation of strict boundaries between Us and Them. They are, in other words, chiefly defined as a group not by their affiliation with the User but quite the opposite: by their closeness to the machine and concomitant distance from the User. It is therefore less likely that the hackers' quest was to demolish boundaries, to make tools for uninitiated users, than it was simply to celebrate the power of the hack. And, at least until the early 1980s, anyone who wanted to use a computer had to share that hacker mentality, since computers were largely distributed in kit form and packaged software was virtually non-existent.[26] The marketing of pre-assembled PCs and packaged software in the mid- and late 1980s might have seemed to represent, as Levy says, the "fulfillment of the hacker dream,"[27] the availability of computers for the masses; but the fact that the new flock of ordinary users were not interested in hacking, were indeed very willing to go into a store and buy hardware and software rather than creating their own, subverted everything that the hackers cherished and stood for.

This conception of hackers as a self-perceived, self-involved information elite is confirmed in Paulina Borsook's exploration of the libertarian spirit of high technology in *Cyberselfish*. Borsook depicts a "geek culture that's antisocial, reductive, paranoid, and celebratory of the virtues of selfishness"—a culture, moreover, in which co-operation and the sharing of information and resources is not very highly valued. According to Borsook,

> Every culture has its Creation Myth; the personal computer industry has as one of its master narratives the story that The People came from the counterculture and were longing for freedom and, lo, the PC freed them up from the oppression of mainframes, the heavy hand of the corporate MIS department, the servitude of Your Father's Computer Company. PCs were all about power to the people.[28]

But, adds Borsook, technolibertarianism is better understood as "the mind-set of adolescents, with their deep wish for total rampaging autonomy" and a concomitant resentment of "the constraints that bind them."[29]

Thus, having liberated computing power from the exclusive control of the data priesthood, hackers now "looked down on the technically benighted."[30] Which is why, according to Crichton, "computer hackers, byte-heads, and other fanatics," began using the term *user* as "a pejorative," implying "somebody who just uses the computer with no knowledge of how it operates."[31]

Today, of course, the word *hacker* is also used pejoratively. Rather than denoting the noble humanitarian depicted by Levy, the term as it appears in media reports typically refers to "an ominous figure, a smart aleck sociopath ready to burst out of his basement wilderness and savage other people's lives for his own anarchical convenience."[32] Best known as a malicious force, today's hacker counterculture is comprised of individuals like the infamous Mafiaboy who seem to delight in concocting the means to exploit users' lack of knowledge and to graphically demonstrate to ordinary users how tenuous their mastery of the machine really is. "Social engineering," for example, is described by Douglas Thomas as the common hacker practice of tricking unsuspecting users into divulging passwords and account information.[33] Hackers have also been known to commit digital bank robberies and identity thefts, and to create tools which allow them to literally take keyboard and mouse control of computers on the other side of the globe, and even to alter and delete its files. But while hackers themselves may lack any sense of connection to a social network, apart from the insular hacker community itself, their elaborate cybercrimes should serve as potent reminders to the rest of us that, as computer users, we do not commune with the machine in isolation but as part of a social network that plays a vital role in constructing the identity of the User.

Whiz-Kid Entrepreneurs: The User as a Non-Technical Entity

The contemporary image of the hacker as a malicious force aside, it is important to keep in mind that the world that we enter as users has been and continues to be constructed, in large part, by hackers. For, despite their loathing for bureaucratic control and hierarchy and despite the principles enshrined in the hacker ethic, hackers soon began to be absorbed into the dog-eat-dog corporate world, described by Karla Jennings as "a free-for-all where engineers sweated out marathon building sessions to edge out rivals, their machines soon made obsolete by other competitors."[34] This was a world where the goal of liberating computing power was as fervently espoused as it was at MIT and other centres of hacker culture, though the corporate mandate of the new generation of whiz-kid entrepreneurs was quite blatantly to expand the customer base. Among these Third Generation hackers, as Levy calls them, "[e]legance, innovation, and coding pyrotechnics were much admired, but a new criterion for hacker stardom had crept into the equation: awesome sales figures."[35]

Ultimately, it was the advances in computing taking place in these highly competitive environments that made the counterculture dream of computing for anyone seem achievable. In short, it was the profit motive, and not the selfless desire to empower all people through unlimited access to information, that spurred the development, in 1971, of the first microprocessor, which put all of ENIAC's massive power on a single silicon chip the size of a fingernail. Ten years later, the microprocessor would provide the basis for IBM's Personal Computer. The hulking monoliths were dying off like dinosaurs, and with the birth of the far more adaptable and versatile PC, the myth of digital evolution gave way to what was widely heralded as a computer revolution.

Hackers greeted the advent of the microprocessor enthusiastically, and none more so than those entrepreneurial spirits who sought to profit from their intimate knowledge of the machine. Chief among these was Bill Gates. As a young man confronted with the advent of the personal computer, Gates grasped what many others did not: that, no matter how small and inexpensive the new PCs might become, they would still remain unusable by the average person as long as the only way one could make them do something useful was to engage in the difficult and time-consuming business of writing instructions in cryptic machine language. According to Gates, "The digital revolution is all about facilitation—creating tools to make things easy."[36] Thus, while everyone else was still caught up in the quest to make the hardware more accessible, Gates went on to build an empire, despite the hacker ethic that information should be free, on the basis of easy-to-use (or, at least, easier-to-use) software, including Microsoft BASIC, MS-DOS, and Microsoft Windows.

Ease-of-use was also the guiding principle behind the formation, in 1975, of Apple Computers, the brainchild of Steve Wozniac and Steve Jobs, two erstwhile hackers who also defected to the dark side of profit and corporate interest. Driven by the desire to make a computer with an intuitive interface that anyone could use and understand, Wozniac and Jobs struggled through several unsuccessful iterations before finally coming out, in 1984, with the icon-based, mouse-driven machine which, eschewing acronyms, they christened the Macintosh. Its very name invited familiarity. The Mac was, according to Rowland, designed to "be an extension of its user," in direct contrast to IBM's DOS-based computer, "which treated its operators as living peripherals who were required to know pages of machinelike DOS command codes and obey machine, rather than human, logic."[37] I recall a joke that circulated in the 1980s, before the advent of Windows, which offered a similar comparison of the two machines: When you start up a Mac, it greets you with a happy face; when you start up a PC, it grouchily demands, "What do *you* want?"

However, jokes such as this couched a larger struggle between the values represented by what had, once again, become two distinct cultures: the IBM, DOS-based paradigm, which had already become well entrenched in the corporate and high-tech worlds, and the Macintosh paradigm, which was eagerly appropriated by writers, graphic artists, educators, and other creative people who tended to dwell on the disempowered fringes of society. It was a conflict that Apple was perhaps eager to foment: the Macintosh slogan, "The computer for the rest of us," seemed designed not so much to celebrate increased access for the ordinary person as to promote an assertion of difference. Although Apple has subsequently been compelled to reduce barriers to use by, for instance, ensuring that the Mac is capable of reading PC disks, its corporate marketing strategy continues to emphasize the gulf between the two computing paradigms. The more recent "Think Different" campaign continues to foster the association of the Macintosh with creative, "right-brain" activities while tacitly relegating DOS/Windows-based machines to the analytical, regimented work of accountants and other number crunchers.

Over the years, as Apple and Microsoft became embroiled in long-standing strategic, technical, and, eventually, legal struggles to assert power and control over emerging forms of hardware and software, users also joined the fray. Two distinct contingents of computer users formed around these different interfaces; and, where once the divide had been between the data priests and everyone else, it now seemed to be between "Mac people" and "DOS people." And the stereotypes, as Fred Moody describes them, soon became well entrenched:

> The two types were as opposite and nearly incompatible as cat people and dog people. Mac people were free thinkers with artistic temperaments, given to reacting emotionally to issues and occasionally following up with more or less rational arguments. DOS people, in their own view, were purely analytical thinkers whose approach to computing problems was scientific, rational, and unclouded by emotion. Each claimed to see profound shortcomings in the other, and the two groups disagreed on virtually everything.[38]

Moreover, members of the two camps seemed to have very different attitudes towards the issue of computer power. Mac people rallied round the banner of the easy-to-use graphical interface, which technically made computer power accessible even to those without knowledge of or the propensity to learn esoteric machine languages. They formed large user groups in order to pool and disseminate Macintosh-related information and skills, thereby theoretically placing all Mac users on an equal footing with respect to computer knowledge. (However, because such user groups were formed in order to buttress the interests of Apple and its operating system, the extent to which they actually functioned to put power in the hands of individual users is debatable.)

Advocates of DOS, on the other hand, tended to be more technically minded individuals who denounced the "Macintrash," as some called it—not only because its interface prevented them from achieving the kind of intimacy with the machine which they craved, but also because it threatened to undermine their power by rendering irrelevant their mastery of the complexities of DOS.[39] Before the advent of the Mac, users with an ability to function in the DOS world might not have been deemed hackers, per se, but their technical competence and tinkering at least placed them somewhere in the same sphere. Now, the new graphical interface would tend to push them to the margins by establishing clear distinctions between experts and novices, between those who had the power to create and manipulate the icon-based software and those who merely used it. "MS-DOS enthusiasts," writes Turkle, "did not want to give up citizenship in the culture of calculation."[40]

Thus, although the arguments of Macintosh and DOS supporters might seem to concern only the relative merits of the mouse and the command line, underlying such office banter was a fundamental difference of opinion regarding the critical issue of access to computer power, and, by extension, of who the computer User would be. Easy-to-use interfaces implicitly defined the computer User as a non-technical person, someone with limited computer skills. Macintosh people clearly regarded this as a positive development while DOS supporters vigorously denounced the dumbed-down point-and-click interface—or "point-and-drool" interface, as it is still disparagingly called by those who continue to lament the virtual demise of DOS.

With the development of Windows, an easy-to-use, Macintosh-like interface which is designed to lie on top of the DOS operating system (and which has been deemed, by more than one observer, as merely "DOS in drag"), the debate has been rendered more or less irrelevant. One still encounters the occasional diehard who is eager to argue the relative merits of the Windows or Macintosh interface, but with each new iteration of Windows, the differences become increasingly trivial. In this way, ease-of-use has become entrenched as a principle of interface design, and with it a new conception of computer users. In fact, it was with the advent of easy-to-use graphical interfaces that reference to "computer users"—diverse people with diverse needs—increasingly gave way to "the User": a faceless, amorphous, monolithic entity whose sole defining characteristic was a lack of technical skills. This was a significant transition, for, as Steve Woolgar observes, reference to "the User" rather than to a "heterogeneous rag-bag" of people serves to emphasize the distinction between insiders and outsiders, between Us and Them.[41]

Thus, while easy-to-use interfaces were marketed and popularized on the basis of their ability to eliminate difference by levelling the playing field, so to speak—by making computers comprehensible to all people, not just the technically minded—the reality has proven to be rather different. In the end, ease-of-use as a principle of software and interface design actually tended to contribute to the formation of boundaries between the "techies" and the User, and this trend continues today. As the machine becomes increasingly less exclusive and more accessible, the high priest attitude is returning in force. (In fact, as I have already suggested, there is reason to doubt that it ever really left, despite the hacker ethic and the rhetoric of a counterculture-led revolution.) Now that we have more or less achieved, at least in the Western world, the kind of universal access to information for which hackers once agitated, the contemporary subculture of computer whiz-kids, cyberpunks, and dot-com entrepreneurs appears to be responding to the encroachment of an ever-expanding user base by retrenching and reverting to the same sort of elitist posture once assumed by the military-industrial cadre that created and zealously guarded ENIAC.

Today, however, technical power has nothing to do with access and everything to do with technical smarts. According to Andrew Ross, hackers now see themselves as a self-defined digital elite, "a privileged social milieu, further magnetized by the self-understanding of its members that they are the apprentice architects of a future dominated by knowledge, expertise, and 'smartness,' whether human or digital."[42] The world increasingly sees them in those terms, too. The stereotype of malnourished, pasty-faced, unwashed young men is giving way before filmic representations of the hacker by such buff young stars as Keanhu Reaves (*Johnny Mnemonic* and *The Matrix*) and Sandra Bullock (*The Net*)—clear evidence, if any is needed, of the hacker's new social cachet. Geekiness is definitely in, a fact which may be regarded, in the words of Clifford Stoll, as "the ultimate revenge of the nerds."[43]

The User, on the other hand, emerges as a nameless, faceless, amorphous entity, defined only, it would seem, by absence and lack: in short, by a sheer inability to comprehend the complex inner workings of the machine. In *The New Hacker's Dictionary*, the user is defined as "[o]ne who asks silly questions," otherwise known as "luser"; and the graphical interfaces designed to make computers usable by ordinary people are variously referred to as being "dumbed-down," "user obsequious," and infected with "menuitis," a "disease suffered by software with an obsessively simple-minded menu interface and no escape."[44] Thus, those who once presumably sought to eliminate barriers to computer power now seek to establish clear divisions between the technically minded and the technically benighted. And those who once presumably struggled to empower the ordinary person are now associated with malicious, covert activities such as seeding viruses, infiltrating hard drives, and other attacks on the user's power and freedom.

The User as a Variable Signifier

The User, then, came into being as a social entity largely as a result of the often ruthless attempts of various individuals and groups, including users themselves, to stake their claims upon the computing frontier. Although we now consider the division between computer users and hackers/programmers to be natural and common sense, that division has in fact emerged from and been shaped by struggles to define the nature and limits of computing power. These were often fierce struggles in which, despite the rhetoric, members of the hacker contingent, who supposedly sought to topple authoritarian structures, were fully participant. And as much as these negotiations had to do with the computer as object, also at stake was the power to define who the User was and should be.

As we have seen, the notion of the User as a distinct social category, an Other, did not have its origins with the data priests, for those digital elites simply could not envision a world in which any but technical experts would desire or be allowed access to the hulking monstrosities that computers were in the 1940s and 1950s. Rather, it was with the emergence of the hacker counterculture of the 1960s and 1970s, and the subsequent development of microcomputers, that the contemporary notion of computer users first emerged, and given the libertarian spirit of the time, the social category potentially encompassed everyone, whether trained technicians or computer-savvy schoolchildren. In the 1980s and 1990s, the notion of the computer user continued to evolve as young entrepreneurs emerged from the hacker counterculture and built, despite the principles entombed in the hacker ethic, billion-dollar corporations of almost grotesque proportions. Rather than lowering the barriers between techies and ordinary users, however, the principle of ease-of-use upon which these mighty empires were formed has tended to buttress the borders between these two groups by reconfiguring the User as a monolithic entity characterized solely by a lack of technical skills.

Thus, when we talk about the User, it is important to keep in mind that the concept is not static, neutral, or natural. Rather, the User is a variable signifier whose meaning is intimately connected with attempts on the part of various stakeholders to determine who will have access to computer power. Those who sit down in front of the computer today are called into being in a vastly different way from those who sat down in front of the computer fifty, twenty, or even ten years ago—and also, no doubt, in a different way from those who will use a computer ten years from now. And, as we shall see in the chapters that follow, the User as a social category continues to be transformed through boundary-forming encounters with the supposedly neutral artifacts of our computer culture: in particular, software, advertisements, user manuals, and even objective studies of user psychology.

3

"Problem Exists between Chair and Keyboard": Producing the User

In the previous chapter, I examined the struggles over computer power that played a formative role in the User's emergence as a monolithic, unknowing entity. Those struggles, of course, are ongoing. And as computer power grows exponentially in accordance with Moore's Law (which predicts that computer processing speed will double every two years or less), attempts to assert control of that power become at once fiercer, since more is at stake and, less apparent, since computers are no longer novelties.

Indeed, having moved out of the air-conditioned backrooms and university engineering faculties, computers are now so entrenched in society as to play a role in many day-to-day interactions, from banking to dating. Each of those interactions is mediated by a set of coded instructions that we call software. The power of these programs, and of those who design and develop them, lies not simply in their ability to make digital devices perform certain functions, but also in their ability to shape computer users' interactions with the programs and thus, by extension, to shape the identity of the User.

For example, my university, like many others, has invested in a software program designed specifically to support the creation and delivery of on-line instruction. This "course management system," as it is called, provides a supposedly neutral structure into which faculty are encouraged to add or import existing course content. Of course, the pressures to move one's courses on-line are intensely political; beyond that, however, the program structure itself insidiously compels faculty to accommodate their instructional practices and decision-making to the imbedded aptitudes of the system. Thus, as I began to experiment with using that system to put some of my course content on-line, I found my commitment to the promotion of higher-level thought processes—a commitment which defines who I am, as a teacher—wavering. I found myself succumbing to the pressure to fit my course content and instructional strategies into predetermined formats which, premised as they are upon the assumption that an instructor's ultimate goal is to deliver information efficiently, accorded with neither my content nor my convictions. Similarly, had I persisted in the process of putting my course materials on-line, my students might have found that use of the program to access those materials played a significant role in structuring their ways of being as learners.

In this way, the power of individuals involved in the production of computer software extends beyond digital realms and impacts significantly on real world activities and perceptions. As Sherry Turkle observes in *The Second Self*, ideas which have their origins in the world of computation "move out; they are popularized and simplified, often only half understood, but they can have a profound effect upon how people think."[1] And, I would add, upon how people think about *themselves*.

However, despite the enormous power of software developers to implement the digital worlds that we enter and the terms of our existence within those worlds, the fact is that, as computer users, we do not tend to give much consideration to the people who are responsible for developing the software that we use. True, against all odds, the cliché of the geeky programmer equipped with bottle-bottom glasses and pocket protector prevails and continues to provide occasional moments of office mirth. (Recently, for instance, an acquaintance e-mailed me an image entitled "Tan Lines from Various Summer Activities." There, amidst the buff, well-tanned figures of water skiers, mountain bikers, and tennis players, stands the awkward, nerdy, and absolutely untanned computer programmer.)

But this stereotype of the programmer is rarely evoked in conjunction with the software that these all-too-human and flawed individuals produce. Why? Because booting up the computer is an act of extreme faith that requires us to believe, absolutely, in the fundamental integrity of the programs that we use to enter, manipulate, and use data. The cult of information in which we are all, as users, fully participant, demands that software speak to us with the anonymous, authoritative, and highly rational voice of science and technical virtuosity. And, as Gary McCarron observes, software programs can only be considered perfect insofar as "the labour necessary for their production [is] clinically excised from public view."[2] Digital perfection—and thus authority—is compromised the moment that we are, as users, allowed to glimpse the lifeworld from which the software product has emerged; therefore, all evidence of human involvement, all traces of the relations of production, must be eliminated. From the user's perspective, the computer itself becomes, of necessity, a black box that represents the inviolable boundaries between the worlds of those who produce and those who use the software.

In this way, a software program is quite different from a film. Few moviegoers actually linger at the end of the film to watch the credits, that long list of the names of actors, producers, camera operators, script supervisors, makeup artists, stunt men, and others who play a role, large or small, in the production of any film. Nevertheless, even without careful reading, the mere appearance of those scrolling credits provides clear evidence of the movie's status as a collectively authored narrative. Consequently, we take for granted the constructedness of a film. Though we may allow ourselves to become immersed, for a time, in the fiction on the screen—and though the movie may indeed actually purport to be "real," as in the case of the popular 1999 horror flick, *The Blair Witch Project*—those final credits always appear at the end to remind us, as the lights come on and we prepare to return to the real world, that what we have just witnessed was a constructed reality, a narrative brought to the screen through the combined efforts of many people.

Software production is also typically a team effort, yet most software programs are entirely anonymous: they offer no scrolling credits to remind us that a computer program, like a film, is authored. We are simply not meant to consider the processes by which designers, programmers, graphic artists, and others have worked together to transform the ephemera of ideas into the equally ephemeral virtual reality of computer software. As a result, even as software increasingly infiltrates our lives along with the hardware upon which it resides, software production remains a process to which most computer users give little thought—just as we tend to give little thought to the processes by which potato chips and running shoes and bath towels miraculously come to be. In this way, we make fetishes of the objects we consume and use by persistently neglecting to consider them as *constructed.*

Those who do, for the briefest of moments, consider software development tend to attribute to the production processes all of the qualities that we attribute to the software itself. That is, if the software is relentlessly logical and orderly in its organization of information, then we assume, without giving it much thought, that so too were the people—the "software professionals"—who brought it into being, as well as the structures within which they worked. Advertisements perpetuate this mythos by depicting computer professionals—in those rare instances when they are indeed depicted—as white-coated scientists, symbols of machine-like efficiency and logic. Intel has carried this symbolism to an extreme in a series of ads that represent its product developers as faceless, unisex beings clad in identical jumpsuits and visors, an outfit which conceals all traces of humanity and thus also suggests the absolute perfection of the Intel chip.

Over the years, individuals with inside knowledge have provided some interesting insights into the rather less-disciplined reality of the software production process. For example, in *I Sing the Body Electronic*, Fred Moody documents his year observing product development at Microsoft, a process beset by chaos, inefficiency, random decision-making, and patchwork programming: "I began wondering how on earth I could ever reconcile the apparent reality of life at Microsoft with the company's public image of strategic brilliance."[3] Similarly, in *Close to the Machine*, Ellen Ullman provides a first-hand account of the quirkiness of programmers, the unexpected bugs, the frantic last-minute bubble-gum patches that underlie the programming process: "It has occurred to me that if people really knew how software got written, I'm not sure if they'd give their money to a bank or get on an airplane ever again."[4] And, in a chapter entitled "Incomprehensible Programs," Joseph Weizenbaum explains why most computer programs eventually become—through the proliferation of patches and subroutines whose interrelationships and effects can never be completely understood—fundamentally unknowable, even to their creators.[5]

And if we need further evidence that software does not simply spring from an ethereal realm untouched by human hands, and thus by the possibility of human idiosyncrasy and error, then we have only to think back to the year or two preceding the advent of the new millennium, when programmers hastened to avert the possibility of a global catastrophe caused by the failure of other system developers to anticipate that life would indeed go on after the year 1999. Yet, because this potential disaster was averted so neatly by technical solutions (more patches!), the story of the so-called Y2K Bug has, in the end, ironically only served to further buttress the persistent mythos of software perfection.

Of course, all of this is not to suggest that users are unaware of the fact that software systems are often poorly designed and bug-ridden.

Indeed, we all *know*, as Heather Menzies puts it, that "technology is notoriously unreliable":

> About 75 per cent of large software systems either don't work the way they are supposed to or aren't used at all. Robots run amok. Systems crash. Files disappear. Software comes riddled with bugs. And viruses spread like wildfire. These things happen . . . . They are talked about over coffee and in office corridors, but they are seldom reported and rarely taken into account in the discourse on technology and its productivity promise.[6]

However, these familiar coffee-break conversations should not be seen as acts of resistance to an intolerable situation. Having participated in many such discussions over the years, I would argue that they are better understood as outlets which allow users to otherwise comply with the dominant perspective perpetuated by the technocrats: the view of software as somehow emerging whole and perfect from an abstract rationality rather than as a product of chaotic production systems and unequal social relations. For example, in a conversation with an acquaintance not too long ago, I learned that she was temporarily without a home computer because her attempts to install a new software package had inexplicably altered or deleted her operating system. I had recently had a similar experience, so our conversation took a familiar turn: we spent the next five or ten minutes lambasting computers and unreliable software (Web pages that cause the computer to crash inexplicably, document conversions that produce files comprised primarily of meaningless characters, downloads that abort halfway through for no apparent reason), and lamenting our dependence on them. However, at no time did we in any way refer to or cast blame upon the people who made the software.

Thus, despite the contrary evidence provided by the scattered insights of insiders and even our own experiences as users of bug-ridden programs, we increasingly fetishize these complex and fundamentally unknowable systems. We refer to software in terms that suggest that it is concrete, a product (or *ware*) that is made up of solid, knowable materials rather than an unruly amalgamation of the ideas and inclinations of flawed human beings. We rarely consider the people behind the scenes (or screens); and, when we do, it is not to blame them for a program's transgressions (we are, as I will suggest later in this chapter, far more likely to blame ourselves). Instead, we vaguely ascribe to their actions and motivations a distanced, objective perspective and a scientific precision which bear little relationship to the apparent reality—as described by Moody, Ullman, and Weizenbaum—of inexplicable bugs, last-minute fixes, and late-night coding sessions during which strung-out programmers are sustained by pizza and Coke. In this way, the fundamental neutrality and perfection of computer software have become firmly entrenched as common sense. All of which makes us, as users, extremely vulnerable to the unspoken values and assumptions embedded within these purportedly "authorless" programs.

But if computer users tend to reify software—and, if they consider its production at all, to conceptualize it as the handiwork of faceless, efficient, unerring, white-coated software professionals—then it is also the case that the developers of software systems—the designers, programmers, and others involved in the process—typically create programs to meet the needs of a vaguely conceived User who exists in their minds only as a mental construct or fiction,[7] a "dream."[8] And it is further the case that the primary and perhaps only distinctive characteristic of this nameless, faceless entity is its technical ineptitude.

This perspective has, as we saw in chapter 2, a historical provenance. The User emerged from struggles for computer power as an unknowledgeable entity with no possible role to play in the highly complex world of software development. But this mental construct of the User also has much to do with the fact that those individuals who are involved in the software-production process, particularly those doing the actual coding, have, largely as a result of cost and schedule constraints, little opportunity to come face to face with end users.[9] In my experience, this is true not just of developers of shrink-wrapped products but also of developers involved in the creation of custom software, that is, programs made specially for use by a group of users (for example, workers in a call centre or loan officers in a particular bank). While it might seem that tailoring a program to the needs of a specific user group would entail working closely with the end users, it is often the case that the communications between custom-software developers and users are confined to managers talking to managers.[10] Indeed, according to Shoshana Zuboff and David Noble, because software developers typically work with and take direction from managers rather than end users, their programs, consciously or not, are designed to perpetuate managers' power and status within organizations rather than to empower and serve the needs of end users.[11]

The lack of contact with end users is not always regarded as problematic. In fact, engrossed in the workings of the machine as they are, many programmers, even those developing custom software, appear to consider encounters with users as neither necessary nor desirable. In *Close to the Machine,* Ellen Ullman details the trauma of having to deal directly with real people for the first time in a lengthy career as a software engineer:

> I started to panic. Before this meeting, the users existed only in my mind, projections, all mine. They were abstractions, the initiators of tasks that set off remote procedure calls; triggers to a set of logical and machine events that ended in an update to a relational database on a central server. Now I was confronted with their fleshy existence. . . .
>
> I wished, earnestly, I could just replace the abstractions with the actual people. But it was already too late for that. The system preexisted the people. Screens were prototyped. Data elements were defined. The machine events already had more reality, had been with me longer, than the human beings at the conference table.[12]

The upshot of this vast divide between software producers and end users is that the point at which most developers and users first meet and engage in a serious conversation is the interface, when the individual user sits down in front of the computer and uses the software program. At its most basic level, a program is a set of instructions that tells the computer what to do. But it is also a formalized package of ideas and assumptions about who the User is and what the User should and should not be allowed to do. These ideas are woven like secret messages into the code; they appear on the screen, underlying the data and menu options and dialogue boxes and error messages. And they are no less potent for being unseen and for being cloaked behind today's "user-friendly" interface designs. In fact, quite the opposite: it is precisely because they are unspoken that the assumptions and values encoded within software have the power, as Allucquère Rosanne Stone puts it, to produce subjects, to compel us to "synchronize our own internal symbology with these structures."[13] It would therefore be entirely accurate, and certainly more pertinent for the purposes of this chapter, to refer to the activities of programmers, system analysts, end-user representatives, and other members of the production team not as software development but as a systematic if unacknowledged process of User configuration.

Dumb-User Stories

Several years ago, when I was working as a project manager in a computer software company, I had occasion to meet with a programmer to discuss the results of the pilot test of a program upon which she had served as the programming lead. When we came to a consideration of a user's apparent confusion over the message presented in a particular dialogue box, the programmer shrugged and said disdainfully, "The User is an idiot." As the primary contact with the end users, and thus the sole representative, on that project team, of the users' needs and interests, I should have been surprised and appalled; in fact, I was neither. It was certainly not the first time that I had heard such an opinion expressed. And who was I, ever concerned to ensure that the text on the screen did not exceed a grade-seven reading level, to disagree?

In fact, for most people who participate in the software-production process, the User *is* an idiot, an amorphous, monolithic entity whose tendency to use the system in ways that it was not intended to be used—to press the wrong keys, click on the wrong buttons, type the wrong information—is a reality that must be kept in mind constantly. A program cannot pass the testing process and go out the door until the programmer has anticipated and planned for as many input errors as possible, errors made by an imagined User who represents the lowest possible common denominator of computer skills and knowledge. Thus, the User's fundamental idiocy is the underlying leitmotif of all software production activities, from design to programming to testing. In the words of Donald Norman, it is imperative that technology developers design for error: "Assume that any error that can be made will be made. Plan for it."[14] Veteran programmer Edward Yourdan agrees. Referring to software development facilities, he remarks that "much of the work that goes on here is based on the assumption that the vast majority of the human race is computer illiterate."[15] And, according to programmer Ullman, "In the designer's mind, gradually, over months and years, there is created a vision of the user as imbecile. The imbecile vision is mandatory. No good, crash-proof system can be built except if it be done for an idiot."[16]

This pervasive awareness of the User's endless potential for error is sustained, among software developers, through the sharing of "dumb-user stories," comic tales of exchanges between moronic users and contemptuous technical-support folk that provide graphic evidence, if such is needed, of the User's technical ineptitude. Dumb-user stories are typically circulated among members of a development team by word of mouth or e-mail; in the latter case, they are likely to be prefaced by such sarcastic comments as "Sound familiar?" Dumb-user stories are also collected and widely available in on-line repositories, such as alt.folklore.computers. There is, for instance, the story about the user who complains that the cup holder on his PC is broken (it turns out to be his CD-ROM drive); the user who tries to fax a document by holding it in front of the computer screen and pressing the Send key; the user who complains that his keyboard no longer works since he cleaned it by soaking it for a day and then removed and scrubbed all the keys individually; the user who cannot understand why, though she repeatedly pushes on the foot pedal, nothing happens (the foot pedal turns out to be the mouse); the user who rolls her disks (the old 5-1/4 inch floppies) in the typewriter to label them; the user who, asked to send in a copy of a disk, runs off a photocopy and mails it in; and the user who jams two disks in his floppy drive in order to double the computer's memory. Then there's the one about the user who, instructed to "just point and click" the mouse, picks it up and points it at the screen, as he would a television's remote control.[17]

The note of disdain underlying these tales is unmistakable. Describing his experiences as a computer-centre assistant at a university, one contributor to the collection of dumb-user stories on alt.folklore.computers "[wonders] how some of these people got into college." He then goes on to offer a number of encounters with dumb users, including the following:

USER: I turned on my computer, and the screen is still black. Where do I get a new light bulb?

USER: My printer doesn't work. Where do I get a new one?
ME: Are you sure that all the connections are hooked up properly?
USER: Oh, I haven't plugged it into the computer yet. Do I need to do that?

USER: I've told the computer that I want to print to the Public laserwriter, but it's just sitting there. What do I do?
ME: Have you gone to the File menu and selected Print?
USER: Well, no . . .
ME: Try it.
USER: Hey, it worked! How did you know?

Another contributor writes, in very similar terms, about "the joys of dealing with the computer illiterati," and offers the following as one of many examples of User idiocy:

> My favorite sort of exchange was, "My function doesn't work."
> "What is it supposed to do?"
> "I don't know."
> "Then how do you know it's not working?"

Many dumb-user stories are based upon the User's complete inability to understand and respond correctly to the prompts and messages that appear on the screen. There's the well-hashed tale of the frustrated user who can't find the "Any" key on his keyboard (the prompt on the screen reads "Press any key"). There's the story about the user who becomes enraged when his computer tells him he is "bad" and "invalid"—terms meant to refer not to the user but to the commands entered. (Recently, I heard a new spin on this one from a colleague, who told me about a disabled student who took particular offense at the latter term and demanded to know "how the computer knew.") And both Karla Jennings and Jim Carroll offer the classic tale of the user who, having put the disk into the disk drive, responds to the command to "close door" (in other words, close the drive latch) by getting up and closing the door to the office.[18]

It is important to understand that many of these stories are apocryphal; one hears them over and over again, usually from programmers, and usually prefaced by the assertion that "This really happened to a friend of mine who works in technical support. . . ." But, whether or not these stories have their provenance in any actual events, what matters is that they are circulated as *real*; and the few actual encounters that programmers and other members of software production teams might have with end users therefore tend to be perceived in these terms, as substantiating and lending credence to the notion of User ineptitude.

The tales themselves are thus a potent means of boundary formation: "Computer thralls see such actions as evidence that outsiders to their universe have meat loaf for brains."[19] Indeed, Steve Woolgar accurately describes dumb-user stories (or "atrocity stories," as he calls them) as "racist talk."[20] Like all racist jokes, the dumb-user stories not only couch, in humourous terms, attempts to reduce the individual differences of members of a particular group to a few specific, exaggerated traits—in this case, technical ineptitude and idiocy—but also thereby to emphasize the inherent superiority of those who are not members of that group, those who are producers of software rather than mere users. We find the same kind of racist (and, in this case, sexist) humour in an on-line guide to "Tech Support Nietzsche Style," whose author refers to the User as "a weakling" and "a loser in the race of the weak and the strong," a "creature" who "[exists] to serve you and not you him."[21]

Even so, we might simply shrug off the dumb-user stories as typical of the kinds of humourous exchanges that take place in most high-stress work environments were it not for the fact that the racist ideas contained in the stories do not stop there. Rather, those same ideas about the User are encoded within the software itself, such that, as you use a program, "you are often made to feel like a complete, hopeless idiot every step of the way."[22] And, not surprisingly, the presence of such attitudes tends to be most evident in the means by which a software system is designed to respond to the clear and indisputable evidence of User ineptitude: error messages.

User Error

"What did I do?" This is the typical refrain of the anxious computer user, confronted with an irate noise emerging from the computer, or a brusque and incomprehensible error message, or a mouse pointer that seems to be stuck in one place. The computer is mad, the computer is hung. Clearly, the user has done something wrong.

No other technology tyrannizes us like the computer. I once had an elderly but generally reliable car that one day, to my horror, made a sudden grinding noise and then screeched to an absolute halt, right in the middle of a busy intersection. Of course, I was upset, but I certainly never *blamed* myself for the car's failure. Yet that is precisely what so many computer users seem to do: to accept blame when digital systems do not perform as expected. Some time ago, an acquaintance shared with me a story about the computerization of her workplace in the early days of the PC. One day, shortly after the introduction of the new computers, she overheard a colleague saying, repeatedly, "Sorry. . . . Oh, sorry." Curious about who or what might have brought this usually confident, even arrogant, man to such a point of abject humility, she peeked into his office, only to see that the humble apologies were being directed towards the new computer on his desk as he tried, with repeated errors, to perform a task.

But it is not only novices who accept the blame when things go awry. Take, for instance, an incident related by Donald Norman in *The Design of Everyday Things*. Asked by a large computer company to evaluate a new product, Norman observed that the system was designed in such a way that it was vital to differentiate between the Return and Enter keys. Pressing the wrong key at any time meant that work would be lost, yet it seemed to Norman to be a very easy mistake to make. When he pointed this out to the system designers, they claimed that it was not a problem since they had received no user complaints about this aspect of the system design. But when Norman spoke to the users themselves, they admitted that they often made the mistake of pressing the wrong key. Why hadn't they reported it? Because "they blamed themselves. After all, they had been told what to do. They had simply erred."[23]

Even experienced computer users thus accept blame for a system's failures because, having bought into the mythos of the technical perfection and neutrality of software programs and the devices upon which they run, we also accept and participate in the configuration of ourselves as the endlessly inept, illogical, and culpable User. "No matter how poor the system," writes the author of *The Trouble with Computers*, himself a systems designer, "users rarely complain that it is badly designed; instead they apologize for their own ineptness."[24]

A proclivity for self-blame is, in fact, coded into the software we use. In that software, the User exists as nothing more than a variable. Moreover, the User is the one variable that is totally beyond the control of software developers—the single unreliable, unpredictable element whose mindless actions can destroy an otherwise perfect program (since a program's perfection is independent of its ability to meet the needs of end users). Indeed, in the world of software production, human users are *problems*. As one programmer put it in a newsgroup contribution which I happened upon many years ago, users are "mysterious beings" who tend to "slow down the computer." Ursula Franklin rightly observes that the real world of technology is characterized by a "basic apprehension of people,"[25] a belief that people cause problems and computers offer solutions.

From the developer's point of view, then, any breakdown of communications between the system and the user must originate not with the software designer's failure to anticipate certain user input, nor with a mismatch between the end-user's thought processes and the design of the program, but with the inability of the User to communicate in the computer's terms. As Edward Yourdan observes, "In most cases . . . the problem is in the design of the user interface, but many software developers make the implicit assumption that an even larger part of the problem is that users are somehow mentally deficient."[26] The assumption, among many software developers, is that technical problems—hung computers, lost data—have nothing to do with the design of the hardware and software and everything to do with the User's inability to use the computer as it was meant to be used. Which is why, according to Theodore Roszak, this notion of human culpability "permeates the technology with a haunting sense of human inadequacy and existential failure. . . . That despairing motif comes with the machines."[27]

In short, the view widely held by software developers, and embedded in the programs we use, is that "computers don't make mistakes, people do." The techie acronym PEBCAK says it all: Problem Exists Between Chair And Keyboard. The same attitude is clearly articulated in the old programmers' gag from which the title of this book is drawn, a parody of a typical DOS error message: "User error: Replace user and strike any key." It is also the theme of *The New Yorker* cartoon below (see fig. 2), which depicts a nonplussed user who is confronted with an error message that makes it eminently clear where all technical problems originate: "Human error. Again."

Both the programmers' gag and the cartoon find their humour not in the remoteness of the error messages from those we usually see on the screen, but indeed in the fact that *all* responses to input errors contain this subliminal meaning, such that every encounter with the computer becomes an encounter with one's own inherent fallibility as a user. The very term error implicitly assigns blame.[28] As Jim Carroll says of error messages in general, "It's almost as if computers have been designed to hit you on the head with some difficult, incomprehensible instruction, message or statement that sets you back every time you use it or attempt to learn something new."[29]

Indeed, in the DOS world, the messages that informed computer users of their input errors were notoriously brusque, abrupt, and unhelpful. Messages such as, "Illegal entry," "Program aborted," "Fatal disk error," "Abort/Retry/Fail," and "Error-1507" evoked hidden processes and obscure, occultish references in order, deliberately or not, to reinforce the status of the system developer as one who knew and

FIGURE 2: *User error: Computers don't make mistakes, people do.*

of the User as one who did not (and who was therefore likely to "crash" or even "kill" the machine). As Michael Crichton asks, "What is one to make of NEXT WITHOUT FOR ERROR? Or TYPE MISMATCH ERROR? Even if the error message appears to be in English, it's not helpful, such as the self-evident CAN'T CONTINUE ERROR."[30] Moreover, the use of absolute words evoking danger, destruction, and even death—words such as *invalid, illegal, abort,* and *fatal*—both reflected and constructed an understanding of the User as one who was prone to making extreme and intolerable input errors. Such vague, unhelpful error messages must be understood not as a means by which software developers communicated with the User, but rather as a sustained form of *miscommunication*: an attempt to create precisely the kinds of user confusion and frustration which are lambasted (even, perhaps, perversely celebrated) in the dumb-user stories.

It is worth noting that such obscure, downright rude error messages appear to have done little to diminish the users' desire to get closer to the computer. Quite the contrary, in fact. Messages of this kind may be off-putting, and may even seem to be, as Crichton observes, "the worst sort of reprimand,"[31] but since users tend to blame themselves for the appearance of error messages—even those originating from system failures—they are also inclined to view those reprimands as an unmistakable sign of the necessity of learning more about the computer's operations. In this way, an abrupt notification that a fatal I/O error has occurred may perversely serve to reinforce the (negative) allure of the machine.

Friendly Programs

Of course, many of these brusque error messages have gone the way of DOS. Today, with the advent of "user-friendly" interfaces such as Windows and Macintosh, we do not have error messages, as such, but rather dialogue boxes in which the system kindly informs us that something is amiss—the message perhaps clarified by the friendly picture of a bomb—and asks us to confirm our agreement with the computer's assessment of the situation by clicking the "OK" button. Whether we like it or not.

What exactly is user-friendliness? We sometimes hear it said that a user-friendly system is one which is not system-centred but designed "with the user in mind." This is an interesting distinction (and one that I will return to later), but its vagueness is typical of much that is written on the subject. Indeed, the term seems to elude clear definition. "Everyone wants to have a 'user friendly' system," laments one contributor to a book entitled *What Is User Friendly?* "but no one can really define what user friendly is."[32] Another contributor to the same collection agrees: "User friendly is one of those valuable concepts that has become such an overworked phrase that it has lost much of its meaning."[33] As it is overused, *user-friendly* seems to be emptied of denotative meaning (if, indeed, it ever had any) while at the same time accumulating positive connotations related to empowerment and accessibility. (We see the same process occurring with many other computer-related words, which, though they may elude definition, are far from meaningless. *Virtual*, for instance, has oddly come to evoke not an approximation of reality but a constructed world that is in fact superior to the real thing.)

In the end, most attempts to define user-friendliness fall back upon a description of the nature and characteristics of the kinds of computer systems that the term describes. Chief among these characteristics is ease-of-use—the quality which, as we saw in the previous chapter, helped to launch the personal computing industry during the 1980s and 1990s. Indeed, since computers first emerged from the cloistered backrooms and the ministrations of data priests, ease-of-use and user-friendliness have gone hand in hand. The new PCS were "friendlier" than the mainframes and minicomputers, not only in the sense that they were more accessible but also in that their operations were rendered increasingly comprehensible to the average person.

Eventually, the push to make computers more user-friendly (or, as I will suggest in chapter 4, more *consumer*-friendly, more accessible to a larger user base) resulted in the development of graphical-user interfaces (GUIS). These interfaces depicted complex processes in terms of icons and other images, thereby, it was suggested, enabling relatively unskilled users to focus on the tasks they wanted to accomplish rather than on the actual complexities of the system. For instance, the Macintosh interface represents the workings of complex systems and processes in terms that are presumably comprehensible, familiar, and "intuitive" to most users: the screen is a "desktop" wherein we work not with zeroes and ones, nor even with computer files and directories, but with documents and folders. Even though the graphical-user interface functions as a sort of screen between the user and the inner workings of the computer, an easy-to-use, user-friendly GUI is said to be "transparent," in the sense that it is no longer governed by opaque, hard to understand commands and processes. The iMac's clear casing is thus Apple's way of marketing its system as the ultimate in user-friendliness. Although a view of the wires and circuits inside the machine can provide no insight whatsoever into computer processes that take place on a microscopic level, the iMac's exposed innards nevertheless function as a potent metaphor for a demystified system.

But even the Macintosh interface, frequently offered as the ultimate in user-friendliness, has its limits when it comes to transparency and ease-of-use. Consider, for instance, the Macintosh convention which requires that, when you are done using a disk, you "put it in the trash"—that is, drag it over the top of the trashcan icon. Since the trashcan is also the place where unwanted files are deposited, this technique for ejecting disks is hardly intuitive and, indeed, typically causes great concern to new users. Even after they have mastered the difficulties of dragging and dropping with the mouse, many novice users are reluctant to eject their disks in this way because they fear, quite logically, that by putting a disk in the trashcan they will lose all the data that it contains.

In fact, speaking both as someone who has made the transition from DOS to GUIS, and who has had many opportunities to teach computer novices the basics of both the DOS and Macintosh interfaces, I would suggest that there is nothing particularly intuitive about most GUI conventions—nor is a GUI necessarily easier to use, or to learn to use, than a command-line interface such as DOS. In both cases, all lip service to user-friendliness aside, it is the human users, and not the "friendly" systems, who do most of the accommodating. For example, in the process of writing this book, I have worked around the limitations of a word-processing program that will only place footnotes at the bottom of the page or at the very end of the document, but not where I want them: before the references. Similarly, I have been compelled to create my table of contents manually because the Table of Contents function insists on treating the chapter number, title, and subtitle as three separate things, each with its own page reference, and cannot by any means be persuaded to do otherwise. And when, one day, I booted up Microsoft Word only to discover that all my preferences had been inexplicably reset to the default, I simply shrugged and reset them. The straightened paper clip, which so many Mac users keep beside their computers (used to eject disks when a system crash or other malfunction makes it impossible to eject the disk via the friendly trashcan), serves as a small but potent reminder of the many ways in which we unconsciously adapt to our "friendly" systems. In short, it is the users who become *computer-friendly*.

According to Donald Norman, if supposedly user-friendly systems are not in fact easy to use, it is because the people who design and develop the systems fail to consider the needs of the end users.[34] Paulina Borsook concurs that the programmers' "lack of empathetic imagination" towards the user "could very well explain *why* computers and networks are still so damned hard to use and understand, so complex and inclined to strange malfunctions."[35] Robert Johnson's verdict is similar: supposedly user-friendly programs, he suggests, are really system-centred because the user is still "far removed from the central concern of the system or interface design," which means that lip service to the idea of user-friendliness merely "[gives] credence to technology-driven initiatives."[36]

Certainly, the "creeping featurism"[37] that we see in so many programs today, and which is parodied in the cartoon below (see fig. 3), attests to the paradox of a user-friendliness that has somehow become divorced from the needs of the user while at the same time it serves as the justification for system complexity, as more and more capabilities are added to programs in the name of empowering the computer user.

Like most *Dilbert* cartoons, this one finds its humour in its accurate depiction of a reality that it reveals to be ridiculous. Scott Adams, the creator of *Dilbert*, might also find some wry humour in the fact that programs inflicted with creeping featurism are increasingly marketed as "software solutions," a term which, as I suggested in chapter 1, implies that the accumulation of features has nothing to do with the drive to expand system capabilities and everything to do with addressing pre-existing user needs.

DILBERT reprinted by permission of United Feature Syndicate, Inc.

FIGURE 3: *Creeping featurism: Adding system complexity in the name of user-friendliness.*

Indeed, many so-called friendly programs are actually becoming unbelievably complex through the sheer proliferation of features, most of which the average user will never use. In *The Trouble with Computers*, Thomas Landauer observes that most programs "are too complex, have too many features, give the user far too many options." Users' "machines and minds are loaded up with a vast junk pile of options, commands, facilities, doodads, and buttons, most of them superfluous to the user and there just because somebody knew how to program it. Having this mountain of stuff available usually means that doing even the simplest operation can be extraordinarily difficult."[38]

Roger Shenk expresses a similar frustration, triggered by the move to a new version of Microsoft Word, which was supposed to be much easier to use:

> The upgrade was advertised as having a "built-in intelligence that senses what you want to do and produces the desired result, making routine tasks automatic and complex jobs easier." But all the new bells and whistles had transformed the program I depended on for basic word processing into a veritable zoo of capabilities that were

> cumbersome to learn, and had slowed down even the most elemental functions, like opening a file and printing, to a painful crawl.[39]

Shenk's frustration has to do with the fact that, while the 1992 version of Microsoft Word had 311 commands, the program had acquired, by 1997, an additional 722 commands—all in the name of ease-of-use.[40] The number continues to grow, giving us more and more supposedly essential commands that few users bother with. Take, for example, the AutoSummarize option. Now, would anyone who has seen what the automatic spelling and grammar checkers would do to a document if left to their own devices actually rely upon the word-processor's ability to pick out the sentences most relevant to the main theme of a document? (The computer-generated summary of this chapter includes a dumb-user story, a couple of randomly selected section titles and picture captions, and the following sentences: *What exactly is user-friendliness? We sometimes hear it said that a user-friendly system is one which is not system-centred but designed "with the user in mind." In short, it is the users who become computer-friendly. Creeping featurism: Adding system complexity in the name of user-friendliness. The office assistant is the essence of user-friendliness, yet the tale it tells about the User is really just one more dumb User story. That, undoubtedly, is the ultimate user error.*)

Ultimately, as supposedly user-friendly programs accumulate features like snowballs plummeting out of control, it becomes increasingly apparent that ease-of-use is a figment. The user is required, today no less than in the days of DOS, to tolerate the needs of unwieldy computer programs, to adapt to the limits imposed by system developers, and to accept blame for the program's failings—to be, in short, computer-friendly. And as the features accumulate, and mastery of a program and all its complexities becomes ever more difficult, the chasm between experts and novices, between developers and users becomes ever more unbridgeable—and the User, by extension, more unknowledgeable.

But is creeping featurism really the result of a failure on the part of software developers to consider the end user? Or is it, rather, precisely *because* software is developed "with the user in mind," albeit an inept User whose attempts to tap into computer power are laughable, that user-friendly programs continue to tyrannize us? I would suggest that the latter is often the case, and I would further suggest that, if most attempts to come to terms with the meaning of user-friendliness fail, it is because they focus on the fundamental characteristics of those systems which the term describes rather than on the underlying assumptions about the computer User. (Consider, once again, that AutoSummarize option: its mere presence on the Tools menu implies a great deal about the relative "smarts" and capabilities attributed to the system and the User.) In the end, given what I have suggested about the mental construct of the User that prevails in many software production facilities, we should question if any program developed with that idiotic User in mind could ever be truly *friendly*.

The User as a Twitching Finger

What I am suggesting is that, among those who develop computer software, the concept of user-friendliness has less to do with ease-of-use than it does with preventing User error—with, as Donald Norman and Stephen Draper put it, creating "idiot-proof" computer programs.[41]

In fact, the term user-friendly was originally coined by hackers and programmers as a derogatory reference to User idiocy: "Since *user* already had disparaging connotations, tacking *friendly* onto it amplified the derogation."[42] This sense of the word is certainly perpetuated in *The New Hacker's Dictionary*, which defines *user-friendly* as "Programmer-hostile. Generally used by hackers in a critical tone, to describe systems that hold the user's hand so obsessively that they make it painful for the more experienced and knowledgeable to get any work done." We are referred, for additional information, to *user-obsequious*, which is defined as an "Emphatic form of user-friendly. Connotes a system so verbose, inflexible, and determinedly simple-minded that it is nearly unusable. 'Design a system any fool can use and only a fool will want to use it.'"[43]

Today, the notion of user-friendliness as it is used in the context of software development still resonates with those derogatory undertones. As a result, individuals who are involved in the production of user-friendly systems tend to confront the technological ineptitude of the User by seeking to minimize the possibility that the User will go astray and do something *wrong* (that is, something that is not within the bounds of possibilities offered by the system).

There are three main strategies by which software developers achieve this tacit end of making it difficult, even impossible, for a user to make input errors. First, they compensate for User idiocy by making their software programs more "intelligent"—that is, by building into the software assumptions about what it is you really *meant* to do. For instance, if you forget to capitalize a sentence, Microsoft Word will automatically correct the error for you. The second way in which software producers minimize the possibility of User error is by limiting the information transmitted to the user to only the essentials, only what the user absolutely needs to know, which means nothing of the processes and algorithms underlying automated decision-making. (This is, rather ironically, a fundamental rule of "dialogue" in the world of user-interface design.) Finally, the possibility of error is minimized by creating programs that present the user with predefined sets of actions, which presumably represent all the things that a user could possibly wish to accomplish with the program. These actions are described, in a vocabulary of choice and empowerment, as *options* and *commands*. A program that offers a predefined range (or menu) of options and commands limits the possibility of human-input error and thus the need for error messages. As users, we are not being continually reprimanded, and this in itself makes the program more friendly.

This would seem, upon first consideration, to be a powerful good for the computer user. Who could possibly object to a software program that reduces the possibility of human error? A program that is, moreover, anthropomorphized as a "friend," an entity whose sole concern is the welfare and happiness of the individual user. But in fact, user-friendliness, as it tends to be conceived within software-production facilities, has nothing to do with tolerance for error, nothing to do with accommodation of individual differences, and everything to do with reducing all user differences to a set of clearly defined inputs, processes, and outputs, with the ultimate goal not of meeting all end-user needs but of thwarting the miscues of the monolithic, technically inept User. There are times when you in fact *want* to begin a new sentence with a lowercase letter (for instance, in a bulleted list), but Microsoft Word is going to make it difficult for you to do so because its so-called intelligence arises from and is based on the User's tendency to err. And even though, according to Jaron Lanier, everyone hates those "annoying features in Microsoft Word and Powerpoint that guess at what the user really wanted to type," it is difficult, sometimes virtually impossible, to disable them, "even though that is supposed to be possible."[44] Hence, William Safire's lament: "Why do I have to wrestle with my word-processing program for control . . . of my own text? Who owns which?"[45]

The answer to this question is that, increasingly, knowledge and thus power inhere in the system and its developers. The concept of user-friendliness emerges from and continues to evolve based on a fundamental disregard, even disdain, for the User's skill, knowledge, and ability to learn and adapt. "Underlying every user-friendly interface," admits one programmer, "is a terrific human contempt."[46] David Noble concurs that the tendency to design systems that preclude human intervention is based on the assumption that such intervention will necessarily involve error rather than, "more positively, a chance for creativity, judgement, or enhancement."[47] Therefore, from features such as AutoSummarize, which rob the user of motive power, to word processors that automatically make typed World Wide Web addresses "hot," to programs that force the user to confirm the deletion of a file three times, to dialogue boxes that offer only the option of agreement (i.e., clicking the "OK" button), user-friendly interfaces are not designed so much to make computing easier but rather to make it "fool proof" and dumbed down for error-prone users. And as the system paradoxically proliferates with features and capabilities, "[t]he human presence is reduced to a twitching finger, spastic body, and an oversaturated informational pump that . . . makes choices within strictly programmed limits."[48]

User-friendliness thus provides the imprimatur for software developers to produce dazzling pieces of interactive multimedia which take full advantage of the capabilities of the computer while ignoring users' minds in favour of conditioned responses. In this way, power is transferred from the User to the system and, by extension, the system developers.

Having already considered one paper clip, let us now consider, in this context, another: Microsoft Office 98's office assistant (see fig. 4). Clippy the animated paper clip is smiling and eager to lend a helping hand. "It looks like you're writing a letter," it will cogently observe. "Would you like help?" Clippy is surely the essence of user-friendliness: it is prompt, pleasant, and helpful. But you cannot get rid of it. True, you can choose not to have it on the screen at all times. And, yes, you can change your office assistant. If you object to being served by a grinning paper clip, you can choose from a variety of other characters, including Bosgrove the butler, F1 the robot, Rocky the dog, and Scribble the paper cat. And you can change the size of the office assistant, set how much it moves around, turn off the sounds it makes. And of course, once the assistant has popped up on the screen, you

FIGURE 4: *Clippy the office assistant: The essence of user-friendliness.*

can click the "Cancel" button to make it to go away. But try as you might, there is no apparent way to prevent that office assistant from appearing on the screen in the first place, in situations predetermined by the system designers.

The office assistant is the essence of user-friendliness, yet the tale it tells about the User is really just one more dumb-user story. Given the ability to manipulate sizes, sounds, and appearances—options that are, in the end, entirely trivial and cosmetic—we are expected to feel empowered by the office assistant, even as we are prevented, by the admonishments of a grinning paper clip, from tampering with the deeper workings of the system. The same is true of other features. We are allowed to customize displays, to add and delete toolbar buttons, and even to decide which toolbars should appear on the screen at a given time; but underlying this capability for superficial customization is a system that is highly resistant to users' innovations and alterations and that conceals the processes and algorithms upon which system decisions are based.

In this way, rather than opening the black box of the computer, user-friendliness paradoxically seals it tighter and further buttresses the boundaries between the software developers and the error-prone User, between the experts and the "idiots who must have the technologies 'dumbed down' to their level."[49] Ultimately, it is not the users who are empowered by user-friendly interfaces; rather, the "intelligent" programs with predetermined menus of options and commands allow the system developers and the systems themselves to become the primary agents of knowledge insofar as they maintain absolute control over user input and define what counts as knowledge.

The individual user, on the other hand, is rendered increasingly helpless, unable—because of a total lack of knowledge of the system's inner workings and logic—to deal with anomalies or system errors,[50] and apt to assume blame when they do occur. Neil Postman thus notes the "curious form of grammatical alchemy" whereby "the sentence, 'We use the computer to calculate' comes to mean 'The computer calculates.'"[51] The semantic transformation reflects a nascent belief that the User is insignificant to the larger operations of the computer, relieved of responsibility and volition. Perhaps this is why, as Theodore Roszak observes, the term user-friendliness is tainted with undertones of condescension and with the underlying suggestion "that the machine is being kind enough to simplify and slow down for less talented users who need to be babied along."[52]

Of course, some users may not *want* to know anything of the inner workings of their digital devices. But it's important to understand that that desire itself likely emerges in the first place from the belief that the computer is too complex for us to comprehend. User-friendly systems create and perpetuate that belief by ensuring that everything that goes on behind the screen remains a mystery to the user, for, ultimately, user-friendliness is the means by which system opacity is perpetuated beneath the guise of transparency. We are continually assured that we do not need to know how systems work, but, according to Steve Mann, the notion that we are "better off 'protected' from having to learn even the basics of computer programming" is merely "the self-serving argument of software monopolists."[53] Mann goes on to make the important point that, whether we wish to know more about the inner workings of our computers or not, we should at least have the option of being able to tinker with the programs we use if we wish to do so:

> Perhaps it is true that many of us don't wish to learn detailed new skill sets simply to function in everyday life. But, then again, if we are not given the option to learn and contribute, if, indeed, we are prevented from viewing how most of our programs work, the argument that this is done for our own benefit seems dubious at best. . . . The distinction between "developer" and "end user" needs to be redefined. We should be encouraged to learn and understand how computers work, and we should be allowed to modify and adjust software and hardware according to the needs of both ourselves and our particular communities.[54]

John Seely Brown agrees that "the classic design goal of designing 'idiot-proof' systems . . . is profoundly wrong," in that ease-of-use paradoxically minimizes users' power and control:

> An implicit design goal in most discussions of human-computer interfaces is that system design should enable users, in particular casual users, to be in control of their technology. Unfortunately, in many instances, this is taken to mean no more than the self-evident

> proposition that people should be able easily to do the things they want to do with computers. . . .
>
> We need to recognize how fully a user's sense of control rests on a robust understanding of how a given system functions, of why the procedures for operation are as they are. . . . [W]ithout at least a common-sense understanding of how the procedures relate to the underlying system, users will be unable to adapt them to new situations, to deal with either system malfunctions or the consequences of their own errors, or to adapt to new or evolving systems.[55]

Imagine a world in which software developers put as much effort into making systems "user-understandable" as they now do into making opaque systems *seem* transparent. Users in that world would have a very clear picture of how their hardware and software functioned, and would be able to control and modify their systems in non-trivial ways in order to meet their unique needs.

By way of conclusion to this section on user-friendliness, it is worth noting that, with the release of Office XP in 2001, Clippy has been forced into retirement. Microsoft's Web-site advertisement prior to the release included the claim that Office XP was "so simple it's going to put Clippy the Office Assistant out of a job." Other ads for "the greatest version of Office software" invited us to "Experience simplicity." But even as we rejoice at Clippy's departure, we should remember that, if the office assistant is now considered expendable, it is only because Microsoft Office has been further idiot-proofed, through the addition of still more features and "intelligence." In the end, it is not the software that has been made more *simple*—in fact, Office XP proliferates with even more features than the preceding version—but the imagined User.

The Ultimate User Error

Thus far in this chapter I have been rather hard on software developers. I have made and drawn upon what many may consider to be unfair generalizations about the attitudes of those who design and program software. Indeed, as I suggested in the Introduction, it may seem that, in lumping together designers, programmers, graphic artists, and other members of the software-production team into a homogenous group of people who all participate in the construction of the User as an idiot, I am party to precisely the process I describe:

the reduction of diverse individuals to a single undifferentiated entity—in this case, Software Developer.

My own experience suggests that the considerations uppermost in the minds of most software developers are, first, the perfection of the program, largely independent of end-user considerations, and, second, a looming schedule and budget constraints imposed by management. Nevertheless, I have no doubt that some designers and programmers are also motivated by a keen desire to work with and empower the end user. After all, the discourse of computer science includes numerous books and articles on the human–computer interface, usability, and other topics related to the creation of software programs that will meet user needs, and many information technology companies have whole departments devoted to finding ways to make their programs more user-friendly. Of course, much of the corporate emphasis on usability can be attributed to an attempt to boost the bottom line. It is unlikely that Microsoft, IBM, and other software companies invest millions of dollars in usability departments because of a sincere wish to make their programs more user-centred—particularly given that those companies are also notorious for rushing to get buggy, albeit feature-laden, systems to market.

However, there are two movements in the domain of computer science that clearly do emerge from a desire to establish a closer link with the end users and their needs: user-centred design and participatory design. These models of software development would seem to transcend some of the problems inherent in the notion of user-friendliness, and to offer hope that attitudes towards the User which are currently deeply rooted within computing culture may be slowly giving way to a recognition of the needs and potential contributions of diverse users.

One of the chief proponents of user-centred design is Donald Norman, author of such books as *The Design of Everyday Things* and *The Invisible Computer*. As the title of the latter work suggests, Norman premises his work upon the conviction that people do not want to have to think about computer use: "I don't want to use a computer," insists Norman, "I want to accomplish something. I want to do something meaningful to me."[56] Setting aside the rather significant fact that user-centred design is premised upon a very simplistic, utilitarian view, which completely disregards the potency of the mythology of computer use, there is every reason to believe, on first examination, that this model of system development offers a potentially effective means of overcoming the wholesale disdain for the nameless, faceless User that underlies the production of user-friendly programs. After all, user-centred design emphasizes the importance of designing software not simply "with the user in mind"—that is, in accordance with a mental construct of the User—but, more specifically, of designing and developing software in conjunction *with* the user, consulting with actual end users during the production process in order to ensure that the final product will indeed meet their needs.

Whereas the rationale for user-centred design is largely functional—to involve end users as a source of information in order to improve system design and, ultimately, user buy-in—participatory design emerges from Scandinavia and a political program to give power to those employed in computerized workplaces: "The focus of participatory design (PD) is not only the improvement of the information system, but also the empowerment of workers so they can codetermine the development of the information system and of their workplace."[57] Users are not merely consulted in the participatory design model; rather, they "actively engage in designing the computer systems they will eventually employ."[58]

So how much influence can these two models be expected to have upon the software-development process and the deep-rooted attitude to the User? Participatory design has certainly had a relatively wide influence outside the English-speaking world, but has yet to make significant inroads into North America.[59] According to Bonnie Nardi and Vicki O'Day, participatory design has failed to move outside North American research labs because it simply does not fit into our mass-production mentality: "Ironically, product developers fear that collaborating with users in a few particular settings would make their software less generally usable by all—perhaps it is better to work closely with no users, so everyone will be at an equal disadvantage."[60]

But there is more to PD's lack of uptake in North America than a concern with ensuring general usability. The principles of participatory design are inherently antithetical to mass-production techniques and to what Ursula Franklin calls "the programming of people,"[61] the creation of a culture of compliance which demands from software developers, as from all individuals working within a system dedicated to the attainment of manufacturing efficiencies, an unquestioning acceptance of production processes and standards. According to David Noble, such closed systems, which reduce workers' knowledge and opportunities for action and judgement, are a necessary part of the management obsession with control and the diminishment of worker power.[62] The point is that, before they participate in the configuration of the User, software developers are themselves programmed. Unless it is somehow shown to increase profits, participatory design is unlikely to flourish within those organizational cultures that give precedence not to human needs but to deadlines and bottom lines, and that provide software developers with neither the time nor motivation to regard diverse individuals as anything but an objectified User.

As for user-centred design, it too is more likely to remain an ideal than to become a reality, for several reasons. First, as Robert Johnson, a proponent of user-centred design, admits, "the system-centered view is so embedded in Western cultural ways of thinking about technology that even the best user-centered design approaches to technology can unwittingly fall victim to the system-centered ideology."[63] This system-centred view gives rise to the tacit and largely unacknowledged notion that the User is the problem, the one uncontrollable variable in a software program. And, as Rob Kling observes in his article on "Computerization and Social Transformations," computer science, the academic discipline from which most programmers emerge, fosters this perspective by seeking to align itself with the scientific—that is, with algorithms, data structures, and the mathematical analysis of computer performance—rather than with the social and the importance of developing a sensitivity to the ways in which computerization can reconfigure social processes and entities.[64] In this way, system-centred attitudes become entrenched, even among developers who may give lip service to the importance of putting the user and the user's needs first.

A second reason user-centred design is unlikely to affect the status quo is because it fails, as a model of software development, to challenge or diminish in any fundamental way the hierarchy of computer knowledge. In fact, user-centred approaches to software design emerge from and reinforce the strict division between those who produce software and those who merely use it. User-centred design may purport to place computer users in the centre rather than the sidelines of the development process, but in fact it continues to foster the construction of the User as a single, objectified entity, clearly differentiated from the knowing insiders. This attitude of exclusivity and exclusion inevitably becomes embedded within the software itself, "user-centred" though it may be. Until such a time as the hierarchy of computer knowledge collapses, then, designers and programmers of software will continue to produce the User by unconsciously encoding, within their programs, assumptions about how we should think and, more particularly, how we should think about ourselves.

A third reason, if Franklin is correct, is that user-centred design represents nothing more than a stage in a discernable pattern of social growth common to most new technologies. In *The Real World of Technology*, Franklin suggests that the user's needs are only a matter of interest—and that interest is largely rhetorical—until such a point as the technology has become well entrenched:

> Carefully selected phrases used to describe new technical advances could generate an image of chummy communities and adventurous users. But once a given technology is widely accepted and standardized, the relationship between the products of the technology and the users changes. Users have less scope, they matter less, and their needs are no longer the main concerns of the designers.[65]

Surely Microsoft's monopolistic business practices, and the history of the resulting antitrust litigation, suggest that the goal of user-centredness will always be sublimated to the more important goal of creating a computing universe that is increasingly *Microsoft-centred*. When the day arrives, not too long from now, when we are incapable of conducting our day-to-day business, of coping and surviving in the world without continual use of computers running Microsoft programs, how important will our needs and desires as users really be? And if user-centred and participatory design persist as fields of endeavour, whose interests will be served by attempts to create the illusion of user control of the technology?

But perhaps the most important reason user-centred design is unlikely to significantly alter either the software development process or the entrenched attitudes towards the User is that it originates not with end users but with a few wayward software developers. Indeed, while software developers have initiated and experimented with both user-centred and participatory design, users remain conspicuously and curiously apathetic. Rather than agitating for more involvement in the development process, we seem quite content to accept a passive, dependent role as users of "friendly" systems. Can we really expect high-tech corporations to concern themselves with our interests when we have thus far shown ourselves to be eager initiates into the mythology of computer use, quite willing to use systems that are only friendly in name?

By way of conclusion, then, I will emphasize that the purpose of this chapter has not been to assign blame to software developers. The responsibility both for the status quo and for change lies not with those who produce software but ultimately with us, the users. As Robert Johnson rightly observes:

> Users are not innocent in this enterprise of idiocy. . . . Users themselves have in many ways allowed the construction of the idea of technological idiocy through an acquiescence to the knowing expert and to the acceptance of the idea that technology is just too complex for the "average" person to understand.[66]

And, having so acquiesced, it is very easy for us to disregard the constructedness of the software we use—software which is, after all, developed in dimly-lit offices rather than large, clanking, smoke-belching factories, and which is comprised of formless bits rather than heavy metal parts. But the fact that ideas and processes are invisible does not make them neutral, only more insidious for being unconsidered. And insofar as we avoid consideration of the software programs we use as constructed environments and avoid taking an active role in their development, we participate in the construction of ourselves as the unknowing User, a voiceless entity which blithely uses "friendly" programs that dictate needs and circumscribe possibilities rather than accommodating human diversity. That, undoubtedly, is the ultimate user error.

4

Caveat Emptor: The Emergence of the User-Consumer

Technology is undeniably trendy. It is hardly possible, these days, to open a newspaper or magazine, or even to turn on the television, without being confronted by an advertisement for the latest digital innovation which, we are assured, we simply cannot live without. Nevertheless, one can still find, amidst all the hyperbole, a number of books and articles that offer sustained critiques of computing culture. Many of these critiques are based on the computer's fundamental *lack* of utility. For example, in *The Trouble with Computers*, Thomas Landauer musters up an impressive quantity of evidence to support his claim that digital devices do not increase users' efficiency, do not make our lives easier and better, and do not "do a sufficient number of sufficiently useful things."[1] In *Silicon Snake Oil*, Clifford Stoll offers a sustained argument, based largely on his own experiences as a long-time computer user, for his view that computers actually get in the way of work and "real" life. And the authors of *The Child and the Machine* take these arguments into the realm of education, asking us to consider whether using computers in the classroom really adds anything to the educational experience that cannot be achieved through teacher–student interactions and the use of traditional media, such as chalkboards and books.[2]

But as I suggested in chapter 1, stories about the measurable, verifiable results of computer use (increased efficiencies, higher grade-point averages, and so forth) should be understood less as real than as *mythical*, a means by which we seek to explain to ourselves the curious allure of high technology. As Lewis Mumford observes in *The Pentagon of Power*, our "over-use of the machine flouts any practical test of efficiency: it has the force of an obligatory religious ritual, a genuflection before a holy object."[3] If the books and articles that attack the utility of digital technologies fail to convince us, it is therefore in large part because our fascination with the computer actually has very little to do with its usefulness. Though we may indeed explain the appeal to ourselves and each other in these terms, the fact remains that what really lures us to high technology is the siren song of pure desire.

I refer, in this context, to the insatiable desire of the consumer. The consumer is, after all, a creature of desire; and the act of consumption, as Jean Baudrillard suggests, has less to do with purchasing objects than with regarding those objects as signs that denote the possibility of achieving satisfaction and the fulfillment of one's desires.[4] Therefore, regardless of whether or not we actually make computer purchases (and many users do not), we are all consumers before we are computer users. Although my thesaurus offers the two words as synonymous, the distinction between them is important in the context of this chapter. *Users* make practical use of a product; *consumers* regard objects as the means of fulfilling desires which have been restructured, via various marketing strategies, into needs—the things one simply *must* have in order to be happy and successful.

Consider, once again, the slogans used, respectively, in the marketing campaigns of Microsoft, Rogers Digital Cable, and Hewlett-Packard: "Where do you want to go today?" and "Where will it take you?" and "Everything is possible." While these slogans ostensibly address users of digital devices, their purpose, as I suggested in chapter 1, is in fact to create consumer desire by offering computer power in magical, flying-carpet terms. And all three slogans further construct the desire to explore digital realms as a fundamental human need, an essential source of well-being and prestige, since the question they pose is not, *Do you need to use digital technologies?* but rather, *How will you use them?* In this way, as Baudrillard observes, the commodity offered ceases to be merely a tool, an object of use, and becomes instead an object of consumption, which is to say an object of desire.[5]

But in the frenzied world of digital consumption, desire goes both ways. If the consumer's desire for computer hardware and software is constantly being pumped, then so too is the consumer him/herself an object of intense desire. This creates a paradoxical situation: as users, we tend to be dismissed by software producers as error-prone and mindless; but as consumers of high-tech, we seem to be highly sought after and cherished. Salespeople sidle up to us; marketers of hardware and software products carefully craft advertisements in order to appeal to our deepest needs; and market researchers, like our newest best buddies, want to know everything about us, from how much money we earn to the kinds of television shows we enjoy watching. If the digital world oozes with friendliness, it is a friendliness that is patently misnamed: not user-friendliness but *consumer*-friendliness.

In this context, it is therefore worth offering some additional thoughts on user-friendliness. In chapter 3, my interest was in examining how the concept of user-friendliness manifests itself in software programs, as a result of the unspoken assumptions and attitudes to the User held by those who design and develop those programs. But the term has an even greater currency outside software-production environments, where it tends to be cavalierly bandied about by marketing folk. In fact, although the term user-friendly was coined by programmers as a disparaging reference to User ineptitude, it was the hardware and software marketers who, having failed to "catch on to its negative implications," appropriated the term and then popularized it by using, or overusing, it as a buzzword to convince potential buyers "that their company's products were easier to use than they really were."[6]

Friendliness thus emerged as the digital mantra of the 1980s: as the PC market underwent rapid expansion thanks to the new, purportedly easy-to-use interfaces, the term *user-friendly* became common currency. It seemed to roll effortlessly off the tongues of salespeople and marketers, who used it in order to claim distinction for their hardware and software products and to seduce potential users with images of empowerment and accessibility. The computer, we were assured, was more than a tool: it was a *friend*. Precisely what that meant was left up to the imagination of the consumer. After all, as Robert Anderson and Norman Shapiro point out in their attempt to come to terms with the meaning of *user-friendly*, friendship itself is an elusive concept. Does user-friendly imply friendship in the sense of a long-standing intimacy (the computer knows everything about you and adapts to your needs and preferences) or a casual familiarity (the computer "likes" you on first acquaintance and is eager to make you happy)?[7] Since it can mean anything at all, the term also means nothing; thus, being greeted by the picture of a smiling computer on the screen when the Macintosh boots up can be taken as sufficient evidence of an ambiguous "user-friendliness."

The origins of the term therefore suggest not only that the implied "friendliness" is a misnomer but also that whatever it connotes is directed not at the User but at a very different entity: the consumer. Thus, while it plays liberally with the mythos of individual autonomy and empowerment, user-friendliness has less to do with helping users fulfil existing needs than with *creating* needs, and thus creating consumers, in accordance with technological and economic imperatives. Indeed, this conclusion applies to the high-tech industry as a whole, which, with its creeping featurism, continual upgrades, and proclivity to market "vaporware" (software that is not really ready to be distributed and used) seems more and more, as Paulina Borsook puts it, "like an industry that creates consumer demand rather than serves it."[8] Dan Weisberg concurs that computers "are primarily created to be purchased, and secondarily and often only coincidentally to make us smarter. . . . Products that make us smarter but aren't profitable disappear, while those that make the buyer stupider and the seller's bottom line blacker thrive."[9]

The computer user, then, is first called into being as a *consumer* of hardware and software, someone who is drawn to the computer not because it is a tool that offers efficient ways to accomplish instrumental ends—though he or she may very well justify the computer's allure in these utilitarian terms—but for reasons of pure desire. The purpose of this chapter is to examine some of the discourses and transactions that invoke the consumer and the role that these play in the social construction of the User.

Consuming Ourselves

Presented with a newspaper advertisement for coffee or cough medicine from a century or two ago, the contemporary consumer might be surprised to see merely a few paragraphs of unadorned text, a simple itemization of the reasons the product is worth purchasing. For instance, a 1791 ad for Freake's Tincture of Bark begins with a list of reasons why the tincture is "far more efficacious than other preparations," and then offers as "a proof of its superior efficacy" a public testimony from a Mrs. Hollinworth, age 68, who "thinks it her duty" to proclaim Freake's healing properties.[10]

In the centuries since Mrs. Hollinworth was purportedly restored to health by Freake's Tincture of Bark, the world of advertising (not to mention medicine) has undergone some significant changes. Most noticeably, the balance between text and image in magazine and newspaper advertisements (and, indeed, in our culture as a whole) has shifted profoundly. Efforts to marshal an intellectual appeal to the rational consumer have given way to the use of carefully crafted images and a minimum of text in order to elicit a visceral rather than intellectual response. Thus, rather than reading Mrs. Hollinworth's endorsement, it is far more likely that today we would be treated to an image of a happy, attractive, healthy-looking older woman dancing with her husband or playing tennis. In this way, contemporary advertisements seek to sell commodities not through an appeal to reason but, more often, through the manufacture of desire.

It is important to understand, however, that most ads do not work by simply creating, as one might expect, a longing for the product being sold—whether it is a deodorant, a sports-utility vehicle, or a laptop computer. Rather, the desire that advertisements construct is narcissistic. As Judith Williamson explains in *Decoding Advertisements*, ads function by establishing a connection between certain products and certain kinds of people: "Advertisements are selling us something else besides consumer goods: in providing us with a structure in which we, and those goods, are interchangeable, they are selling us ourselves."[11] Heather Menzies agrees that, essentially, what we consume is not so much products as the "image of ourselves" which ads offer.[12]

Advertisements, in other words, are not designed to sell a product directly; rather, they function by creating an identity and attaching that identity to their product. The ad, for instance, that associates a particular brand of soft drink with youth and vibrant energy, or the ad that associates a specific chewing gum with an active, happy love life, succeeds insofar as it manages to "attach the desired identity to a specific commodity, so that the need for an identity is transformed into a need for the commodity."[13] Indeed, since the products themselves are generally not necessities (before, that is, the ads convince us that they are), and are often not very different from competitors' products, their commercial success or failure depends largely upon the extent to which marketers are able to tap into the psyche of the buying public and to associate their particular product with an identity that has mass appeal.

When it comes to computers, then, purchasing a particular digital product means "buying into" that company's image of who the User is, accepting the identity that an advertisement or marketing campaign confers. As Weisberg observes in his critique of advertisements for high-tech products, "in technology ads, as in all ads, the value of the product equals the values of the viewing audience. In other words, advertisers show us exactly what they think we want to see, not just in the product, but in ourselves."[14]

What do hardware and software vendors think that we want to see in ourselves? The answer, of course, varies from advertisement to advertisement, each of which is carefully crafted to sell a particular aspect of self to a particular audience. Beyond that, however, it is possible to make a few generalizations, since the answer also seems to depend very much upon whether we are talking about ads for Windows-based computers or for the Apple Macintosh. As we might expect, the historic dichotomy between these two computing camps, which I introduced in chapter 2, carries over into the world of marketing, where they tend to employ very different advertising strategies that function to create desire and, ultimately, to construct the consuming User in seemingly contradictory ways.

First, then, there are the advertising strategies typically used to promote IBM and other Windows-based machines: True to their historical provenance, these computers are most often marketed as business—or, in today's jargon, *e-business*—tools, designed to meet the needs of dynamic enterprises in our fast-paced, high-tech world. Found in the kinds of magazines and newspapers high-powered executives might peruse, the advertisements tend to follow a presentation formula that features the image of an empowered businessperson or entrepreneur. For instance, an advertisement for the IBM ThinkPad depicts a woman standing in what we assume, from her confident stance, to be her own framing shop (see fig. 5). The ornate gold frames hanging on the wall behind her evoke a traditional world of high culture and gentility; yet, beneath the frames, both inconspicuous and unavoidable in its place on an antique desk, sits an open ThinkPad.

Similarly, a Compaq advertisement depicts a woman standing in her office (see fig. 6). Again, a computer sits on a nearby desk, its presence there both emphasized and de-emphasized by the fact that, because the camera lens is directed at the woman, the computer is slightly out of focus.

In both advertisements, the presence of the computer is deliberately downplayed (although in such a way as to paradoxically draw attention to it) while the computer user is constructed as the object of interest and desire. Both also offer images of empowered, confident businesspeople (significantly, in both cases, business*women*, reflecting, perhaps, the changing demographics of the corporate world), each standing in her place of work. These women are not supermodels; indeed, they are clearly meant to look like "real" people in their thirties or forties—trim, well-dressed, and immaculately groomed, yet, for

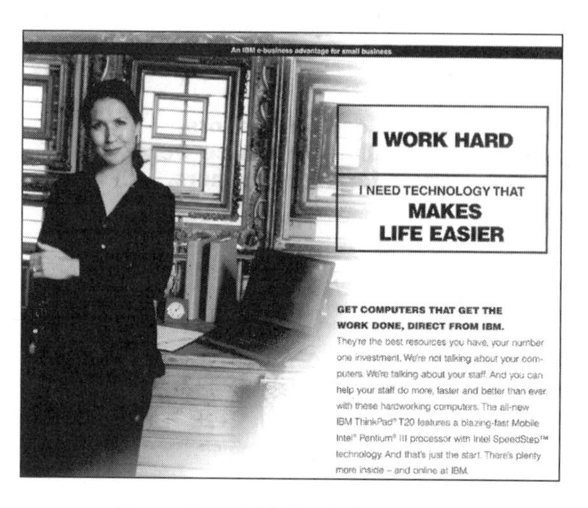

FIGURE 5: *IBM ThinkPad advertisement*

FIGURE 6: *Compaq advertisement*

all that, very ordinary. Nevertheless, they are objects of desire because, gazing at them, we are meant to aspire to be what they are: confident, happy, attractive, and successful. And, if all goes as planned by the marketing folk, this desire for an empowered identity will transfer itself to computers and specifically to the brand of computer being advertised, which will thereby become perceived as a need.

A second common feature of many ads for Windows-based computers is that the text accompanying such images of empowered users shifts from first to second person. "I work hard," reads the IBM ad. "I need technology that makes life easier." The smaller text that follows foregoes the use of first person to address the reader directly: "your staff," "your data," and so forth. The Compaq advertisement follows precisely the same formula: the large text, once again, is in the first person ("I run my office. My office doesn't run me"), with the smaller text beneath it in the second person ("You got where you are by working smart. . . .").

Invoking philosopher Louis Althusser, Judith Williamson observes that grammatical shifts of this kind "hail" readers, pull them into the ad and compel them each, as individuals, to become its subject,[15] in much the same way as people walking down the street might all turn their heads in response to the exclamation: "Hey, you!" Furthermore, having accepted that persona, readers also accede to being constructed as individuals whose primary concern is efficiency and enhanced productivity. Thus, the IBM ad assumes that the reader's primary concern is to "help your staff do more, faster and better than ever, with these hardworking computers." The same advertisement also includes the following phrases: "work fast, work smart"; "improved productivity"; "high performance anywhere the day takes you"; "empower your employees"; "packed with power and essential business productivity software"; and "give your employees the tools they need to get the job done." Similarly, Compaq markets its technology as the means to "help grow your business" as a result of an implied increase in worker productivity: "Want to revise a spreadsheet in a taxi? Go for it." The purpose of this textual emphasis upon productivity and business efficiencies is clearly less to make a claim regarding the inherent qualities of the computer being advertised than it is to tell a story about who the reader is or should strive to be: precisely the kind of person (efficiency-oriented, bottom-line-minded) who will purchase an IBM or Compaq computer.

Finally, both the IBM and Compaq advertisements are typical of ads for Windows-based machines in that they also offer, beneath the larger image or on another page, small pictures of the particular digital devices being marketed, each accompanied by price and other details. In the case of the IBM ad, the reader is invited to "Look inside" for more information. Obediently lifting the flap of the adjoining page reveals a two-page spread offering small, exceedingly non-descript images of IBM computers, with accompanying prices and details on RAM, processing speed, monitor size, and so forth. Similarly, the Compaq ad provides icon-sized pictures of its machines, each accompanied by the kind of bottom-line information that businesspeople need in order to make and justify purchases: speed, memory, and other factors represented numerically, as absolutes that can be easily compared and plugged into spreadsheets. The highly technical, code-like form in which this information is offered (500MHZ, 64MB SDRAM, 6GB HDD, 6x–2x DVD-ROM, and so forth) will have very little concrete meaning for most readers; for many, it will be nothing more than technobabble. Nevertheless, it is provided as evidence of full disclosure, the suggestion being that, as someone who is as successful and knowledgeable as the businessperson pictured in the advertisement, the reader must not only find such data comprehensible but must also consider it entirely sufficient as the basis for an informed decision to purchase. In this way, such advertisements function not only to construct the computer User as someone who is concerned primarily with efficiency and the bottom line, but also to subtly train those who read the ad in the proper way to consume computers.

Anyone so trained will doubtless tend to regard advertisements for the Macintosh as distinctly frivolous and unhelpful, since Apple's marketing strategy is quite different from that which prevails in the Windowed world. While ads for IBM, Compaq, and other "business machines" tout corporate efficiencies and offer bottom-line information, Apple's ads represent a deliberate rejection of the values of the corporate world (of which, of course, it is a member). For one thing, Apple's advertisements rarely appear in the kinds of magazines and newspapers to which high-powered executives might subscribe. Rather, its marketing strategy involves an emphasis on the creation of eye-catching, artsy billboards, bus signs, and posters. (Many of the latter can only be had for a price—may, indeed, sell for hundreds of dollars on e-Bay. Thus, Mac zealots who use these ads to decorate their office walls must pay for the right to promote their computer of choice.) And whereas ads for Windows-based machines emphasize business efficiencies and the presentation of bald, unadorned data, Macintosh ads are designed to subtly provoke us to consider the purported appeal to the rational user as manipulative and dishonest. The Mac ad seeks to disarm by its deliberate rejection of the subliminal in

FIGURE 7: *Apple's "Yum" poster: Scintillating the senses.*

favour of what we are meant to regard as an unabashed, refreshingly honest scintillation of the senses.

The "Yum" poster offers a classic example of the kind of sensory appeal for which Apple strives in marketing the Mac (see fig. 7). Juxtaposed against a white background, the circle of iMacs in five tempting colours (or flavours, since the colour names are blueberry, strawberry, tangerine, grape, and lime) offers a rich feast for the senses. The brightly coloured computers are clearly not meant to be regarded as tools to promote efficiencies. In fact, since we view them from above, all traces of utility (the screens, the keyboards, the mouses) are invisible. All we see is eye candy: five colourful shapes, sensory stimuli that appeal viscerally to our senses of sight and, as invoked in the single-word caption ("Yum"), taste. That caption speaks briefly but irresistibly to the fact that these computers are being unapologetically offered as objects of pure desire. Hence the fact that the poster offers no information about the computer's processing speed, hard drive capacity—not even its price. The advertisement deliberately shifts the consumer's focus from the interior and from factors such as memory and speed to the exterior and the realm of digital aesthetics.[16]

Macintosh ads also flout the values of the corporate world by consistently presenting the Mac as the centre of attention rather than as a socially embedded artifact. Whereas advertisements for Windows-based computers tend to feature, as we have seen, an image of the computer in a place of work, many advertisements for the Mac follow the pattern of the "Yum" poster in that they consist of two elements presented against a plain white background: a picture of a computer (or computers) and, beneath the image, a clever pithy caption ("I think, therefore iMac"; "Chic. Not geek") in a bold font. Indeed, not only do such ads present the iMac, iBook, or other Apple product in isolation from its contexts of use, they also present the computer in isolation from images of people with whom we might be expected to identify.

While the point of such advertisements would therefore seem to be to invoke desire for the product directly, they in fact function, like the ads for Windows-based computers, to associate Macintosh computers with a particular, implied identity. That identity is not the number-crunching executive, but, quite the contrary, someone who rejects that lifestyle and ideology: a free spirit, as unique as the colourful computers, who lives in touch with his or her senses and emotions, who has the wisdom and confidence to ascribe importance to non-quantifiable aspects of human existence, and who, as one of the most recent Apple slogans would have it, is able to "think different," to think outside the stultifying box of corporate culture and to imagine alternative possibilities for life and, of course, computer use. Ultimately, the paradox of Macintosh ads that depict only the computer and no human forms whatsoever is that the message they seek to convey is an alignment between the Mac and a more human-centric computing experience than, the ads would have us believe, is available to users of Windows-based machines.

Of course, magazine ads for computers are in a constant state of flux. Compaq, for instance, is beginning to shift its emphasis to the realm of digital aesthetics, with the result that some of its ads are becoming, like the Windows interface itself, more "Mac-like." A recent advertising campaign for the Compaq Presario, for example, emphasizes the machine's appearance more than its capabilities: "Black stands out. Its black, elegant styling complements its bold attitude." And an ad for the Compaq Armada M notebook computer tells us that "As for style, it'll give your Armani suit a run for its money."

However, two elements remain consistent in the ads, regardless of the kind of computer they are promoting and the strategy used. First, as we have seen, computer ads consistently seek to address the consumer as an *individual*, for it is only as individuals that we can receive and buy into the identities constructed for us by these mass-advertising campaigns. Ads for Macs thus associate the uniqueness of their product with the free spirit and liberated intellect of the individual consumer, while ads for Windows-based computers hail the individual consumer as "you." According to Judith Williamson,

> The "you" in ads is always transmitted plural, but we receive it as singular. Although the aim is to connect a mass of people with a product, to identify them with it as a group, this can only be achieved by connecting them with the product as individuals, one by one.[17]

Second, both computer camps seek, by means of the advertisements, to associate their products with the identity of a *smart* user, someone who knows his or her mind and is able to make the "right" computer purchase. In the Windows world, being smart implies being technologically savvy, knowing about the internal functions of the computer and being able to speak with acronymistic authority about RAM and ROM, processing speeds, and screen resolutions. As Sherry Turkle puts it, "Becoming fluent in this language, participating in this world, is part of what people are buying" when they purchase a Windows-based computer.[18] In the Apple world, conversely, being smart means rejecting that language, because, far from being anally fixated on such quantifiable data, the liberated, free-thinking Mac user recognizes it as nothing more than technobafflegab that is used to create desire through a psuedo-appeal to the reader's rationality. Although *smart* is thus defined very differently, its significance is identical. In both cases, smartness implies an identity which associates so profoundly with the values represented by the computer platform in question—either Mac or Windows-based—that the possibility of purchase outside that computing camp becomes more or less out of the question. Thus, an appeal to the consumer's "smartness" is one way of ensuring the consumer's "loyalty" to a particular product.

Downgrading the User

Advertisements, then, play a significant role in invoking consumers' desire for computers and, more specifically, for the confident, technologically savvy identity that their use confers. But the desirous consumer is also the positive product of fear and apprehension about the possibility of *not* achieving that enviable identity—of, in fact, becoming obsolete and socially irrelevant. After all, people who stubbornly refuse to use computers are often dismissed as "dinosaurs," doomed to extinction.

The result, as we saw in chapter 1, is that we purchase computers in order to ward off the threat of social obsolescence and to appear "smart." This is, however, only a temporary measure, since the computers themselves seem to obsolesce before our eyes, becoming passé before they even leave the store: "Computer technology grows faster than fly specks on a clean windshield, and your computer will be out of date the moment you purchase it."[19] True to the dictates of Moore's

Law, computer processing speed continues to double every two years or less, thereby rendering otherwise fully functioning systems obsolete. Upgrades are inevitably necessary: new operating systems, new software, and, ultimately, new computers and peripherals to replace systems that function perfectly but are no longer socially sanctioned as evidence of technological competence. (You only own a 386? You don't own a Palm Pilot? How can you expect to participate in the world or to be taken seriously?)

The continual release of new, cutting-edge computers and improved versions of software therefore has more to do with fashion than function. Indeed, Apple's new emphasis on machine aesthetics must also be understood in large part as a clever means of obsolescing its hardware even faster, since, having shed the non-descript beige that they wore for so many years, Macs will now, like clothing, begin to *look* out of date—perhaps even before their hard-drive capacities and processing speeds are perceived as inadequate.

In this way, the user becomes trapped, through a fear of personal obsolescence, within a revolving door that compels ceaseless consumption, each purchase of hardware or software reaffirming his or her identity as someone who is truly participant in the information society: "One decision—to use a computer for word processing, for instance—leads inexorably to further expenditures and upgrades, each transformation prefigured in the nexus of digital discourse as an 'improvement.'"[20] Consumption, in its original sense of "using up" manufactured goods, becomes ironically transmuted, in this age of ceaseless upgrades, into a never-ending process of self-melioration.

The rise of the Internet has exacerbated this situation. The initial fear of being left in the dust of the information highway compelled many of us to go out and purchase modems, new operating systems, and finally, new computers. And now that we are all connected, the rate at which our hardware and software obsolesces has actually accelerated, since computers that function satisfactorily as stand-alone entities may be unable to "communicate" with other, more sophisticated machines. Recently, for instance, I reluctantly consigned my twelve-year-old Macintosh SE to the closet—not because this little workhorse was slowing down or because it no longer met my word-processing needs, but because it was not capable of participating within the computing network within which I was increasingly pressed, both personally and professionally, to engage. And having purchased a new iMac, I am compelled to keep upgrading my e-mail software, Internet browser, and operating system. As Mark Poster observes,

> [T]he Internet promotes its own use, and a sordid relation of codependence entwines the user in endless upgrades. New versions of operating systems require more memory and more hardware purchases. New hardware purchases come with new versions of programs that require the consumer to buy updates for other programs. A self-perpetuating cycle of purchases and time-consuming installation procedures absorbs the potential Net user in coerced, time-consuming computer fiddling.[21]

In this way, we become entangled within a "technological web"[22] of continual so-called improvements that are offered, and purchased, in the name of making computing "better"—of boosting the efficacy of the computer as a "tool" for writing, business, learning, and so forth. But if the merits of Version 3.0 over Version 2.0 often seem indiscernible, it is because what we are really purchasing when we buy hardware and software upgrades is a renewed sense of belonging and a confidence, however short-lived, in our right and our ability to participate within an increasingly technological social order. And what is peddled by Microsoft and other high-tech companies—which, let it be understood, make most of their profits on upgrades—is not so much hardware and software but information anxiety: the fear of being left behind.[23] The effusions of technophiles train us to rationalize our entrapment in terms of personal empowerment and autonomy, but upgrading is really all about a never-ending struggle to ward off social obsolescence.

Upgrades thus function not only as "the lifeblood of the information industry"[24] but also as a primary means by which the User is constructed as someone who is, of necessity, also a consumer. The User-consumer not only purchases digital devices, but also buys into the view that one can only sustain the social cachet and "smartness" associated with being a computer user by continually spending money to replace fully functional systems with "better" versions.

Paradoxically, this continual cycle of self-improvement subtly downgrades us. It dumbs us down by making it impossible for any individual, even the most seasoned computer user, to remain up to date. Just when you have mastered one version of Windows, along comes another much-hyped release with all kinds of new protocols and features that make you feel like a "newbie" again. And just when the quirks of the new operating system have become familiar—just when you have upgraded your own skills to accord with the capabilities of the new system—along comes something else: you've got to master a new e-mail system, learn how to design Web pages, figure out how to put your agenda on-line, in order to maintain your social and professional cachet. In this way, we are pumped up as consumers even as we are maintained in an inescapable state of User incompetence. We are, in short, compelled to pay for the privilege of being continually put in our place.

Moore's Law, then, should be understood not simply as a prediction about the steady doubling of computing power every two years but also as a means of constructing the computer user as, to borrow from Louis Althusser, "always-already" a consumer. Of course, although it is labelled a "law," and is considered by technophiles to be as accurate and objective a description of reality as, say, the law of gravity, Moore's principle of computing power began life as nothing more than a prophecy. That prophecy, however, became self-fulfilling. Certainly, as a co-founder of Intel Corporation, Gordon Moore was in a position to ensure that his prediction operated with the force of law within the high-tech industry. But Moore's prophecy could not have been transmuted into an unquestioned law without a consumer base ready to capitulate to the myth of obsolescence—that is, quite willing to view hardware and software that functioned as intended, and precisely as it had at the time of purchase, as insufficient and in need of replacement.

Can we break out of this self-perpetuating cycle of upgrades? There is some evidence that users may be seeking to do just that. In July 2001, a *Globe and Mail* article offered the startling news that the "worldwide market for personal computers contracted for the first time ever in the second quarter—and may continue to shrink the rest of this year—as the global economy softens and major markets hit the saturation point."[25] This first-ever decline in computer sales, followed by a continued decline in the PC industry's profits, suggests a growing resistance to the pressure to upgrade, and the emergence of a new principle of "good-enough" computing that stands in direct opposition to the pressures of Moore's Law.

However, much as I deplore prophecy, I will offer a prediction of my own: the coming of an exciting new development, probably from Microsoft, which obsolesces all existing systems and effectively disarms all consumer resistance to upgrading. Such a development is absolutely necessary because, unlike other goods—be it cars, televisions, dishes, shoes, light bulbs, batteries, and most of the things they power—computers don't tend to wear out very quickly. Wal-Mart profits because, as obedient members of a capitalist society, we blithely accept both our "duty to consume" and the manufacturer's concomitant duty to produce "products weak enough and shoddy enough . . . to lend themselves to rapid replacement."[26] But the computer industry succeeds only to the extent that it traps us within a revolving door whereby we are compelled to replace fully functional systems and components as a means of reaffirming, through continual hardware and software upgrades, our identity as individuals who are truly participant in the information society. As Jacques Ellul puts it in *The Technological Bluff*, technology "can continue its triumphant march only if the public follows, buying the maximum number of computers, tape recorders, videos, photocopiers, high-definition televisions, microwaves, and compact disks. For every new technical advance there has to be a public that is ready to buy the latest product."[27] And, moreover, willing to believe that it is the "smart" thing to do.

The Shopper's Network

Earlier in this chapter, I said that *before we are computer users we are consumers*. Clearly, that statement now requires some elaboration, since it is not accurate to suggest that there is a temporal distinction between the two identities, that we go in the door of the computer store as one thing and emerge sometime later as another. Indeed, some users may never actually enter a computer store but will use hardware and software purchased for use at their place of work. Nevertheless, to those who market digital products, we are all potential consumers before we are users in that the former identity takes precedence over the latter, and the hardware and software marketing strategies that stroke and woo us are cleverly designed to maintain us in that consuming state of mind.

Moreover, if technology advertisements and the ceaseless production of hardware and software upgrades provide the impetus for the merging of the identities of the User and the consumer, then that union is fully realized with the advent of the Internet. This assertion, of course, is contrary to the claims of some techno-enthusiasts that the rise of the Net is actually rendering the consumer, as a social category, obsolete. Alvin Toffler, in particular, contends that information networks are fusing producers and consumers into what he calls *prosumers*, individuals who "[contribute] not just money but market and design information vital for the production process" and who may even, someday, "also push buttons that activate remote production processes."[28] Mark Poster shares Toffler's enthusiastic view of the Internet as a postmodern force which blurs the boundaries between those who create and those who consume goods:

> Information technologies place into the hands of the consumer the capacity to become a producer of cultural objects. The line dividing the two functions increasingly is blurred. . . . The Internet also offers the consumer such a vast domain of information for easy and cheap reproduction that one no longer thinks of Web surfers as consumers.[29]

Such glowing accounts of consumer empowerment are not, however, born out by actual on-line experiences. In fact, *prosumers* are figures of myth; they do not exist in the real world of technology because, as I suggest throughout this book, the identity of the computer User emerges through the struggles of various individuals and interest groups to stake their claims to computer power. Those who currently produce information will not readily relinquish their exclusive right to do so. More importantly, however, the commercial interests which have seized control of information networks (and of many information producers) do not appear to be particularly enamoured of Toffler's model of the actively involved prosumer. (Consider the fate of Napster, the Web site which promoted and facilitated the sharing of music files between users. In 2000, as Napster's popularity skyrocketed, the recording industry mobilized to shut it down under charges of piracy and illicit trade in on-line music.) These powerful commercial interests are now reconfiguring both the function and form of the Internet "from a network for the exchange of information to a marketing platform"[30]—one in which the increasing prevalence of ever-helpful shopping agents or "bots," programs that go out and search the Web for deals, further reduces the user to a passive consumer rather than someone who is actively involved in creating the on-line world. In other words, rhetoric aside, commercial interests are not constructing a virtual realm that encourages users to make meaningful contributions to the content and culture of the Net but one that structures, controls, and limits consumer behaviour.

Thus, despite the hype about the ease with which on-line individuals can now become both producers and consumers of culture, the reality is that the Internet has developed into little more than a vast cybermall. Even enthusiast Douglas Rushkoff is forced to admit that the "Internet's original promise as a medium for communication is fast giving way to an electronic strip mall that will trade the technology's potential as a cultural catalyst for a controlled and monitored marketplace."[31] Increasingly, moreover, going on-line resembles nothing so much as window (or Windows) shopping: browsing, selecting from existing options, and submitting one's credit-card number at the appropriate time. This is true regardless of whether or not one is actually making a purchase. As the Net becomes the virtual site for more and more commercial transactions, other on-line activities, such as communicating, learning, and researching, are increasingly required to conform to a commercial model of interaction in which, writes Howard Besser, "most people will be relegated to the role of information consumer."[32]

Hence, what we are witnessing is not the much-heralded dawn of Toffler's *prosumer* but the emergence of a less widely recognized entity: the *User-consumer*. The User-consumer is, in fact, a central character in Bill Gates's manic vision of a Microsoft-centred world, in which not only is every purchase transacted on-line but also every on-line transaction has the potential to lead to a purchase:

> If you are watching the movie *Top Gun* and think Tom Cruise's aviator sunglasses look really cool, you'll be able to pause the movie and learn about the glasses or even buy them on the spot. . . . If a movie has been filmed in a resort hotel, you'll be able to find out where it's located, check room rates, and make reservations. If the movie's star carries a handsome leather briefcase or handbag. . . .[33]

You get the idea.

The Customer is Always Right

Having established, then, that the identity of the computer User is closely and unavoidably allied with that of the consumer, it is necessary to conclude this chapter by seeking a more precise understanding of what a consumer is. I have already suggested that consumption is not merely a matter of purchasing goods but of regarding those goods as objects of desire. In *Keywords*, Raymond Williams points to another important element of the meaning of *consumer*. Williams notes that the term must be understood as conveying something quite different from *customer*: the latter word implies "some degree of regular and continuing relationship to a supplier, whereas *consumer* indicates the more abstract figure in an abstract market."[34] In other words, while a customer is a well-known individual, a consumer is an abstract, faceless entity who is enticed to purchase mass-produced goods through mass-marketing strategies.

To clarify this distinction, let me compare my own book-buying experiences with those of Helene Hanff. Hanff was perhaps the ultimate customer: a resident of New York, she routinely purchased books from Marks & Co., a London bookseller, for twenty years, from 1949 to 1969. Her correspondence with Frank Doel and other Marks employees is documented in *84, Charing Cross Road*. I, on the other hand, have been for the past few years a sporadic and somewhat reluctant user of Amazon.com's on-line book distribution services. There are several notable similarities between our book-buying experiences. First, none of our transactions are face to face (despite an often-expressed wish to meet her correspondents, Hanff did not actually make the trip to London during the period in which she purchased books from Marks & Co.). Second, the vendor often attempts to anticipate our needs—although Marks & Co. employees were much more successful in this regard than Amazon.com's shopping bot, which greets me by name and offers personal recommendations based on my previous purchases: "Hello, Ellen Rose. We have recommendations for you. If you are not Ellen Rose, click here." Finally, both Hanff and I buy our books from a remote source for similar reasons: namely, convenience and selection. As Hanff explains:

> Why should I run all the way down to 17th St. to buy dirty, badly made books when I can buy clean, beautiful ones from you without leaving the typewriter? From where I sit, London's a lot closer than 17th Street.[35]

Here, however, the similarity ends; for whereas Hanff was a customer, I will never be, to Amazon.com, anything more than a consumer, a node—albeit a necessary node—in a "single integrated loop"[36] of commerce and profitability. On-line, I am continually reminded that I am there not to be served as an individual by an individual but to serve the needs of this particular e-business, and of the market as a whole. The Amazon.com Web site is carefully structured to control and limit the kinds of information that I can provide: essentially, either word-limited reviews of books, item ratings (on a five-point scale, from "Don't like it" to "I love it"), or, of course, credit-card numbers. Moreover, any information that I choose to enter will immediately become data that will enable Amazon.com's shopping bot to further target the screen presentation to my particular needs and interests. This blatantly superficial form of technology-enabled "personalization" is really just another "arm of mass marketing—little more than an additional inducement to buy."[37] Similarly, despite the hype surrounding the new use of customer relationship management (CRM) software, which is designed to help vendors attract and retain highly valued customers, this so-called revolutionary development that moves away from mass-marketing techniques is merely another way to ensnare and control as many faceless *consumers* as possible.

The old adage that "the customer is always right," a legacy of the days of owner-operated neighbourhood businesses, conveyed a sense of individual choice. There was a keen awareness, among vendors, that an individual could decide, based on lack of service, selection, or price, not to shop at a particular establishment, or not to make a purchase at all. Much has been made of the power of the consumer, but in an era of supposedly unlimited and hitherto unknown choice, the computer consumer is increasingly being deprived of the ability to make the most basic choice of all: to step outside of that limiting subject position. The onslaught of advertisements, of hardware and software upgrades, and, finally, the rise of the Internet and on-line shopping have intensified the process of commodification and created a situation in which we are increasingly powerless to escape our entrapment within what Baudrillard calls "the collective ritual of consumption."[38] It is precisely this powerlessness that defines us not as customers but as consumers: the customer is always right, but the consumer, quite simply, always *is*.

The difficulty of opting out of this subject position is brilliantly parodied in a mock high-tech ad that appeared in *The New Yorker* magazine. The ad is for the KL-1000, an amazing new device which, though "no larger than a domestic olive," is able to perform "all the photographic, data-processing, and information-retrieval functions you yourself do—automatically." The hyped description of the KL-1000's capabilities concludes by informing the powerless User-consumer that "A device of state-of-the-art convenience, the KL-1000 has already projected your technological needs and, with funds transferred from your checking or savings account, has purchased itself. It has already expedited its own delivery."[39]

Some individuals resist entrapment within the subject position of User-consumer by simply refusing to purchase and use high-tech devices. However, as I have already suggested, and as the ad for the KL-1000 also suggests, it is no longer practical nor, indeed, possible for most of us to opt out of computer culture. Therefore, responsible action, in this context, does not involve refusing to make purchases but taking small actions by which we reassert our status as customers rather than as a faceless mass of User-consumers. Of course, that is not to suggest that we should not take time to consider whether we truly need that turbo-charged computer, that scanner, that Palm Pilot, cell-phone, or what have you; but then, having decided that we must own and use the item in question, responsible action involves, for example, purchasing from a dealer with whom it is possible to communicate face to face, as one human being to another, rather than as faceless entities caught in a data stream. Such dealers still exist in most communities; however, as we increasingly accept the role of User-consumer, we also become more inclined to purchase computers, peripherals, and other high-tech devices via those devices themselves, from large, remote dealers who are able to offer variety and significant cost savings. The local dealers are finding it increasingly difficult to compete in a culture—a *consumer* culture—that emphasizes initial cost savings over personal customer service.

Writing in 1976, Raymond Williams observed that "to say *user* rather than *consumer* is still to express a relevant distinction."[40] Over a quarter of a century later, as we are increasingly pressured both to purchase high technology for use and to use high technology to make purchases, it may be less meaningful to distinguish between these two subject positions than to acknowledge their amalgamation in the single identity of the emergent, socially produced User-consumer whose technological desire sets in motion an endless cycle of self-consumption. It would be overly optimistic to expect that cycle to be broken by responsible action on the part of users, but perhaps we may hope that, over time, the cumulative effect of many small acts will be to slow the cycle, thereby resolving the blur of ceaseless consumption into something visible.

5

User Documentation: Telling Stories about the User

In the parlance of those who work in the field of software and hardware production, the reference and instructional manuals that accompany a program or a computer are known as *user documentation*. The term itself, as Theodore Roszak points out, is "a sign of technical mystification"[1]—indeed, rather paradoxically, precisely that kind of mystification that the documentation itself is meant to help dispel for the user.

Apart from its complexity, however, the term is worth considering because of its grammatical ambiguity. User documentation purportedly refers to printed material provided *for* the computer user, but this meaning is somewhat muddled by the fact that other similar constructions are generally used in such a way that the first word is the object of the second—as in *road construction* (construction of roads), *water purification* (purification of water), *meal preparation* (preparation of meals), and *interior decoration* (decoration of interiors). This established grammatical pattern would seem to dictate that manuals be referred to as *software documentation* (documentation of software) or *computer documentation,* and that the term *user documentation* be used to refer to something quite different: written materials, such as this book, in which the subject is not the software itself but the software user.

But, like many grammatical ambiguities, this one is revealing. For user documentation does indeed function as precisely what its grammatical structure suggests it is: a story about the User, which it is the purpose of this chapter to explore.

From Bad Manuals to the Documentation Set

When user documentation first emerged upon the scene, however, it told a story in which the User figured only marginally, if at all, and the protagonist was the software program itself. The term *documentation* harks back to the era, described in chapter 2, when the computer was a large, mysterious device that was carefully tended and guarded by white-coated initiates, its only users. *Documentation* in those days referred primarily to technical explanations of a machine's or a program's features and functions which one programmer wrote for other programmers who might use or modify the hardware or software. Many of these explanations were (and still are) actually embedded in the code itself. And as long as only the data priests used the programs, these terse, highly technical explanations sufficed.

As the personal computer proliferated in the early 1980s, however, hardware and software companies began to pay heed to users' demands for less technical instructions that would help them understand how to use complex systems. It was perhaps inevitable that the task of writing the newly required user documentation would fall to those who were already documenting system functions and who, moreover, knew the systems best: the technicians and programmers themselves. These individuals, needless to say, were less than thrilled with the new task. They tended to view user documentation "as a necessary evil that must be created for the 'idiots' who cannot figure out the system through their previous knowledge or trial and error."[2]

As a result, the first user manuals that appeared in the late 1970s and early 1980s were last-minute productions dashed off by programmers who were accustomed to simply elaborating the inner workings of their programs and who had little interest in helping or understanding the needs of the befuddled user. Hence, users had to cope with manuals that contained numerous errors and such unhelpful instructions as: "The function of this key should be obvious"[3] and "Restore operates like its name implies."[4] This kind of non-instruction was not merely the result of a condescending attitude towards the unknowing User: to the creators of a program, its functions were obvious, and only a simpleton required the assistance of a manual to understand how to use what was clearly a masterful piece of coding. The manuals written up to and during the early 1980s were therefore notoriously unhelpful, and many a computer languished in the basement alongside dusty exercise bikes and cast-off clothing because, as John Barry writes in *Technobabble*, the owners "could not understand the documentation."[5]

Rather than making the technology more accessible and understandable, then, much early user documentation merely tended to muddy the waters even more. Writing in 1984, Craig Brad observed in *Technostress* that most computer manuals are "impenetrable" and "full of technical instructions that sometimes seem designed primarily to drive people crazy."[6] And because the manuals were system-centred and written in a language that actually excluded users—through unexplained references to variables and functions, buffers and compilers, executables and I/O errors—they not only failed to effectively bridge the gap between the two knowledge communities but instead exacerbated it. Now, User ineptitude was revealed not only by an inability to use the technology but, even worse, by an inability to make sense of the supposedly clear and helpful instructions that accompanied the system.

Given their failure to provide the necessary instructions in an understandable language and format, software and hardware manuals became a last resort in the minds of many users, something to be turned to only when trial and error, human assistance, and all other options had been exhausted. In short, the credo of the computer user became: *When all else fails, read the instructions*. Those few users who were able to make sense of the documentation emerged as "power users" or "gurus," individuals who were regarded by their friends and colleagues as experts on the use of a particular system. Thus, among users, the hallmark of expertise became not so much an ability to use a system, per se, as an ability to comprehend the user documentation and use it to find solutions to specific problems.[7] Accordingly, a guide to PC use describes the "true guru" as someone who may not immediately know the answer to a program problem but who is able to "sift through the manuals and discover it quickly."[8]

If a guru was not available to provide assistance, users seemed to be more inclined to place a call to technical support than to consult the documentation themselves. Paradoxically, the growing realization that users often did not even bother to consult the manuals did nothing to diminish software and hardware developers' disdain. User demands for manuals may have merited the scorn of programmers, but users' notorious reluctance to use the documentation was perceived by technical folk not as a sign that the manuals were lacking but rather as further evidence of User ineptitude—the kind of mindlessness that prompted a user to pick up the phone to talk to a technical support person (source of many of the dumb-user stories cited in chapter 3) when the question was answered in the manual, as any intelligent person could surely see. It's hard to miss the undertone of irritation lurking in the following quote from *The New Hacker's Dictionary*:

> It is true that users ask questions (of necessity). Sometimes they are thoughtful or deep. Very often they are annoying or downright stupid, apparently because the user failed to think for two seconds or look in the documentation before bothering the maintainer.[9]

It would seem that, rather than freeing programmers from the necessity of dealing with users, the manuals actually compounded the users' demands and inanities. Hence, the similar attitude of annoyance and resentment expressed by a colleague who, in the late 1980s, was responsible for providing telephone support to those using a custom software program he had taken the lead in developing. After dealing courteously with a caller, he would hang up and loudly exclaim, "RYFM!" Pronounced as "riff-em" and short for "Read Your Fucking Manual."

Bad user documentation thus became oddly self-perpetuating. Users avoided consulting the poorly written manuals and instead sought help from power users or technical support lines. Managers of software and computer companies consequently saw little value in spending time and money on producing documentation that no one seemed to consult, and continued to allot the last-minute task of writing manuals to technicians with few writing skills and even less tolerance for or understanding of users' needs.

What seemed to be a downward spiral was halted by the ease-of-use movement described in chapters 2 and 3. User documentation was increasingly viewed as a critical factor in achieving the new ends of user-friendliness and ease-of-use—and, of course, the ultimate end of increased profitability from an expanded user base. As the makers of the Commodore 64 computer put it in 1982, "Commodore is known as The Friendly Computer company, and part of being friendly is giving you easy to read, easy to use and easy to understand instruction manuals."[10] Not only did good instructions offer a relatively uncomplicated and inexpensive means of compensating for program complexity, but "easy" manuals also served as an effective marketing tool in that they imparted at least the appearance of ease-of-use to the products they accompanied.[11] The result, from the mid-1980s on, was that user documentation was increasingly taken out of the hands of the technicians and programmers and made the exclusive job of technical writers. In a 1985 guide to writing user manuals, Edmond Weiss commented,

> These are interesting times for user documentation. Writing user documentation—especially software manuals for users and operators—is the subject of several new books and graduate courses. It is emerging as a distinct profession, incorporating elements of computer science, training, graphic arts, and traditional principles of rhetoric and composition.[12]

Still, despite Weiss's enthusiasm, documentation writers were generally perceived by programmers as user advocates and stand-ins, and therefore tended to have little status or credibility within software and computer companies. As one technical writer lamented, "[Y]ou're always at the end of the feeding chain."[13] This feeling is clearly shared by Tina the technical writer, the quirky character in Scott Adams's *Dilbert* comic strip, who chafes at the lack of respect typically accorded those in her line of work (see fig.8).

FIGURE 8: *Tina the technical writer: She gets no respect.*

Writing user documentation continued to be a peripheral activity for many years, considered by most developers to be both unrelated to and far less important than other software and hardware production tasks. A 1992 article on the subject quotes Beth Holmes, who comments on the "status problem" experienced by technical writers, many of whom were, like herself and Tina, women working within a traditionally male-dominated industry. Says Holmes, "Doing the manual is a necessary evil at the end of the project. [The programmers] are not very receptive to your input because they're finished as far as they're concerned."[14] Having worked as a fledgling documentation writer myself during the early 1980s, I well recall the reluctance with which programmers tore themselves away from their coding in order to provide me with the information I needed in order to complete, what was to them, the trivial and unnecessary task of explaining how to use the software.

During the 1990s, however, computer companies continued to place greater emphasis on providing useful, competently written user documentation. And those responsible for creating this documentation began to be acknowledged as *professionals*, still lower in the hierarchy of computer knowledge than the developers themselves but no longer completely beneath notice.

With the growing influence of documentation writers, it became increasingly likely that a computer or software program would be accompanied by a professionally written collection of manuals—or "documentation set"—that might include, for instance, a "quick start" guide, a weighty reference manual, and a step-by-step "getting started" tutorial. Providing a whole library of texts to users who were notoriously uninclined to consult written instructions may seem the height of perversity, and it was not entirely clear that users were indeed more likely to seek help from the many pages of a documentation set than from the slapdash manuals that prevailed during the previous decade. In fact, users tended to regard the sheer weightiness of the documentation that now accompanied software packages as merely another obstacle to usability. As one disgruntled user commented, "The writers are apparently paid by the word."[15] Similarly, in *The Trouble with Computers*, Thomas Landauer wondered why "[t]he user manuals accompanying even the smallest and simplest user-oriented systems are thick volumes."[16] And, in *Silicon Snake Oil*, Clifford Stoll grumbled that the documentation for Microsoft Word weighed more than the average laptop computer:

> Microsoft needs a thousand pages to describe a popular program written for ordinary people? Am I expected to know all this just to write a letter to my friend Gloria? Are computers so complex that they cannot be described simply?[17]

Nevertheless, it was also the case that most users—indeed, the same users who complained about the sheer weightiness of the documentation set—would be more likely to purchase a piece of hardware or software if it was accompanied by printed support materials, and the more the better. And so it became accepted wisdom in the field of documentation writing that, when it came to user manuals, one could never have too much information.

Thus, the user manual emerged as perhaps the defining "literary" form of the 1990s—and, rather paradoxically, the primary means by which technically unskilled individuals could achieve the ephemeral goal of "computer literacy." Canadian media specialist Marshall McLuhan might have suggested that the phenomenon of the documentation set represented a means of bridging the turbulent frontier between two distinct cultures: the print culture that had prevailed since the development of the Gutenberg press in the mid-fifteenth century and the emerging culture of electric technology. That certainly seemed to be the primary goal of the weighty documentation set: to ease the transition into the digital world by buffering us with the familiar medium of text. It seemed that, in order to become users, we must first be readers.

Stories for and about the Reader

Beyond the sheer weight of the instructions provided, the user documentation that emerged during the late 1980s and 1990s was notable for its new emphasis on the needs of the User, as opposed to the functions of the program itself. This was a literal as well as a philosophical shift, for best practice in the emerging field of documentation writing now required that the use of the program be described in concrete, precise terms that included the direct, succinct second person: *you*—as in "When the opening screen appears, *you* will see an empty application window"; "*You* are now ready to create a new document"; "Choose Save from the File menu to save *your* work."

The User, in short, was not only the reader but also the stated *subject* of software manuals. Texts that had once merely offered terse technical descriptions of the features and functions of programs had, over the years, become something quite different: precise and detailed stories about the User and the User's interactions with the program. This shift would seem, finally, to justify the grammatical ambiguity of the term *user documentation,* since the manuals are now indeed both for and about the User. But if contemporary software and hardware manuals are essentially about the User, then we should ask ourselves: What kinds of stories do they tell? What subject positions do they ask the User/reader to assume? And what are the limits of knowledge and action ascribed to the User/reader who is the subject of these texts?

Of course, all texts are in a sense addressed to an implied reader. Newspaper articles, for instance, with their inverted pyramid format and (purportedly) value-free presentation are written for a hasty reader who wants to absorb only the main facts about current events over a quick cup of coffee. This book, on the other hand, has been written for the reader who is willing to spend time considering the underlying premises of cultural phenomena, such as computer use, which we tend to accept as natural and neutral.

User manuals are also written with an implied reader in mind. But though it is an axiom of technical writing that "A good manual should be developed with a clear definition of the intended user,"[18] computer documentation is often designed, as Robert Johnson, a professor in the field of technical communication, admits, "to conform to predetermined notions of users and use," which may in fact have little to do with the intended audience and its needs.[19] This lack of correlation between the implied reader and the actual readers may seem odd, given that most contemporary guides to technical and documentation writing stress the importance of conducting a preliminary audience analysis. Yet the fact is that, despite the thoroughness suggested by the word *analysis*, the documentation writer typically considers, in fairly superficial terms, only one dimension of the intended readership: knowledge level. Little if any consideration is given to the social contexts of use. Therefore, as documentation writers plan and write user manuals, they tend to carry with them a one-dimensional image of an implied reader who has little or no technical knowledge of the system in question, and whose only purposes, interests, and needs relate to the immediate desire to rectify that knowledge gap. The reader, in short, is conceptualized as little more than an unskilled tool-user.

But in the case of user documentation, as I have said, the reader is also invoked as the *subject* of the text. This means that the potency of the implied reader—problematic as that image may be—is amplified, since readers are more or less compelled to assume a particular subject position. Consider the novel *Going Down Swinging*, in which author Billie Livingston also uses the very potent second person as a means of compelling her readers to adopt a certain subject position and the values that accompany it. As readers, we *become* the struggling alcoholic, Eilleen Hoffman. And by casting the reader as the subject of the story—"Sunday afternoon and you're on your way to the bootlegger, walking down the Danforth"[20]—Livingston eliminates the objective distance that might allow us to sit in judgement upon Eilleen's struggles and degradations.

Despite Livingston's use of the second person, however, the association with Eilleen Hoffman only goes so far. The reader of *Going*

Down Swinging need not actually perform all the actions ascribed to the subject, but can remain seated in the comfort of his or her easy chair while Eilleen visits the welfare office or tarts herself up for a night on the town. User documentation, however, is unique in that it is written not only to be read but to be *performed* by the subject/reader/User. In this way, the literary form it most closely resembles is the script. Both script and user manual offer a precise description of actions, and both forms are best understood when they are performed rather than read in isolation from actual use.

Several years ago, as a project manager in a software company, I asked a new employee to learn how to use a software program. The next day, she proudly informed me that she had taken the software manual home and spent the better part of the night reading it from cover to cover—and therefore had "learned" the program. But this, I hastened to explain, is not how user documentation works. User documentation—and particularly the "Getting Started" portion of the documentation set—is meant to be read in front of a computer, where we alternately read and enact the prescribed steps ("Press the Control key"; "Click OK"; "Type your password") in the prescribed order. We need a computer in order to understand and use the manual as much as we need the manual in order to understand and use the computer.

Unlike a script, however, user documentation allows for no creative license, no deviation from the rigidly detailed, step-by-step process. As unknowledgeable actors, we are required to follow the instructions precisely. Which is perhaps why, in the early 1980s, when the convoluted language of user documentation included instructions to "depress" rather than simply press a key such as Enter or Escape, some users considered it amusing to loudly berate the key in question ("You're *ugly*, Escape key"), thus demonstrating, if only to themselves, the absurdity of being required to follow the instructions to the letter. In the cult novel *Zen and the Art of Motorcycle Maintenance*, author Robert Pirsig (himself a writer and editor of computer manuals) offers a more soberly framed objection to the fact that most technical manuals, whether for software or rotisseries, allow for no deviation from the mandated procedures:

> What's really angering about instructions of this sort is that they imply there's only one way to put this rotisserie together—their way. And that presumption wipes out all the creativity. Actually there are hundreds of ways to put the rotisserie together and when they make you follow just one way without showing you the overall problem

> the instructions become hard to follow in such a way as not to make mistakes. You lose the feeling for the work. And not only that, it's very unlikely that they've told you the best way. . . . And when you presume there's just one right way to do things, of course the instructions begin and end with the rotisserie.[21]

What Pirsig is suggesting is that, far from empowering users, user manuals actually disenfranchise those who read them because they compel us to act almost mechanically—less as skilled, autonomous beings than as robots—and to approach computer use in the same piecemeal way in which the manuals themselves present it. Deprived of a sense of the whole and the context of our actions, we are therefore also deprived of knowledge and choice. Although the User is the subject of the text, and though the text is written with the assumption that we will not only read but perform the prescribed steps, all knowledge about the system resides entirely within the authoritative pages of the manual—which is what Pirsig means when he refers, elsewhere in his book, to the paradoxical "spectator attitude" implicit in user manuals.[22] In *User-Centered Technology*, Robert Johnson concurs that the tendency of user manuals to construct readers as mere tool-users, without any epistemology of their own, reduces readers/users not simply to rote practitioners but to "awestruck spectators, thus perpetuating the view that users are idiots."[23]

It is important to emphasize, however, that as users, we participate in this devaluation of our own knowledge. For instance, we commonly deem the strategies we develop for accomplishing tasks or overcoming the hurdles encountered during system use as the "wrong way," since they are not acknowledged in the official documentation. Some years ago, I supervised a project that required the use of a particular software program to input text and images. The limitations of the program were such that text and images could not be placed side by side, only above or below each other. Most of the team members adapted to this annoying constraint, but one woman found an ingenious way to overcome it. However, when I asked her to explain how she had managed to place text and images side by side, she grew embarrassed and described the approach she used as "cheating," since it was nowhere described in the user documentation.

User documentation thus emerged, during the 1990s, as a supposedly empowering medium, and the primary means of bridging the gap between those who know and those who do not know. Despite this overt purpose, however, software and hardware manuals have tended to maintain the existing hierarchy of computer knowledge by telling a story that constructs the User as a mere tool-user in search of knowledge. Moreover, the very format of the story, as well as the authoritative and highly prescriptive tone in which it is told, limits what we can know. In this way, like many materials designed to promulgate knowledge, user manuals serve to maintain existing social power structures, and they do so by defining the limits of knowledge available to the User.

Documentation for Dummies

I have briefly traced the development of user documentation from the early manuals, which tended to be highly technical and even error-ridden, to the weighty documentation sets that emerged a decade later. Over the years, one thing did not change very much: the belief, shared by many computer users, that most user manuals were fundamentally unusable, written in a language that suggested a profound disregard for the needs of users and a contempt for the intellectual capabilities of anyone who might need to consult those pages. Most user manuals, in other words, were written for dummies.

This tacit construction of the computer User as a "dummy," someone at the very bottom of the hierarchy of computer knowledge, was made explicit with the publication, in 1991, of *DOS For Dummies*, a beginner's guide to the operating system that ran most personal computers at the time. From the beginning, it seemed unlikely that the book would achieve any kind of success: many publishers rejected it; IDG Books, the publishing company that finally decided to take a chance on the book, issued a small, cautious initial run; and when *DOS For Dummies* finally did come out, a number of bookstores refused to stock it. Yet, to the surprise of everyone—and particularly of the skeptics, who believed that the book's insulting title would ensure its rapid demise—sales skyrocketed. After eighteen months, *DOS For Dummies* had sold 1.3 million copies.[24] Over a decade later, the *...For Dummies* series has expanded to hundreds of titles, covering not only a broad range of computing topics (including *Windows For Dummies*, *Word For Dummies*, and *The Internet For Dummies*), but also including how-to guides on such diverse subjects as wine, gourmet cooking, sex, figure skating, cats, home improvement, and classical music.

As the characteristic bright yellow *...For Dummies* cover becomes a familiar sight on bookshelves everywhere—and as Macmillan leaps into the fray with the *Idiot's Guide* series—we are faced with a conundrum: Why is it that users who are reluctant to consult the pages of the manuals that accompany their hardware and software are willing to spend extra dollars on a book that probably contains the same information and, what is more, that is based on the premise that they are *dumb*? If computer use, as I suggested in chapter 1, is all about proving oneself to be "smart" through an alliance with the intelligent machine, then why is it that, far from being insulted by the assumptions implicit in the title, readers are actually flocking to join the new club of computer users who are not embarrassed to admit that they are, as the flyleaf of every *...For Dummies* computer book puts it, "intimidated and confused by computers"?

Clifford Stoll views the *...For Dummies* phenomenon as merely further evidence of the condescending attitude towards the User that has plagued user documentation since its inception. If users "dread plowing through documentation," he writes, we "[c]an't blame 'em. . . . Look at the titles of introductory computer manuals: *DOS for Dummies* or *The Complete Idiot's Guide to the Internet*."[25] However, viewing the *...For Dummies* books as merely an extension of the existing user documentation trajectory, rather than as an attempt to break from it in important ways, is a mistake and certainly does nothing to explain the remarkable success of the series.

In fact, many attempts have been made to explain the unexpected popularity of the *...For Dummies* books. The author of one article posits, "The initial attraction is in the titles, which accurately imply that they are aimed at computer users who feel overwhelmed by the technology, and are not ashamed to admit it."[26] Another writer claims that the *...For Dummies* publishing phenomenon "is a sign of the times":

> Price wars have created a mass market for personal computers, yet they remain maddening machines, difficult to use and humbling to encounter—and that's the empathetic insight behind the success of "DOS for Dummies," an irreverent primer for the perplexed.[27]

The flyleaf text of every *...For Dummies* computer manual explains the appeal in these terms:

> *"...For Dummies"* books are written for those frustrated computer users who know they aren't really dumb but find that PC hardware, software, and indeed the unique vocabulary of computing make them feel helpless. *"...For Dummies"* books use a lighthearted approach, a down-to-earth style, and even cartoons and humorous icons to diffuse computer novices' fears and build their confidence. Lighthearted but not lightweight, these books are a perfect survival guide to anyone forced to use a computer.

There is no doubt that the chatty, informal style in which the books are written makes them far more accessible than the typical user manual. *...For Dummies* computer guides offer no end of cartoons, puns, and bad jokes. What is a printer? "The thing that sits to one side of the computer and prints information on paper, which is the reason that it's called the printer. We mention it here because some people think that the printer is a kindly old gent wearing an ink-stained apron who runs an offset press for a living."[28] Can jokes of this calibre really explain the success of the series?

In fact, all of these attempts to explain the unprecedented success of the *...For Dummies* computer manuals merely skirt the real reason for the series' popularity: they are the first books that not only dare to acknowledge the existence of the hierarchy of computer knowledge but, what is more, persistently belittle those individuals whose digital prowess places them in its topmost reaches. For instance, the authors of *PCs For Dummies* continually make jokes at the expense of the "nerd programmers," variously denigrated throughout the book as "geeks, "technoweenies," "technogeeks," "Dorito-breathed geeks," and "computer dweebs"; and they further exploit all the stereotypes in order to emphasize the difference between the nerds and "normal people."[29] Thus, in describing how to use a mouse, the authors are quick to provide the following gratuitous information: "Computer nerds grab potato chips with the middle finger and thumb of their right hand. That way their index finger won't get greasy stuff on the mouse button."[30]

Moreover, unlike traditional manuals, which offer computer knowledge in authoritative tones, the *...For Dummies* guides do not hesitate to represent that knowledge as both trivial and arbitrary, and to ascribe the complexities of computer use to the eccentricities and failings of the "technogeeks" responsible for creating "the beast." Why are there so many computer terms? So that "computer geeks can confuse more people with less effort." Why are the symbols in a graphical user interface also called icons? "Because computer geeks often name everything twice." Why do we press the F1 key for Help? Because "[w]hen computer dweebs transferred the typewriter keyboard to the computer, they added plenty of goodies. But, in all the excitement . . . they forgot the most important key of all: Help."[31] Finally, the "tech-noweenies" are further belittled by the fact that their unique knowledge is set aside in boxes with such labels as "Technical drivel on the BIOS," "Technical tidbits I'd skip if I were you," and "Boring technical details on the differences between RAM and ROM."[32]

Judging from the information provided in the About the Authors section of *PCs For Dummies*, both Dan Gookin (who wrote the original *DOS For Dummies* manual) and Andy Rathbone could easily be deemed technoweenies themselves, but they are careful to set up and maintain the "us" against "them" dialectic which is the heart of the *...For Dummies* appeal. It is, after all, as the cover of every book in the series proudly proclaims, in a deliberate echo of the early Macintosh slogan, the "reference for the rest of us!"

At the same time that they acknowledge the hierarchy of computer knowledge, the *...For Dummies* guides also implicitly acknowledge what most other user manuals ignore: the social contexts of computer use. In the lexicon of the *...For Dummies* world, a dummy is someone who is, say, an accountant, a parent, a stamp collector, a spouse, a cook, a manager—but who is not, in his or her own mind, first and foremost a computer user. A dummy is someone with a healthy balance of interests and roles; someone who is not obsessively preoccupied with digital devices but who is, indeed, "forced" to use them. The real boobs, at least from a social point of view, therefore emerge not as the normal people who read and use the books but as those socially inept, single-minded technoweenies who have no purpose or interests in life other than the creation of a perverse, arbitrarily designed digital universe that users are right to find confusing.

However, popular as the series' sustained attack on the hierarchy of computer knowledge has proved to be, we should ask ourselves how effective or meaningful it is to shout taunts up to those perched securely at the top of a ladder—to those who are, what is more, unlikely to peruse the pages in which those taunts are found. In the end, despite their irreverence, the *...For Dummies* books do not even manage to so much as give the ladder an impudent shake. Moreover, given their unrelenting emphasis on the distinctions between those who produce and those who use, the stories the *...For Dummies* books tell tend to perpetuate the hierarchy of computer knowledge and the notion that the User is a unique entity who must be told what to do while being insulated from arcane technical information. As I suggested in chapter 3, this kind of "friendly" reassurance that we need not concern ourselves with the inner workings of the machine or with boring technical details ultimately does not serve users well. Having accepted the notion, perpetuated in the *...For Dummies* books, that use and knowledge of digital devices need not—indeed, should not—go hand in hand, we willingly accede to a situation in which those who use the devices relinquish all control over their inner workings.

A Clash of Intelligence

Of course, user documentation continues to evolve. Anyone who has recently purchased a software program is doubtless aware of the current trend, which involves putting more and more of the instructional information on-line. For instance, the version of Microsoft Word that I am using to write this book offers, in addition to a reduced documentation set, balloon help, on-line Microsoft Word Help (which accesses the ubiquitous office assistant), on-line Contents and Index, and a link to Help on the Web.

The move away from paper is, for software manufacturers, a cost-cutting measure, but it is offered as a boon for the user, who is thereby liberated from the necessity of thumbing through a manual. Rather than getting in the way of computer use, on-line documentation is supposed to become an integral part of the program. And rather than being compelled, as users, to pore through thick volumes, we can now presumably access information with the touch of a key or the click of a mouse whenever we need it. The move to on-line documentation thus constructs the contemporary computer user as someone who is no longer tied to text—or, at least, to paper.

However, it is not entirely clear that on-line documentation differs in any meaningful way from the help information found in books. Indeed, according to Johnson, it is often the case that the "on-line documentation is nothing more than the print documentation re-entered into on-line Help with little or no attempt to alter the information to fit the use of the new medium."[33] And according to John Seely Brown and Paul Duguid, the same problems persist: "Anyone who has had trouble with a piece of information technology (surely that is everyone who has a piece of information technology) has trawled through manuals and indexes and help systems and never found the problem in front of him or her described."[34]

The most recent manifestations of on-line help incorporate elements of "intelligence," in the way of context-sensitive tips and advice that pop up on the screen (like the friendly paper clip I bent out of shape in chapter 3) in order to lend support for specific tasks. Indeed, according to digital prophet Nicholas Negroponte, the intelligence of the computer is such that, today,

> [t]he notion of an instruction manual is obsolete. The fact that computer hardware and software manufacturers ship them with product is nothing short of perverse. The best instructor on how to use a machine is the machine itself. It knows what you are doing, what you have just done, and can even guess at what you are about to do. . . . Add some familiarity with you (you are left-handed, hard of hearing, and have little patience with mechanical things), and that machine can be a far better aide (the *e* in *aide* is purposeful) to its own operations and maintenance than any document.[35]

However, despite Negroponte's enthusiasm, so-called intelligent online documentation is not without its drawbacks. The fact that these systems are on-line creates a significant hurdle, for there is no getting around the fact that the user requires a basic familiarity with computer functions in order to use on-line help. Hence the absurdity of introductory tutorials that purport to teach the user how to use a mouse, select from a menu, and so forth—all functions required in order to access and progress through the tutorial in the first place.

The "intelligence" of on-line documentation may also pose unexpected problems. In a study of a simulated "SmartHelp" facility, John Carroll and Amy Aaronson discovered that programs which anticipate users' difficulties and provide unrequested tips actually annoy, frustrate, and distract users—no matter how useful the help messages might be. What Carroll and Aaronson describe is a "clash of intelligence," in which users ignore messages that seem unrelated to their goals, or that tell them *what* to do without telling them *why*.[36] This clash of intelligence occurs because, rather than transferring power and knowledge to the user, on-line documentation ascribes intelligence to the machine itself, thereby further cloaking it within an aura of mystical power and obscurity. The clash of intelligence also occurs because, rather than giving voice to the user, intelligent help systems continue to speak for us, to tell stories *about* us, just as user manuals have since their emergence in the 1970s and 1980s. Like all forms of user documentation, on-line systems ultimately render the User mute.

Thus, as we move from paper-based manuals that the user consults to intelligent systems that act as on-line consultants, it is not clear that user documentation has indeed progressed very far. After all these years, users still seem reluctant to consult documentation and still resent the intrusions of "intelligent" help systems. This reluctance has a great deal to do with the fact that, as we have seen, most user documentation does not and never has served its ostensible purpose, which is to demystify digital artifacts for non-technical users. Rather, documentation, in whatever form, actually serves to maintain existing knowledge and power structures.

Nevertheless, despite our subliminal awareness of the ways in which user manuals construct us, and despite our long-standing dissatisfaction with user documentation in general, few users do more than grumble and find ways to work around the limitations. Indeed, as more and more aspects of our lives are transferred on-line, thereby becoming the provenance of system processes and decisions, we seem content to remain "dummies," reluctantly consulting manuals that tell us what to do while revealing nothing of the inner workings of the systems we use nor, more importantly, of the values and assumptions upon which the systems are based.

Once again, it is not the users but the writers of user manuals who are beginning to articulate the problem and take steps towards improving the situation. In recent years, a number of technical writers have become acutely aware of the role they play in, as Michael Salvo puts it, "reinforc[ing] the passivity of technological consumers" and "re-inscribing the dichotomy between technical producers and consumers."[37] In his discussion of graduate curricula for technical communicators, Salvo talks about the importance of redefining the technical writer's role, from that of "a scribe transferring technical information from one group to another (usually from a powerful group of technology producers to a relatively powerless group of technological consumers)" to that of someone responsible for "articulating issues and concerns of users."[38] Similarly, Bernadette Longo takes a cultural studies perspective on her field, which allows her to perceive technical writing as a "control mechanism" which—though "often characterized as a simple collaborative effort in which writers mediate technology for users"—still functions to uphold the importance of the kinds of knowledge possessed by technology producers while marginalizing "users' naïve know-how."[39]

Commendable as such efforts are, however, Salvo, Longo, and other similarly minded technical communicators are exposing and challenging ideas with a long history. While user documentation continues to change in form, becoming ever more "intelligent" and embedded within technological systems, its underlying premises are likely to change much more slowly—unless, perhaps, users begin to demand for themselves a more active role in its creation.

6

Anxiety Attacks: Pathologizing the Technophobic User

Do your palms grow moist at the thought of using a computer? Does your heart race? Do you feel fearful and confused? Dizzy and nauseous? Do you often experience frustration when using a computer to perform everyday tasks? Or have you—be honest, now—ever had the overwhelming impulse to wreak some kind of damage on your keyboard, mouse, or monitor? If you answered "yes" to any of these questions then chances are that you are suffering from *computer anxiety*. First diagnosed as a psychological condition in the 1980s, as the personal computer began increasingly to infiltrate offices, classrooms, and homes, computer anxiety—also known as computer phobia, computer alienation, computer aversion, cyberphobia, technophobia, technostress, tech rage, and even *logizomechanophobia*[1]—is defined as "a person's tendency to experience uneasiness or stress over the use of any technology related to computers."[2] The condition is estimated to affect as much as one-quarter to one-third of the population of the Western world.[3] Indeed, according to Craig Brad, author of *Technostress*, "[i]n a society already plagued by stress-related illnesses, from hypertension to cancer, technostress may well be the most crucial disease we have ever had to face."[4]

Whatever we choose to call it (and as I will presently suggest, what we choose to call it *does* matter), computer anxiety is, according to the many scholars who have conducted studies and written on the subject, a real phenomenon, not simply a piece of folklore sprung from the darker side of our technoculture. During the past twenty years, these scholars, working primarily in the fields of psychology and education, have produced hundreds of books and articles that attempt to probe the parameters of this emerging condition.

However, amidst all the published research studies, one can find very little in the way of consensus on computer anxiety—not surprising, perhaps, given the fact that researchers cannot even seem to agree on a name for the condition. Some researchers claim to have established a conclusive link between negative feelings about computer use and the anxious computer user's gender or age[5] while others whose studies have produced different results conclude that "the belief that older people and women will have less affinity for computers is more myth than reality."[6] Nor does there seem to be conclusive evidence that technology-induced stress bears any relationship to other demographic characteristics such as computer experience, math anxiety, years of education, and ethnicity, though over the years many researchers have tried to establish such correlations. In the end, despite the concerted attempts to devise rating scales for computer anxiety and other instruments for accurately predicting who will experience the condition, we have nothing but "contradictory findings on the relationship between computer anxiety and demographic variables."[7] As Valerie Worthington and Yong Zhao put it, the fact that "different researchers come to different conclusions about computer anxiety in different studies," means that they are "ultimately unable to make meaningful statements" about the phenomenon.[8]

This situation, however, does not appear to stem the tide of computer-anxiety research; quite the opposite, in fact. Michael Gos begins his report on a two-year study of computer anxiety by bemoaning the fact that, although "much work has been done in the study of factors correlated with computer anxiety . . . the empirical evidence is, at best, inconclusive,"[9] a situation he clearly hopes to remedy.

But even though researchers can offer us very little in the way of definitive information about computer anxiety and its correlates, the mere fact that they have identified it as a phenomenon, and one which is worthy of extensive study, is important, for this research plays a significant role in the social construction of the computer User. True, research on computer anxiety tends to be conducted primarily within narrow academic circles, to which most computer users do not belong, and the published findings tend to appear in scholarly journals which most computer users do not read. However, a researcher's role is not merely to understand phenomena but, more importantly, to *produce knowledge*: to determine what is worthy of investigation in the first place and then to name the phenomenon and define its parameters. The knowledge so produced finds its way into the popular press, where journalists participate in the social construction of the anxious user by reproducing the knowledge in widely read newspaper and magazine articles—such as "New Illness of High-Tech Age," "Dealing with Tech Rage," and "Who's Afraid of their Own Palm Pilot?"[10]—and in books intended for a wide readership, such as *Computer Phobia—How to Slay the Dragon of Computer Fear*.[11]

Thus, while scholarly research that yields rotated factor analyses of computer phobia items and taxonomies of technostress may seem to bear no connection to the assumptions and attitudes held by the mass of humanity, the fact is that, far from being irrelevant, scholarly research functions as a potent form of knowledge production. And as such, it plays a pivotal role in shaping the way in which a phenomenon such as computer anxiety—and, hence, the anxious computer User—is understood and regarded by society.

Moreover, published research studies about computer anxiety contribute to the objectification of computer users as a single entity. Of course, the tendency to reduce human subjects to undifferentiated objects of study is not a unique feature of research in the area of computer anxiety. Research in general tends to lump those who participate in controlled studies into a single "sample" or "cohort," thereby minimizing or ignoring individual uniquenesses—or at best, treating them as a finite set of variables. As Lewis Mumford observes, it is the tendency of much research to avoid human complexity, to "cancel out the differences of individual experience and private history," for the sake of findings which can be deemed error-free and generalizable.[12] Heather Menzies agrees that "the language of objective rationality" functions to replace lived experience with objectified facts: "This language translates people from being subjects of their own story and culture into objects. They cease to be people in social and moral contexts and instead become statistics in abstract categories. . . ."[13] Thus, even those computer-anxiety researchers who are especially concerned with differences—particularly with the relationship between technostress and differences in age, gender, and computer experience—ultimately construct the User as a homogenous entity through the prevalence of research methodologies which seek "to reduce the occurrence of computer anxiety to . . . a single demographic characteristic."[14] In this way, supposedly neutral studies of computer anxiety play a significant, if largely unnoticed, role in constructing individual computer users with unique needs and abilities as a homogenous mass of predispositions and tendencies: the anxious User.

The Invalid User

Despite their failure to arrive at a shared understanding of computer anxiety and its correlates, the authors of published research on computer anxiety *do* appear to agree, for the most part, upon two key points. The first is that "[t]here is no question as to the seriousness of the problems caused by computer anxiety."[15] The consensus is that computer anxiety is a debilitating condition that impairs the quality of life of those who experience it by reducing their job security,[16] depriving them of access to the "legitimate benefits of computers,"[17] and—as a host of studies on computer self-efficacy suggest—diminishing their ability to undertake with confidence tasks that involve the use of a computer.[18]

The second point upon which researchers tend to agree is that computer anxiety—or technophobia, or whatever they choose to call it—is a fundamentally *irrational* response to high technology, a "fear of impending interaction with a computer that is disproportionate to the actual threat presented by the computer."[19] There is, in other words, no logical reason for an individual to experience feelings of nervousness or frustration when using, or when confronted with the necessity of using, digital devices.

In fact, neither of these beliefs has a basis in research. Since most computer-anxiety research is devoted to discovering correlates for the condition, with relatively little effort devoted to an exploration of its consequences,[20] there is no objective reason to believe that the user who quakes at the sight of a computer, or who clutches the mouse with a sweaty palm, will suffer a corresponding decrease in general quality of life. Nor does the research support the assumption that anxious computer users are less rational as a group than users who approach computers with eager confidence. Rather, both of these assumptions have their provenance not in research findings but in the mythology of computer use, which I elaborated on in chapter 1. In a society wholeheartedly devoted to the twin deities of Technology and Progress, the only rational response to technology is perceived to be a zealous commitment to its use. Therefore, anyone who fears to climb aboard that joyous bandwagon must necessarily be viewed as both socially disadvantaged and psychologically disabled.

Since they agree on these two points—that computer anxiety is both debilitating and evidence of some kind of psychological imbalance—it is not surprising to find that researchers tend to pathologize computer anxiety. They do so by using a pseudo-medical language ("phobia," "neurosis," "condition," "symptoms") similar to that with which I deliberately introduced this chapter, a language that implicitly characterizes computer anxiety as an aberrant state, and the anxious computer User as not simply uneasy but *diseased*. Most often, such language appears to be used unreflectively, with no consideration of the power of metaphor to structure, as George Lakoff and Mark Johnson suggest in *The Metaphors We Live By*, "how we perceive, how we think, and what we do."[21] The author of *Technophobia* is perhaps an exception; however, while Mark Brosnan admits towards the end of his book that his decision to refer to the phenomenon as a *phobia* may be somewhat problematic, he nevertheless defends from the start his use of the diagnostic label: "Whilst not a phobia in the classic sense (such as agoraphobia), there are many similarities in aetiology and 'treatment' which warrant the term 'technophobia.'"[22]

The notion that computer anxiety is a sickness is further emphasized by the frequent references, in books and articles on the subject, to the need for "treatment interventions,"[23] which will help anxious users overcome their psychological disability. In fact, treatment seems to be an overwhelming concern, judging by the numerous references to programs for managing and controlling computer anxiety that have sprung up over the years, and by the researchers' interest in assessing the effectiveness of those programs. For example, Larry Rosen, Deborah Sears, and Michelle Weil evaluate the success of a Computerphobia Reduction Program which, they happily conclude, "successfully changed nearly 150 people from being computerphobic to being eager to seek further positive computer experiences."[24] Similarly, Brosnan describes the implementation of his own technophobia reduction program specifically designed to help the anxious new user feel comfortable during his or her first encounters with the computer.[25] Gerard George and M.R. Camarata offer "one possible cyberanxiety learning approach" that will overcome teachers' "behavioral resistance to the introduction of technological sophistication in the classroom" and "ensure that faculty feel committed to the change."[26] And the essence of Mark Pancer, Margo George, and Robert Gebotys's study is to establish the efficacy of "persuasive communication"—what we might, elsewhere, deem propaganda—as a means of inducing people to use technology.[27]

Even the authors of books and articles which explore the correlates and causes of computer anxiety without explicit reference to treatment interventions seem compelled to offer, if only in passing, some words of wisdom about "the best way" to cure people who suffer from this serious, socially debilitating condition.[28] In this way, these researchers also participate in the characterization of the anxious computer User as being somehow unsound, beyond the pale of what is considered "normal" and socially acceptable.

The commonly expressed assumption about treatment is, as Michael Gos observes, that computer experience is the best "cure" for computer anxiety.[29] This assumption constructs the anxious User as not only unhealthy but also unknowledgeable, the one undesirable state springing from the other. The assumption persists that anxiety diminishes as users become more familiar with and knowledgeable about the technology, despite the fact that this correlation is not borne out by research findings,[30] and despite the fact that the belief conflicts with the view of computer anxiety as a pathological condition—for it's a strange disease indeed in which the sufferer is best served not by shunning the cause of illness but by seeking further exposure to it! But by representing computer anxiety as a condition "that needs to be overcome"[31] and by describing treatment as a process whereby the technostressed User becomes desensitized to digital technology and able to accept it as an inevitable part of life, these studies tacitly construct the anxious computer User not simply as an invalid, someone who is disabled by actual interactions or the prospect of interactions with computers, but more particularly as someone who is socially *in-valid* and who must be "cured" in order to function as a productive member of society.

Representations of the anxious computer user as someone who engages in irrational acts of destruction further drive home the necessity of treatment interventions. According to Nina Ray and Robert Minch, "extreme user reactions" have included pouring honey into a terminal and running over a computer with a forklift.[32] Chris Wood tells similar tales of users throwing their laptops at walls and otherwise "violently abus[ing] computer equipment. The most common targets: keyboards, followed by mouses and monitors."[33] Such tales serve the same function as the videoclip that made its appearance in computerized workplaces several years ago. Presumably taken from an office surveillance video camera, the videoclip—ironically, circulated largely via e-mail and the World Wide Web—showed a man in an office cubicle using his keyboard like a baseball bat to smash his computer to the floor while a shocked co-worker peered over a nearby partition (see fig. 9). Such stories function to emphasize the irrationality of computer anxiety, and thus the importance of providing treatment interventions that will bring anxious users around to the "proper" way of seeing and behaving.

FIGURE 9: *Smashing machines: The anxious computer user.*

What lies behind all this concern with effecting cures? In *Ideology and Curriculum,* Michael Apple observes that labelling people as being in need of treatment "is a moral and political act, not a neutral helping act." Referring to the ways in which schoolchildren are given labels (for example, "slow," "underachiever") that call forth apparently neutral forms of treatment, Apple observes that "such language hides the more basic issue of inquiring into the conditions under which one group of people consistently labels others as deviant or applies some other taken for granted abstract category to them."[34] In *Discipline and Punish,* Michel Foucault makes the similar point that an "immense 'appetite for medicine,'" such as that manifested by computer-anxiety researchers, has less to do with a humanistic impulse than it does with the exercise of a normative power, which "has become one of the major functions of our society":

> The judges of normality are present everywhere. We are in the society of the teacher-judge, the doctor-judge, the educator-judge, the "social worker-judge"; it is on them that the universal reign of the normative is based; and each individual, wherever he may find himself, subjects to it his body, his gestures, his behavior, his aptitudes, his achievements.[35]

Individuals who demonstrate reluctance, discomfort, or anger when it comes to the use of digital devices become objects of study and manipulation by the "computer anxiety-judge," who gains, by virtue of that anxiety, the power to promote, develop, and institute therapeutic treatments for those who deviate from the norm, as well as the authority to speak on their behalf.

And there is no doubt that the norm, in the view of computer-anxiety researchers, is an unquestioning acceptance of and even eagerness to use digital technologies. Anything else—fatigue, complaining, avoidance, anger—is deemed to be an acting out of anxiety and, ultimately, a form of resistance which must be overcome. As the authors of one article on computer anxiety put it, it is important to understand the correlates of computer anxiety because "people's willingness to accept such technology . . . may be profoundly affected by the attitudes they hold."[36] The authors of another article contend that "[i]f individuals are to embrace computer technologies . . . they must feel confident and comfortable using them."[37] This kind of language, reflecting the unquestioned assumptions that we *should* embrace computer technologies and that computer use is invariably beneficial, is commonplace in the computer-anxiety literature. It would seem that, having submitted to the mythology of computer use and the hyperbole of its prophets, the researchers are diligently engaged in supposedly objective, scientific efforts to eliminate all forms of resistance to the deities of Technology and Progress by branding as abnormal, and altering through treatment, those individuals who do not share their enthusiasms.

Meanwhile, there is a relative paucity of inquiries into computer addiction, which is simply not viewed as a social problem or, though it well might be, as a sickness in need of treatment. Consider, for example, the recent suicide of a twenty-one year old player of *EverQuest®*, Sony's popular dungeons-and-dragons on-line game. Even those who contend that the suicide can be attributed to problems arising from addiction and resulting sleep deprivation are inclined simply to blame the manufacturer for the unfortunate event rather than to regard it as

Computer Angst

While researchers rally round the theme of treatment, they appear to have surprisingly little interest in establishing the causes of computer anxiety, beyond the quest for demographic correlates. Most seem to assume that the phenomenon is simply a direct result of interactions with a technology which is not, despite the rhetoric of advertisements and technocelebrants, really all that friendly and easy to use. As Chris Wood puts it in his article on tech rage, "When smart technology makes people feel dumb, some snap."[41] A University of Florida psychologist agrees that computer phobia is often caused by even a single negative experience with using a computer and the user's resulting conviction that he or she is not mechanically inclined.[42]

Certainly, despite all the claims for user-friendliness, there is no denying that general difficulties with using the computer can cause users a great deal of stress, anger, and apprehension. Indeed, it's a truism to say that people often feel clumsy, ill at ease, and frustrated when using computers. Over the years, I have worked with many new computer users, otherwise confident people who flinch at the sound of the computer's warning beeps and remonstrate loudly with themselves when the computer hangs for no apparent reason. The tendency towards self-blame may diminish over time, but as someone who has used a computer daily (and sometimes nightly) for twenty years, I know that the frustration does not. Like most experienced users, I can often be found cursing my machine and gnashing my teeth when files become inexplicably lost or corrupted—particularly, as so often seems to be the case, when a deadline looms. It is precisely because we have all experienced such feelings of exasperation with the apparent whims of digital devices that we play and replay with shocked, vicarious delight that videoclip of the cubicle worker's violent spasm of rage against the machine.

But while the frustrations of day-to-day computer use are certainly real, the assumption that computer anxiety arises from the cumulative effect of difficulties that individuals have interacting with their machines tends to normalize the values and practices of our technological society. Indeed, it is as simplistic and futile as viewing a phenomenon such as road rage as merely resulting from, say, flat tires or other problems drivers might have with operating their cars, and thus omitting from the analysis any consideration of the social contexts of part of a larger social problem. And while stories about the social consequences of *EverQuest*® addiction proliferate in Internet newsgroups such as EverQuest Widows and spousesagainsteverquest, those experts on addiction and mental health who were interviewed for a recent *Maclean's* article about on-line games consistently downplayed the seriousness of the phenomenon. According to one researcher, "The vast majority [of gamers] have it under control."[38]

Herein, then, lies another clue to the emphasis on treatment. Computer anxiety is regarded as a problem, and more specifically as a *sickness*, not because those who exhibit "symptoms" are truly ill but because they are engaging in something that certain segments of our society, which are deeply invested in the mythology of computer use, simply cannot condone: a *resistance* to technology. The thriving research industry that has grown up around the unquestioned assumption that "resistance is futile, we will be assimilated" is surely of far less importance to individual users than it is to the digital elites who strive to dictate the terms of our membership within society. For, clearly, the greatest hazard posed by computer anxiety—which goes hand in hand with not only "avoidance of computers" but also "attempts to cut short the necessary use of computers"[39] and "ownership avoidance"[40]—is its potentially disastrous effect on the fortunes of hardware and software manufacturers alike. As the treatments devised by the computer-anxiety researchers increase our level of comfort with the technology, so too do they decrease the likelihood that we will even contemplate alternatives to computer use.

Of course, I am not suggesting that those who study computer anxiety are all in the pockets of high-tech corporations, but only that their research is based upon a well-entrenched, unquestioned mythology of computer use which comes from and serves the interests not of individual users but of those who construct the digital world in which we live. And I am further suggesting that, rather than continuing to pathologize the anxious User, and to implicitly construct the "sufferer" as a useless burden upon society, researchers might do better to take a closer look at their own labours and labels, and the interests they serve.

automobile use. In fact, road rage arises less as a response to the malfunctioning of a specific car than as a response to the social conditions to which years of dependence upon the automobile as a mode of transportation have given rise: long commutes, traffic jams, fast food, suburbs, strip malls, drive-through banks, polluted freeways, and so forth.

In the same way, although we may—like the well-known cartoon duck caught forever in the act of preparing to bring down a hammer upon his computer—take out our anger on a specific machine, computer anxiety does not simply arise from specific difficulties encountered while using digital technology. Rather, according to computer-anxiety researchers Valerie Worthington and Yong Zhao, the phenomenon should be seen as a response to our society's increasing dependence upon the computer and the social conditions to which that dependence gives rise. Thus, the man in the cubicle may have attacked his computer, but the real source of stress in his life was likely not that individual machine so much as it was the entire dehumanizing culture of efficiency and productivity—the cubicle culture—which surrounds the computerization of work and which transforms those who labour within that culture into isolated and infinitely replaceable information processors.

Computer anxiety, in other words, can be seen as an existential response to digital technology—not to particular difficulties with using it but, as Worthington and Zhao suggest, to "its symbolic aspects":

> To the extent that the fears raised by these participants deal not simply with interactions with a computer, but also with the broader implications of computer use for participants' senses of self and of the "social order" . . . these fears are existential in nature.[43]

The notion that computer anxiety is actually less a reaction to the deficits of a specific hardware or software system than it is an *existential* response to the broader implications of computer use for our lives, our sense of self, and our society, is certainly borne out by the fact that one need not actually *be* a computer user in order to experience computer anxiety. As Sherry Turkle observes in *The Second Self*, "Computers call up strong feelings, even for those who are not in direct contact with them. People sense the presence of something new and exciting. But they fear the machine as powerful and threatening."[44] It is also borne out by the fact, noted earlier, that, contrary to the predictions of some researchers,[45] increased computer experience and societal exposure to computers appear to do little to diminish feelings of anxiety. Perhaps—like road rage, which is not lessened but indeed exacerbated as our society becomes increasingly reliant upon the automobile—incidences of technostress can actually be expected to increase with the increasing prevalence of the computer and our ever greater dependence upon it. (Perhaps, too, we can expect an increase in incidences of both road rage *and* technostress as cars become increasingly computerized.) Indeed, Mark Poster speculates that the Internet will exacerbate technostress: "If the human-computer interface may induce anxiety, how much greater might be that feeling when the computer part of the assemblage is connected to a network including tens of millions of people around the world."[46] All of which lends a certain piquancy to IBM's "Emotion Mouse," which is currently being designed to gauge the user's level of technostress based on factors such as heart rate and skin temperature.[47] If existential angst is the problem, then more technology, of whatever kind, is certainly *not* the solution.

Regarding computer anxiety as a form of existential angst is clearly at odds with the continued conceptualization of the anxious User as someone in need of treatment in order to be restored to a "normal" psychological state. Indeed, Worthington and Zhao speculate that digitally inspired fear and rage may constitute an important and necessary stage, in which we are forced to confront our uncertainties about technological progress and our increasing powerlessness as computer users. A view of computer anxiety as an existential response to technologies that no longer seem to serve human purposes is also at odds with constructions of the anxious (or angst-ridden) User as unknowledgeable and inexperienced in the use of computers, since it's very possible that feelings of anxiety and powerlessness will actually increase with use. Experienced users are, after all, more likely to be dependent upon the technology to accomplish everyday tasks, and are therefore also more likely to feel that they lack choice and power in a world in which computer use is increasingly both a condition of survival and, in the stories told by the popular press, an autonomous force over which the individual user has no control. As the author of *Technostress* suggests, computer anxiety may very well begin with the ominous sense that, when we sit down at the computer, we relinquish something of ourselves in exchange for the convenience and speed of computing: "A common anxiety among those who operate computerized equipment is that the machine will literally end up controlling them."[48]

I agree with Worthington and Zhao that computer anxiety has less to do with irrational feelings of timidity or terror inspired by direct interactions with unfriendly machines than with the larger social contexts and implications of computerization. Apart from that, however, viewing computer anxiety as an existential fear inspired by what appears to be a self-directing technology still leaves us where the computer-anxiety research begins: with a fearful User who is, by virtue of that learned apprehension, easily classified and victimized (in the research, as in life). As Andrew Yeaman observes, "The myth of computer anxiety teaches people they are helpless. It tells people they are ineffective and incapable and that they need special lessons to overcome their disability." Computer angst is thus no less a futile gesture and, as Yeaman suggests, "an oppressive act,"[49] than computer anxiety, since labelling the phenomenon as *fear*, and particularly fear of an out-of-control technology, merely legitimizes the feelings[50] and undermines the user's ability to act wisely and responsibly.

Moreover, studies that replace anxiety with angst still perpetuate the notion of the User as an undifferentiated entity—an entity, what is more, that operates within a social context that is regarded as outside the realm of inquiry. True, Worthington and Zhao offer an increased emphasis on the social contexts of computer use, but only to point out that technology may be experienced as an out-of-control dynamo rather than as a beneficial tool. In other words, like most computer-anxiety researchers, they fail for the most part to transcend a simplistic understanding of a unitary User engaging with Technology within an invariant social context. Indeed, user diversity is of so little significance in this research that studies of computer anxiety in undergraduate students, managers, clerks, and other user groups are premised upon the assumption that the research is comparable and applicable across populations.[51] These studies neither acknowledge nor connect with a whole other body of research that suggests that technology use has diverse meanings which are contingent not only upon the needs and interests of the individual users but upon the social contexts of use and local decisions about whose interests the computers will serve.[52] Studies that attempt to link computer anxiety with specific demographics do not make this leap, for they persistently emphasize such factors as age, gender, and math skills rather than the specific situations and social contexts of use.

In the end, existential angst in the face of a largely uncontrollable and determining technological force is no more satisfactory an interpretation and label than anxiety. Both must give way to an emphasis on responsible action within a social network made up of human beings who themselves determine the uses and meanings of technology. Users who take action and make choices are more likely to view technological developments as the cumulative result of human decision-making rather than as a runaway force—and therein, perhaps, lies the "cure."

7

Songs of Innocence and Experience: The Youthful User

Unlike adult users, children would seem to experience no anxiety whatsoever about computer use. On the contrary, the generally accepted view is that children have a natural affinity for the complex digital devices that intimidate and infuriate their parents and teachers. As one commentator puts it, "technology is second nature" for today's youth: "It's as if they come into this world with a game controller in one hand and a mouse in the other."[1] Another observes that "[o]ne of the internet age's most widely held myths has to be the belief that young people . . . [possess] some innate computing skill that anyone who reached adulthood before around 1980 could never possibly develop."[2]

What is the root of this affinity? Karla Jennings suggests that it is simply a matter of familiarity: "Children growing up playing computer games will be as comfortable with computers when they reach adulthood as their parents are with television, the technology of *their* early years."[3] The author of *Surviving the Information Age* speculates that children's innate confidence with using digital devices has to do with the fact that they are unaware of the computer's origins as a hulking presence in cloistered backrooms. It was "the essence of the mainframe—dark, mysterious, overwhelming—that shaped perceptions that are still with us,"[4] but children have never known the computer as anything but a magical device, a sophisticated toy, with which they can play games and view bright, fascinating images. And, according to Mark Poster, if children "often tend to respond more openly to the new technologies, accepting them more easily than their elders as part of the social landscape," it is because they have no pre-existing ways of knowing or positions of authority which are threatened by the advent of the machine.[5]

Later in this chapter, I will throw all such explanations into doubt by suggesting that the stories about kids' affinity for computers is a rhetorical strategy whereby computer use is constructed as an inevitability for both children and adults. For the moment, however, what is important is the unquestioned belief in that affinity through which "today's children and digital technologies are aligned as natural bedfellows."[6]

Indeed, it would seem that one has merely to plunk a toddler down in front of a computer and in no time at all he or she will be keyboarding comfortably and mousing around the Internet like a seasoned user. As Larry Cuban observes:

> Since the early 1980s, photos of diaper-clad babies facing computer screens and using a mouse have appeared in popular media and delighted (or alarmed) many Americans. The rapt engagement of the very young with software—one company even puts out CD-ROMS for 9-month-old infants—reminds adults not only that the electric millennium is upon us but that very young children are virtual learning machines.[7]

So prevalent is the assumption of the affinity of children for computers that it has even become fodder for cartoonists. I have before me a cartoon that depicts two women walking in the park, one pushing a stroller from which protrude the top of an infant's head and an open laptop. Turning to her companion, the mother remarks, "We gave her the laptop last Christmas and she's already gotten a job offer from Microsoft!"[8]

Of course, like many myths, the notion that children possess an innate ability to use computers has a basis in reality. How many times have you heard a doting parent eagerly offer stories of his or her child's digital proficiency? Recently, I watched a two-year-old clamber up onto a desk, turn on his parents' home computer, and then confidently click and double-click his way to a favourite on-line game: "Mr. Potatohead." However, rather than taking this remarkable feat as a sign that children are natural computer users, I take it as evidence of something we have always known: that children are natural *learners*, and that they will learn to do what they see others around them doing. Thus, computing may indeed become second nature for children in middle-class households, but those growing up in less privileged surroundings will be less likely to develop an affinity for high technology which they encounter only infrequently at school.

However, the mythology of children's innate ability to use high technology disregards all such issues. Concerns about discrepancies in access according to socio-economic status, and even questions about the real implications of access (is a two-year-old who interacts with a digital Mr. Potatohead learning something quite different about the world than the two-year-old who manipulates the actual toy?) are washed away by the waves of celebratory rhetoric that repeatedly insists *all* children take to computers naturally and effortlessly, regardless of their socio-economic background. As techno-enthusiast Nicholas Negroponte proclaims, "The haves and the have-nots are now the young and the old."[9] This is also the tacit message of educational computing guru Seymour Papert's book, significantly entitled *The Children's Machine*, in which he proclaims, "Across the world children have entered a passionate and enduring love affair with the computer," which they view "as 'theirs'—as something that belongs to them," and which they learn to use "more easily and naturally" than their parents.[10] Communications specialist Don Tapscott agrees that "[m]ost kids love the technology," which is for them a natural part of their environment. Tapscott goes on to offer a number of stories about youngsters who install software for their parents, train their teachers in the use of the technology, and help their parents shop for computers.[11]

Advertisers also capitalize on and perpetuate the view, as Bill Gates puts it, that "[k]ids and computers get along just great."[12] The image of the child staring at a computer screen in wide-eyed engrossment has become stock fare in software and hardware advertisements, particularly for those companies seeking to tap into the lucrative "e-learning" market. For instance, some time ago I received in the mail an advertisement for a "Computers 4 Kids" program, which offers parents a computer bundled with an "interactive learning library" of software specifically targeted to children. The ad features an image of a young boy gazing with total absorption at a computer screen while his mother looks on, clearly delighted that her son is so spellbound by the machine as to be impervious to her own presence. Of course, we know that in the real world, if not the fairy-tale world of advertisements, such single-minded fascination with the screen would tend to suggest that the child is using a video game, not a challenging program on long division. Nevertheless—and despite the occasional appearance of cogent objections to the technologization of children's lives and learning[13]—our conviction that children have a natural ability to use digital devices, and that this affinity is a boon both for the children themselves and society as a whole, remains relatively unshaken.

The purpose of this chapter is to explore the dimensions and significance of this myth of the "techno-friendly child."[14] If children really do take to the use of digital devices like fish to water, then can we expect that, in a generation or two, as young people grow up to become confident computer users, the hierarchy of computer knowledge will simply disappear and computer anxiety and the social construction of the idiotic, inept User will become cultural phenomena of the past? Or is the assumption that kids and computers go together like peanut butter and jelly perpetuated by technophiles and digital elites who seek, by tapping into the mythology of computer use, to appeal to our deep-rooted needs and insecurities as both parents and users of complex and fundamentally unknowable technologies—and to construct those who do not use computers themselves and purchase computers for children's home and school use as out-of-step with the times?

The Social Construction of Childhood

I suggested in chapter 2 that the computer user is not a natural category but one that emerged through and continues to be sustained by the struggles of individuals and social groups to lay claim to computer power. In *The Disappearance of Childhood,* Neil Postman reminds us that childhood is also an artificial social construct:

> Unlike infancy, childhood is a social artifact, not a biological category. Our genes contain no clear instruction about who is and who is not a child. . . . In fact, if we take the word children to mean a special class of people somewhere between the ages of seven and, say, seventeen, requiring special forms of nurturing and protection, and believed to be qualitatively different from adults, then there is ample evidence that children have existed for less than four hundred years.[15]

We may be taken aback by the odd-looking, solemn-faced children depicted in medieval paintings, but as Postman points out, the artists were simply rendering young people as they were actually seen at the time: as small adults, with the same physical proportions, facial expressions, mannerisms, and dress as adults.

In fact, the medieval tendency to regard children seven and older as, for all intents and purposes, adults who were able to participate fully in all community activities, including work, persisted well into the nineteenth century.[16] A high birth rate and conditions of extreme poverty contributed to a perception of children as economic entities whose value as family members related primarily to their earning potential: "Parents regularly treated their children not only as their private property to do with as they wished, but also as chattels whose well-being was expendable in the interests of family survival."[17] Such a view of childhood may be difficult to fathom today, but, as Lionel Rose suggests in his study of child labour from 1860 to 1918, in order to understand it we must first try "to visualize streets and tenements, villages and courts, teeming with child life."[18] Children, in other words, represented a plentiful, endlessly renewable, and therefore expendable resource which employers readily exploited, first in fields and domestic service and later, with the coming of steam power, in mines and factories. Rose cites the 1861 census returns for England and Wales, which indicate that approximately one-third of boys and girls aged five to nine, and about half of boys and girls aged ten to fourteen, were employed, many in textile factories.[19]

It should be noted, however, that the appeal of children as factory labourers was not simply a matter of their sheer proliferation across the industrial era landscape, nor even of their willingness to work cheaply. In *The Children of Frankenstein*, Herbert Muller points out that, during the Industrial Revolution, many factory owners preferred to hire young people because they were better able to master and adapt to the use of the new techniques and technologies of mass production. Muller offers the example of Richard Arkwright, a textile manufacturer who employed mostly children because they could be more easily taught, as he put it, "to conform to the regular celerity of the machine" while, says Muller, "men with skills were apt to make poor machine-tenders."[20] Arkwright's preference for technologically adaptable child labour certainly sheds an interesting historical light on the enthusiasm with which we now contemplate children's "natural" affinity for digital devices.

The nineteenth-century outcry against industrialists who, like Arkwright, exploited the labour power of young people reflected an emerging view of childhood as a special time of life, distinct from adulthood. It became increasingly unacceptable, both socially and morally, to regard children as economic entities and to use them to perform arduous, poorly paid work. Rather, people began to perceive youngsters as a separate category of social beings in need of special considerations and protection. This transformation in the attitude towards childhood stemmed from a variety of social factors, including new medical and birth-control technologies and the rise of literacy. The former developments had the effect of promoting deeper attachments between parents and offspring, as families became smaller and children more likely to survive past infancy. And the emergence of the printing press, and therefore of literacy as a criterion for full participation in life, meant that increasingly young people could not simply enter the adult world when, at the age of seven or thereabouts, they had mastered spoken language.[21] Now, they must spend their childhood years in school, learning to read and write.

The schooling that began to emerge as early as the seventeenth century functioned to set children apart physically from the rest of society. It also contributed to a new definition of childhood as an intermediary stage of life that involved *preparation* for adult life rather than gainful employment itself. As Muller observes, "[T]he idea began taking hold that youngsters were entitled to a childhood of school and play, freedom from adult responsibilities."[22] And as young people began to associate increasingly with each other in educational institutions, they began also to form a subculture, characterized by games, songs, books, and other activities and artifacts unique to the distinct social group known as children. Thus, once established as a social institution, public education served to entrench notions of childhood, such that it grew to seem—as it does today—not an artificial social construct but an entirely natural biological category.

Well into the Victorian era, however, the mode of schooling tended to be based on a view of children as corrupt souls in need of enforced moral guidance. Discipline was frequent, and often harsh: "Since children . . . were thought to be corrigible though wicked, strict and prolonged discipline from infancy was considered obligatory lest the Devil get them and the family come to harm."[23] Discipline was also an effective means of breaking a child's spirit as preparation for a passive life of routinized factory labour.[24]

In *Centuries of Childhood*, Philippe Aries discusses the significance of this "insistence on humiliating childhood, to mark it out and improve it." According to Aries, "birching" was the most common form of school discipline, and this degrading form of corporal punishment was administered to all members of the school population. The fact that school masters meted out the same discipline to adolescents and much younger students alike tended to "diminish the distinctions between childhood and adolescence, to push adolescence back towards childhood," and, moreover, to construct childhood as a state "characterized by deliberate humiliation. . . . The concept of the separate nature of childhood, of its difference from the world of adults, began with the elementary concept of its weakness."[25] Thus, as Michel Foucault might observe, rather than regarding the harsh school discipline that prevailed even a century ago as a negative exercise of power over children, we should consider the concept of childhood itself as the positive product, at least in part, of the methods of discipline by which youngsters were trained to become "docile bodies."[26]

In the eighteenth century, however, Enlightenment thinkers began to offer more humane conceptions of childhood which would, in subsequent centuries and even up to the present day, play a vital role in transforming popular views. Jean Jacques Rousseau, in particular, "called for a break with the old notion that the child was depraved until redeemed by strictest moralistic disciplining."[27] To Rousseau, and to Romantic poets such as William Wordsworth and William Blake, the child was not inherently sinful but innocent; and the natural childhood state of purity, joy, spontaneity, and natural goodness was eroded with each passing day of growth, worldly experience, and education in the ideologies and practices of an unnatural and corrupt society. Thus, in *Ode to Immortality*, Wordsworth very clearly describes the child's progression towards adulthood as a fall from grace: "Heaven lies about us in our infancy!" but "Shades of the prison-house begin to close/Upon the growing boy."

From the Middle Ages to the eighteenth century, then, children evolved, in the popular view, from streetwise, grimy-faced factory workers, to depraved souls in need of saving, to innocent beings requiring protection from a corrupt world. And now we are confronted with what is offered, by many technophiles, as the next, inevitable stage in the evolution of the concept of childhood: the computer-savvy child, who seems as comfortable in the virtual realm of digital bits as he or she is among the playground trees and grass. Indeed, according to Douglas Rushkoff, "screenagers"—children who live their lives in front of television and computer screens—represent the key to the evolution of humanity as a whole since, unlike most adults, they readily accept the need to adapt to technology. Rushkoff attempts to prove in *Playing the Future* that this adaptation is necessary if our species is to continue to evolve intellectually and spiritually.

Innocence and Experience

Contemporary ideas about childhood may seem to owe the greatest debt to the more humane conceptions of Enlightenment thinkers such as Rousseau; however, the matter is not quite so clear-cut. Earlier constructions of children as fully functioning members of society, and as innately sinful beings in need of a harsh moral upbringing, still survive. We see their traces, for instance, in the persistence of child pornography, in the current debates on spanking, and in the new tendency to try minors who commit heinous crimes, as adults.

The complex historical legacy—which I have, of necessity, grossly oversimplified—may go a long way towards explaining why the idea of childish innocence that prevails in the Western world today exists side by side with an apparently contradictory perspective that regards children as competent, rational members of society, and workers of the future. Thus, according to Philippe Aries, we seek to safeguard youngsters "against pollution by life," while at the same time attempting to build the character and reason they will need in order to function successfully in the adult world: "on the one hand childhood is preserved and on the other hand it is made older than its years."[28] Neil Postman refers to these two contrary perceptions of childhood as the Romantic and Protestant views: the former constructs the child as an innocent who "possesses as his or her birthright capacities for candor, understanding, curiosity, spontaneity," which should be celebrated and nurtured, while the latter perceives the child as an "unformed person" who must, by stern direction and harsh discipline, "be made into a civilized adult."[29]

This paradoxical construction of childhood is nowhere manifested quite so clearly as in popular representations of the youthful computer user. As I suggested at the beginning of this chapter, a common theme of books and articles about kids and computers is the child's affinity for digital devices. Many texts thus tend to represent the child as a "natural" user and the computer as a safe playground in which, as one enthusiast puts it, "kids can be kids."[30] But running parallel to such stories of childhood innocence are tales of childhood experience. Although also based on the child's affinity for technology, experience narratives emphasize not the innocence of the children and the naturalness of their relationship with computers but, instead, the absolute importance of directing children's use of digital devices and of ensuring that they acquire the information-technology skills needed for survival in the adult world.[31] The former story is one of simplicity and ease, in which doting parents merely sit by, as in the "Computers 4 Kids" ad, and let nature take its course; the latter tale is one of regulation and preparation, in which educational reformers, policymakers, and digital elites call for and institute initiatives that will regulate children's access to and use of computers.

In the first instance, then, stories about the child's "natural" attraction to and ability to function within an idyllic digital playscape represent a means by which the ideology of childhood innocence is extended into the new, high-tech millennium. Consider, for example, George Leonard's 1968 classic, *Education and Ecstasy*, in which the author depicts the computer as a part of the child's landscape that is as natural as trees and flowers. In Leonard's imagined school of 2001 AD (which, like most imagined futures, foretells nothing so much as the futility of prophecy), children "are absolutely free to go and do anything they wish"[32]—and what most of them wish to do, in Leonard's utopian vision, is to sprawl among the pillows in the "great dome" and plug their brains into the "laser learning displays."[33]

Writing thirty years later, Don Tapscott takes Leonard's idyllic vision of a future replete with machines in the garden one step further. The machine *is* the garden for Tapscott's "Net Generation" of youngsters who grow up using computers: "By necessity, cyberspace has become an N-gen playground and hangout. It is a place where they can play and have fun."[34] Compare this rhetoric to a magazine advertisement for Macintosh computers which appeared several years ago. The ad offers an extreme close-up of a child's blue eyes and asks us to "Imagine a special place filled with magic. A place where you can explore, and discover. A place where you can do amazing things. A place where you can see the world through a child's eyes." In the ad, as in the books, the assumption is that the computer is a safe, "natural" environment in which the innocent child can explore, discover, and learn in ways that accord with his or her innate inclinations.

Experience narratives also align children with computers, but now the relationship is represented as something that should be promoted, monitored, and regulated through pedagogical practices, policy interventions, and strategic purchases in order to ensure that the workers of the future, and thus society as a whole, are adequately prepared to function within an information-based economy. This story is found in many government policy documents, where it rationalizes the use of millions of taxpayer dollars to wire schools and equip youngsters with laptops. It is also found in advertisements, as in a magazine ad for Compaq computers, which depicts an adolescent boy sitting in a subway, gazing with interest at the businessman who sits across from him. In large red print beneath the image are the words, "Compaq computers give students the skills they need to survive in the real world. (Like working on Compaq computers for instance.)" The smaller text that follows includes the observation, "Students need to be prepared for the rough and tumble of real life. Getting them PCs that are used in more Fortune 1000 businesses than any other can help. It makes sense." The ad's clear message is that only the acquisition of computer skills, and specifically Compaq computer skills, will enable this youngster to make the transition to adulthood and successful participation in the "real world."

A similar message is conveyed by the aforementioned advertisement for the "Computers 4 Kids" program, which warns parents that they must begin now to prepare their children for a successful future: "If our children are to succeed in the world of tomorrow, they must be able to handle the rapid exchange and assimilation of information through computer technology. One of the best ways to equip our children for the future is by making the entire family computer conversant." In the same way, Tapscott—who, as we have seen, also promotes the ideology of childhood innocence—insists upon the importance of getting computers into the schools because "fluency with the new media is required for productive life in the new economy and effective citizenship in the digital age."[35]

In fact, the narratives of childhood innocence and experience are by no means mutually exclusive. They exist side by side, for instance, in the advertisement below (see fig. 10), which paradoxically emphasizes both the child's innocence, in the freshness of his face and the wide-eyed wonderment of the gaze he directs upon the computer screen, and his technical competence—the suggestion being that the tyke is well on the way to becoming a wealthy, powerful tycoon by virtue of the computer skills he is developing now.

The themes of childhood innocence and experience are similarly juxtaposed in a cartoon that appears in Heather Menzies' *Computers on the Job*. The cartoon depicts a plump, chubby-cheeked little girl sitting on her bed, beside her teddy bear, and announcing to her stupefied mother her solemn plans to become a productive member of a technological society: "I've been thinking about what to do with the rest

FIGURE 10: *BMO Nesbitt Burns advertisement: Themes of childhood innocence and experience.*

of my life. Systems analyst sounds good to me. What do you think?"[36]

Passive Consumers of Technology

These texts, in themselves, probably play a fairly insignificant role in limiting and constructing the possibilities of computer use by children. In fact, all of the books and advertisements to which I have referred are specifically intended for an adult audience and are actually intended to disarm adults' resistance to computer use. As the authors of a British study suggest:

> [T]he discursive production of the child as a natural and competent user of new technologies . . . is primarily employed as a rhetorical device to ensure the uptake of ICT [information and communications technologies] use by adults rather than in relation to discussions of children's own use of computers.[37]

In other words, books, articles, and advertisements that align kids and computers are explicitly designed to promote a view of computer use as being mere "child's play." Artifacts which might otherwise seem sophisticated, threatening, and unknowable, become transparent and beneficent by virtue of their affiliation with innocent youngsters.[38] The intention is to erode adult resistance to and anxiety about computer use by making such a position seem both unwarranted and indefensible. As Ursula Franklin puts it in *The Real World of Technology*, the advertisers' depiction of young computer users "is aimed at creating an atmosphere of harmless domesticity around the new technology to ease its acceptance. Who could fear these cute and clever things that make life so interesting at home when the kids play games on them?"[39]

But these narratives of childhood innocence and experience function on another level—to construct adults not merely as users but, more particularly, as *consumers* of technology. For, ultimately, the stories about the alignment of kids and computers told in books, articles, and advertisements offer the same moral, which can be summed up in a single word: *access*. If we regard children as innocents whose alliance with technology is entirely natural and beneficial, then it is the responsibility of the caring adult not to protect children from their undisciplined urges but to provide them with what they intuitively crave: access to computers. And if we regard children as future productive members of our technological society, then what becomes important is their ability to function as information workers—which, once again, suggests that the adult's responsibility is to prepare the child for a successful future by providing access to computers now.

Adults are therefore compelled, by both narratives, to become computer consumers. And as a moral obligation, the imperative of access effectively disarms discussion about the value or benefits of computer use by children. Indeed, we tend to assuage any qualms or concerns we might have about young people's use of computers by reverting to, and thus further buttressing, the narratives: "by pointing out the children's own open-armed acceptance of computers, as though nothing could be more natural,"[40] or by reiterating the importance of preparing children to function effectively in a high-tech world. Stories about kids' affinity for computers may begin as a mode of constructing social reality, but by the time they pass into common parlance and common sense, they appear to be nothing more than accurate reflections of the "natural" relationship between children and digital devices.

As they are appropriated as moral imperatives by parents and educators, the narratives of innocence and experience impinge indirectly, but irresistibly, upon the options available to children when it comes to computer use. Youngsters are offered two fairly limiting narratives within which to situate themselves as computer users: as innocents or as knowledgeable workers of the future (or, paradoxically, as somehow partaking of both qualities). But children themselves do not necessarily acquiesce in these social constructions. Whereas the form of resistance most prevalent among adults is simple avoidance of the technology (as we saw in chapter 6), children today, even less than adults, simply do not have the luxury of choice in the matter of whether they will or will not use computers: the narratives themselves have prompted us to construct a world in which more and more school activities and lessons involve the unavoidable use of the computer for research, communication, and so forth. (An acquaintance recently told me that she had to buy her son a CD burner because he was unable to complete his homework without one.) And any resistance to the use of computers that cannot be overcome by the demands of schooling is likely to crumble before the sheer onslaught of peer pressure. Consider, for instance, how socially disadvantaged those children will be who haven't the technological wherewithal to participate in such popular modes of communication as instant messaging and cellphone "texting."

For children, then, resistance tends to involve not avoidance but appropriation. In other words, children seek to challenge the authority of parents and teachers by transforming the meaning of their own computer use. Thus, children's actual modes of engagement with technology suggest a deliberate attempt to subvert the constraining subject positions imposed by the adult narratives of innocence and experience. Children resist the ideology of innocence by using the computer to access regions of experience from which youngsters are traditionally shielded—in particular, sexuality and violence—and even by posing as adults in on-line exchanges. Adults may put in place filters designed to protect children from the pornography and pedophilia that lurk in the dark corners of the Net, but it is in such dark corners that the true lure of the Net lies for many young users, and they will therefore do anything in their power to find a way to "break" such filters, and thus challenge adult authority.

Conversely, children resist the narrative of experience by reverting to childlike behaviour—that is, by using the computer primarily as a "toy," a forum for playing games. The fact that, as David Brown observes in *Cybertrends*, the most popular games are those which present extremes of violence, suggests that children have found at least one way to resist the imposed subject positions of innocence and experience in a single act of rebellion: by playing "entrenched digital fantasies, such as Sega's Mortal Kombat" in which "kids are invited to rip off heads and tear out the hearts of their adversaries."[41]

In the end, however, these modes of engagement—which merely cement the bond between kids and computers, youth culture and technoculture—achieve little in the way of subverting the social construction of the youthful User as one who, whether innocent or experienced, is more or less in thrall to digital devices. For whether they are downloading music files, e-mailing friends, surfing the Net, or playing games (the most common on-line activities of nine- to seventeen-year-olds, according to a 2001 study by the Media Awareness Network),[42] young computer users remain essentially passive in the sense that they willingly enter into and accept the conditions imposed by pre-constructed worlds in which they have no authority to "modulate, change, or produce 'information.'"[43]

Thus, while youngsters may gaze at computer screens with engrossed fascination, it goes without saying that each child's wide-eyed gaze is fastened on a screen that is of someone else's making. And while they may explore on-line environments, they do so not as constructors of knowledge but, on the whole, as consumers of information, since the Web is increasingly designed, as even techno-enthusiast Rushkoff admits, to "lull young users into passive complacency so that they may be herded away from interactive exchanges and toward the 'buy' button."[44] Even play, that most creative of childhood activities, which typically involves the invention of imaginary realms, becomes transmuted, on-line, into the passive experience of entering into a constructed world in which the rules and interactions are mediated and delimited by someone else's code. The child's role, as a player, is merely to assume a pre-defined, one-dimensional identity: Ninja fighter. Gladiator. Superhero. User.

Of course, to say this is to fly squarely in the face of a great deal of hyperbole as well as more thoughtful inquiry on the subject of youthful users. Sherry Turkle, in particular, has spent many years conducting field work with computer-using youngsters, and contends, in both *The Second Self* and *Life on the Screen*, that digital devices have become so thoroughly entrenched in our culture that children increasingly think about themselves in computational terms and use computers and on-line environments as "evocative objects" for identity exploration and formation. In fact, Turkle's thesis that children "find themselves" in the machine is not so different from my own; but whereas

Turkle optimistically regards the glass as half full, I tend to see it as half empty. That is, where she views children as engaged in an active exploration of self, whether they are playing video games, surfing the Net, or chatting with each other on-line, I regard youthful users as readily submitting to the rules, limits, mindsets, and ways of being that are imposed on them by the pre-programmed realities that prevail in a point-and-click digital universe. And where she views computers as "objects-to-think-with,"[45] I see them as artifacts that are increasingly used, by both children and adults, in rote, compulsive ways which are inherently antithetical to the possibilities of self-knowledge and responsible action.

Having willingly entered into these pre-packaged realms, then, children also relinquish control over the kinds of beings they become when they sit down in front of the screen; and thus, in a process that remains largely unnoticed and unexamined by both the children and by their parents and teachers, youngsters learn not only to use the mouse, find information on-line, and destroy alien life forms, but also to become passive, well-disciplined users and consumers of pre-constructed programs. Of course, there will inevitably be some children for whom resistance will involve learning to create digital worlds, and it is indeed upon such individuals that most of Turkle's research focuses. Her purpose, as she states it in *The Second Self*, is to attend not to "'average' computer users" but to "ideal types," youngsters who spend most of their time delving into the inner workings of computers, who use programming languages and chatrooms as a means of interrogating the implications of virtuality.[46] However, as a recent survey of young Canadians' computer use suggests,[47] such youngsters represent the exception rather than the rule. Most kids are mindlessly downloading music, surfing the Net, and playing games—and we can expect this majority to grow from youthful users to adults well prepared to inhabit pre-constructed worlds and to accept the identities that those worlds confer.

The social construction of children as inevitably aligned with high technology—either because it is their "natural" environment or because it is the realm in which they, as the digital generation, must learn to function—thus reduces youthful users to a homogenous mass of indistinguishable, albeit wide-eyed, technology users. Should we, then, regard the computer-savvy child as the next stage in the evolution of the concept of childhood? Or would it be more accurate to view contemporary conceptions of computer-friendly youngsters as a throwback to the days when factory urchins were required to relinquish individuality and engage passively with technology, and to the days when harsh discipline was the primary means of achieving what inducing total absorption in the simulated, sensory-stimulating world of video games accomplishes today: the formation of "docile bodies"? It behooves us to consider whether contemporary representations of childhood do indeed represent a positive step forward, because, as Postman points out, social constructions of childhood are also, by default, social constructions of adulthood, and therefore of society as a whole: "In saying what we wish a child to become, we are saying what we are."[48] As we celebrate the evolution of childhood into a "natural" alliance with cybernetic systems, what are we also saying about the nature of humanity and its future?

Conclusion

The Future User

In chapter 2, I offered an alternative history of computers that emphasized how the development of digital devices was paralleled by a struggle for computer power from which, as we have seen, the unknowing, homogenous User emerged. That struggle, needless to say, has not ceased. Indeed, I sought, in subsequent chapters, to suggest the ways in which various discourses and transactions, from software production to advertising, continue to embody that struggle for the power to determine the nature of the computer User and the meaning of computer use.

My purpose in this Conclusion is to extend that historical perspective with a brief look at that minor but powerful deity in the technopantheon: the Future. This is not to say that I intend to engage in the kind of crystal-ball gazing which passes, among technophiles, for a serious contemplation of the social and human implications of rampant computerization. I have already suggested that such prophecy is, as the author of *Futurehype* eloquently asserts, tyrannical in the sense that it closes down other avenues of thought and thus often becomes self-fulfilling. Such prophecy is also, I believe, morally deficient in that it focuses—and, in its use of hyped language, promotes a continued emphasis—upon what technology can and will do while pushing its human users right out of the viewfinder. Humanity thus appears, if at all, as a blur of flesh at the perimeter of an otherwise glowing picture of an "empowering" technology.

Social critique offers a powerful and much-needed antidote to the hyped visions of a technologically enhanced future. Critics such as Roszak, Stoll, and Dublin continually remind us that the prophesies are no more than "high tech mumbo jumbo,"[1] largely motivated by self-interest and greed; but they also emphasize that, rather than merely dismissing the future hype as such, we must recognize that the power of the "rhetoric of prediction"[2] is such that it can help bring about the anticipated future by closing down alternative avenues of thought and action. However, as I also suggested in the Introduction, some of the critics who seek to counter the hype perpetuate the assumption that technology is an unstoppable force, changing everything as it steamrolls its way across the social landscape. Although their commendable purpose is to rouse us from the state of passive acceptance into which we have fallen, the danger of the bleak prognostications offered by Ellul, Postman, Roszak, Stoll, and others is that the underlying rhetoric of inevitability may actually tend to reinforce that passivity by also shutting down the possibilities for action and meaningful response. Whether we ride the technological bandwagon with mindless delight or with a grim awareness that it is careening out of control, the future appears to be equally out of our hands.

What we need as we confront the future, then, is certainly not more prognostication, either of the gleeful or grim variety, about the future of technology. Rather, what we need is to begin to come to terms with what such forecasts mean in terms of the social construction of the human beings who engage with that technology. In what follows, I explore three visions of the future commonly offered by technoprophets: artificial intelligence, ubiquitous computing, and transhumanism. Each vision is based on assumptions, generally unstated and unquestioned, about who the User is, and commensurate with these, assumptions about who the User will become. Following a brief discussion of each prophesied technological future and its implications for the social construction of the computer User, I conclude by offering a fourth possibility—not a hyped prophecy based on the inexorable logic of technological advancement, but a simple hope, with no guarantees.

It should be noted at the outset that each of these prophesied futures—artificial intelligence, ubiquitous computing, and transhumanism—is typically offered by its proponents as an unavoidable development that will prevail over other versions of the future and that will affect all human beings in the same way. My treatment of the three technological futures as separate possibilities, each with its own implications for the social construction of the computer User, runs the risk of perpetuating these underlying assumptions. Let me clarify, then, that—although each camp of future-thought appears to be intent upon ensuring that its own version of the future becomes reality, at the expense of other prophecies—these forecasts are by no means mutually exclusive.

My decision to treat each future separately has more to do with an inability to begin to imagine how artificial intelligence, ubiquitous computing, and transhumanism might play out in relation to one another in the years to come rather than with a belief that one camp will obliterate the others in the struggle to invent the future. Certainly, the *Star Trek* television series and its sequels provide one very optimistic conceptualization of how all three elements might be seamlessly integrated. The shows depict a futuristic world of androids, of holodeck virtual reality experiences indistinguishable from real life, and of computation so pervasive that it is fair to say that the entire starship *Enterprise* is one massive, super-intelligent computer. But this made-for-TV future is situated in a fictional world in which technology develops through an evolutionary process (survival of the best) and is diffused evenly throughout society, while in reality the ways in which a technology develops and is used arise largely from ongoing social choices and negotiations. Although the totalizing visions described below would suggest otherwise, there is not a single future towards which we are inexorably headed but multiple futures, which will emerge from our own decisions and actions as social agents.

Artificial Intelligence

In 1950, computers were large, impressive machines covered with mysterious flashing lights. They were often referred to as "electronic brains," and the question on everyone's mind was "Can machines think?" One man who sought to address this question was Alan Turing, a brilliant, eccentric mathematician who first conceived of the binary computer. In an influential 1950 article entitled "Computing Machinery and Intelligence," Turing dismissed the question "Can machines think?" as too vague, "too meaningless to deserve discussion,"[3] and rearticulated it in unambiguous, behavioural terms: "Can a computer win the imitation game?" The imitation game—or the Turing Test, as it came to be known—involves placing an interrogator in a room with a teletype terminal, which is connected to a computer in another room. The interrogator's task is to pose questions on any subject via the terminal and decide, according to the responses given, whether the output comes from a computer or a human respondent in the other room. If the interrogator believes that he or she has been communicating with another person, or is uncertain whether the questions have been answered by a machine or a human being, then, according to Turing, the computer can be considered "intelligent."

In the same article in which he described the imitation game, Turing predicted that most computers would be able to pass the test within fifty years—that is, by the year 2000. That prediction has not been borne out, but the challenge set forth by the imitation game has nevertheless played a critical role in launching and sustaining the field of artificial intelligence (AI). Today, AI encompasses a broad range of endeavours, including robotics, research into natural language (systems capable of recognizing and responding to inputs in an "ordinary" language, such as English), optical character and voice recognition (computer comprehension of written and spoken language), and expert systems (programs that emulate the decision-making processes of human experts). As they debate the meaning of *intelligence*, AI researchers are also compelled to delve into such issues as knowledge representation, pattern recognition, the nature of human thought processes, and, ultimately, what it means to be human.

In recent years, ideas about machine intelligence have moved out of the laboratory and into everyday language and thought, thanks in large part to media reports that play up the fascination and drama of computers capable of defeating chess champions and robots which behave like sentient beings. Some AI researchers have also helped to popularize their field by offering provocative forecasts about the imminent creation of intelligent machines that will rival human capabilities. Hans Morovac, for instance, has no doubt that robot intelligence will surpass human intelligence well before 2050, and that our artificial progeny "will outperform us in any conceivable area of endeavor, intellectual or physical."[4] Similarly, Ray Kurzweil confidently predicts that an average, $1,000 personal computer will possess the brain power of a single human brain by 2025, of a small village by 2030, of the entire population of the United States by 2048, and of a trillion human brains by 2060.[5]

The result of such hyperbole, according to Sherry Turkle, is that we have become so invested as a society in the concept of artificial intelligence, and so accustomed to conceiving of our own thought processes in mechanical terms, that we increasingly use AI as a metaphor for thinking and talking about who we are.[6] Consider the proliferation of films—from *Blade Runner* to *A.I.*—in which sentient machines compel a re-examination of what it means to be human. Consider, also, the way in which the image of the computer's synaptic matrix has in recent years become almost a visual shorthand for our own heightened postmodern sensibilities.

But if the idea of machine intelligence is indeed seizing hold of the public imagination, it behooves us to ask what underlying attitudes and values are thereby working their way into our "common sense" understandings about who we are in relation to our machines. What subject position, in other words, does the "naturally intelligent" human user assume in relation to artificially intelligent computers?

Turing's "game" was premised on a fundamental mind-body split; on a definition of intelligence that privileged the capabilities of the computer (brain power, in Kurzweil's simplistic terms, is concomitant with the ability to perform calculations); and on the tacit assumption that, in the confrontation between humans and their machines, the outcome would not be a harmonious relationship among all players but the emergence of "winners" and "losers."[7] Despite lip service to the notion of intelligent machines that exist solely to serve humanity, these assumptions have more to do with simply pushing the limits of what is technologically possible while pushing people right out of the picture. According to Steve Mann:

> A common goal in the field of artificial intelligence (AI) is to create "smart" machines that can replace human functions, perhaps to the point where we will no longer be able to do things for ourselves. . . . We are robbed, then, of our ability to interact and respond to the decisions technology makes about what we want.[8]

Although the discourse of AI emphasizes the ways in which intelligent devices will empower human beings, much current research in the field appears to be motivated by the desire to create machines that can transcend human error and ineptitude and, eventually, exceed human capabilities. Consider, for instance, the work at MIT's Media Lab on the creation of intelligent agents. According to the BotKnowledge Web site, an "agent," or "bot," is a software program that, once executed, "can autonomously accomplish a task for a person or other entity."[9] Most bots are currently limited to single functions, be it performing on-line searches or filtering Internet data. The vision offered by Media Lab director Nicholas Negroponte, however, is of an intelligent agent capable of functioning as "a well-trained English butler" who "answers the phone, recognizes the callers, disturbs you when appropriate, and may even tell a white lie on your behalf."[10]

Negroponte touts these intelligent software programs as a means of empowering and liberating the human users whom they will someday serve, but surely the quest to develop software programs that think and filter information for us springs in large part from notions of User ineptitude. As Paulina Borsook suggests, lurking behind the work on intelligent agents is a "specific discomfort with people" and a "fear, contempt, and devaluation" of the subjective. Borsook goes on to describe a conference she attended in 1994, in which the future cheerily envisioned by many individuals involved in AI research and development was of "[a] world where technology in general and software in particular has taken over all higher human brain functions," a "happy land of a world serviced by agents" and thus no longer reliant on the whims and weaknesses of unpredictable human beings.[11] In this "happy land," the agent's role seems to be to provide, as one MIT Media Lab professor puts it, "intelligence augmentation"[12] for human beings whose cognitive abilities are clouded by emotion, imagination, and the relentless cravings of the body.

As they direct us to information, filter out unnecessary data, and otherwise compensate for the human mind's inability to cope efficiently and rationally with the onslaught of information, intelligent agents ultimately push the stumbling, error-prone human User aside. The agents themselves become a new breed of users, totally integrated with the technology. In the end, I find it difficult to conceive of a digital world populated by intelligent agents, robots, and other artificially intelligent entities in which the human User is not further deprived of power and control.

In the same article in which he introduced the imitation game, Turing made a remarkable prediction, which has remained relatively overlooked: he anticipated that, by the end of the twentieth century, "the use of words and general educated opinion will have altered so much that one will be able to speak of machines thinking without expecting to be contradicted."[13] In other words, Turing believed that, regardless of whether machine intelligence, as he defined it, had been achieved, the concept of AI would have so thoroughly infiltrated the public imagination that people would not only have accepted the possibility of machine intelligence but would also tend to valorize the logical perfection of the computer and seek to recreate themselves in its image.

Turing's prediction has been borne out by actual events. Increasingly, the machine's capabilities are considered prototypical of intelligence while humans are regarded as possessing a "natural stupidity" for which a technological solution is required. (Indeed, there is apparently a branch of AI known as "artificial stupidity," which involves the creation of computer programs that replicate human errors.)[14] Thus, Jaron Lanier contends that, if the Turing Test is to be won, it will not be because an inherently flawed software program achieves "intelligence"—an unlikely proposition in Lanier's books—but because its human users will "make ourselves stupid in order to make the computer software seem smart." And, adds Lanier, since we do this everyday, whenever we place our trust in ill-designed, buggy programs, we have already, in effect, "caused the Turing test to be passed."[15]

Now that we no longer ask, "Can machines think?"—now that we take it as a given that computers have superior intelligence and the evolutionary potential to vastly exceed human capabilities in the near future—it behooves us to reconsider the question that Turing so smoothly dismissed: "Can machines think?" Far from being meaningless, the question couched a number of existential queries, such as "Can machines think *for us*?" "Do our hopes for a utopian, leisured existence in the future lie with the capabilities of intelligent machines?" and "What of ourselves, do we relinquish if we give much of the control for day-to-day decision-making to our machines?"[16] All of these important questions, however, got lost in the reduction of the question "Can machines think?" to a game, an overt demonstration of computing power, which effectively shifted attention from human ends to technological means. I agree with Lanier that it's a game that the computer has already won, since merely by consenting to submit to the terms of the game, we also accede to an understanding of intelligence that excludes much of the richness of human thought and experience—all of those elements, in fact, which defy computation—and that therefore threatens to cast us, as users, into a state of perpetual self-enforced stupidity and reliance upon our super-intelligent machines.

Ubiquitous Computing

In 1949, when the ultimate in computing power was the 30-ton ENIAC with more than 17,000 vacuum tubes, the author of a *Popular Mechanics* article made a daring prediction: that "computers in the future may have only 1,000 vacuum tubes and perhaps weigh only

$1\frac{1}{2}$ tons."[17] In this era of laptops and Palm Pilots, such feeble forecasts seem ridiculous. However, if some more recent (and far less modest) prognostications hold true, today's cutting-edge technologies will soon seem as clunky and outmoded as ENIAC. Marching to the irresistible drumbeat of Moore's Law, the computing industry manages, year after year, to condense ever-more computing power into a smaller and smaller package; and some enthusiasts now foresee a time, in the not too distant future, when chip components will be microscopic, the size of an atom.[18]

As computers grow so small that they can be embedded in shoes and jewellery, interwoven in fabrics, and built into bricks, the anticipated result will be what is known as *ubiquitous* or *pervasive computing*. Ubiquitous computing means that "all 'things' can be digitally active"—from teacups and teddy bears to books and fruit bowls.[19] According to James Gleick,

> Pervasive computing is both a buzzword and a new field of study within computer science. It means computers in the walls, in tables, and chairs, in your clothing. Computers in the air, when engineers can figure that one out. (A group at Berkeley is working on "Smart Dust," financed by the Defense Advanced Research Projects Agency.) Computers fading into the environment.[20]

In the future, ubiquitous computing might bring us dishwashers that will calculate the most cost-efficient time to turn themselves on, door latches that will let in the dog while refusing admittance to the neighbour's pet, clothes that will clean themselves, shoes that will change colour according to the outfit one is wearing, food packaging that will recite instructions for the preparation of the package contents, eyeglasses that will automatically adjust according to what the wearer is looking at, and—this one doesn't bear too much contemplation—toilets that will monitor their users' diet, caloric intake, and general health.[21]

If digital miniaturization is fundamental to the vision of ubiquity, so too is connectivity—the notion that all these computerized devices will be interconnected in a pervasive unseen web, which will allow them to "communicate" with each other. In *The Age of Spiritual Machines*, Kurzweil foresees a not-too-distant time when the computers that people carry in their clothing, wallets, and briefcases are networked with "body LANS" (local area networks).[22]

In addition, all of our possessions—household appliances, walls, cars—will be in constant communication with each other, forming "a huge distributed network consisting of thousands of interconnected embedded systems that surround the user and satisfy needs for information, communication, navigation, and entertainment."[23] Thus, Negroponte anticipates a foreseeable future in which your toaster will be connected to an information source, enabling it to brand your breakfast bagel with the closing price of your favourite stock, and in which your refrigerator will be able to notify your car that you are out of milk, so that the car can remind you to pick some up on the way home.[24] (Kitchen appliances are star performers in many ubiquitous computing scenarios.) The head of IBM's Pervasive Computing department predicts that "[i]t's going to be more and more machines talking to machines, things talking to things, without human interaction."[25] The vision seems to be of a sort of "collective mind,"[26] an all-encompassing social intelligence embedded in the environment and in which the role of human beings is rather vaguely conceived.

Ubiquitous computing represents an attempt to make computers so easy to use that the notion of use simply disappears with the technology. You do not *use* the computer that is embedded in your car or in the walls of your home; you simply drive and otherwise live your life. In *The Invisible Computer,* Donald Norman writes that computers, which are embedded within everyday objects (what Norman refers to as *information appliances*), "can perform their valuable functions without the user necessarily being aware that they are there," so that computer use is indistinguishable from the performance of day-to-day tasks.[27] And as the user interface dissolves into the world of objects, the concept of the User also presumably disappears, since it is no longer necessary to know how to operate complex systems. One simply goes about one's business, while being continually monitored and aided by an army of invisibly interconnected objects. Hence, MIT's research in pervasive computing is called "Project Oxygen," suggesting that the goal is to create an atmosphere of information which is as unnoticed, ubiquitous, and presumably necessary to existence as the air we breathe.

Ubiquitous computing is the logical extension of the goal of user-friendliness, a fact which, given the analysis of the concept of user-friendliness offered in chapter 3, should certainly give us pause. Like the development of user-friendly interfaces, research in ubiquitous computing proceeds in the name of empowering people; but the research ultimately embodies the underlying values of user-friendliness as well as the tacit conceptions of the User upon which it is based. The fact that the User's incompetence and inability to interact with the computer on its own terms spawned the ubiquity movement in the first place goes a long way towards explaining why so many visions of this possible future are replete with computers functioning autonomously, while the people whom they presumably exist to serve seem to recede into the background, their capabilities and responsibilities, even for their own maintenance and well-being, seriously diminished. What is the human being actually *doing* while her toaster notifies the coffee maker that it's time to start perking and her refrigerator busily scans its contents and sends a grocery list to the car? Steadily regressing, suggests Christopher Dewdney, to a larva-like state of stasis in which an ambience "invested with more and more consciousness and, eventually, more autonomy" encloses her "like a proto-intelligent cocoon."[28]

We saw, in chapter 3, that the goal of user-friendliness currently justifies the creation of complex programs that compel us to become "computer-friendly," adaptive to interfaces in which hundreds of unnecessary features proliferate in the name of ease-of-use. If the anticipated world of ubiquitous computers emerges from the existing trajectory, then surely it will be a complex world indeed, and one which will render the individual increasingly powerless. If user-friendly systems compel us, for example, to capitalize the first letter of a new line of text, whether we like it or not, then how will user-friendly houses, cars, and appliances, with their multitudinous but unseen features, constrain and manipulate our behaviour? Will we learn to accept that we cannot purchase farm-fresh produce because the fridge becomes out of sorts when we bring home food lacking barcode identifiers? Will we adapt to the fact that the car balks when we try to take the most scenic, instead of the most efficient, route between two points? And will we be compelled in other ways to accept the assumptions built into the nano-machines in our homes, clothing, and appliances because the functioning of embedded computers will have moved completely outside the range of our comprehension?

Ubiquity, as a social goal, involves further depriving individuals of an understanding of the premises underlying the design of pervasive devices, and therefore putting them more than ever at the whim of the elite cadre of specialists who produce the gadgets that automate daily existence. It therefore involves reducing the hierarchy of computer knowledge to two clear-cut levels: those who know and those who do not. And ultimately, as one researcher in ubiquitous computing enthusiastically puts it, it involves the invention of a future in which members of the latter group will simply "stop talking about technology"[29]—let alone about the ways in which we are constructed as social beings through our participation within a social network increasingly populated not only by human beings but by the multitude of devices designed to monitor and serve us.

Transhumanism

According to Christopher Dewdney, we are "about to enter the transition period between the human and the posthuman eras—the transhuman age. The goal of transhumanism is to surpass our current biological limitations, be it our life span or the capabilities of our brain."[30] Whether as the amalgamations of human and machine parts known as cyborgs (short for cybernetic organisms) or as jacked-in virtual life forms who exchange biological bodies for the avatar of choice, human beings are, in Dewdney's view, evolving to a new plane of existence in which ideas about what it means to be human will be fundamentally transformed. The blurring of boundaries between the human and the machine is the essence of transhumanism.

As a relatively new area of research, transhumanism certainly does not possess the mystique of artificial intelligence, nor the practical appeal of pervasive computing. In fact, transhumanism researchers tend to be regarded as kooks. There's cyborg researcher Steve Mann, who admits that he draws many peculiar glances when he habitually dons headwear distinctly reminiscent of *Star Trek*'s the Borg and goes out into the world.[31] And there's Kevin Warwick, head of the University of Reading's Cybernetics Department, who has implanted silicon chips into his arm. In one experiment, Warwick had the chip connected directly to nerve fibres, so that brain impulses to his hand—for instance, signals that make the pinkie wiggle—could be stored and later reactivated. Warwick also plans to experiment with storing brain signals for pain and emotions.

Such experiments in transhumanism may strike most of us as bizarre and even distasteful, but the enthusiasts are at pains to remind us that the merging of humans and machines is already commonplace. According to Rodney Brooks, the director of MIT's AI Lab, transhumanism is happening now: We "are already starting to change ourselves from being purely biological entities into mixtures of biology and technology." Brooks offers as examples the electronic inner-ear implants that are replacing external hearing aids, and the research being done to treat paralysis with electrodes implanted in the brain.[32] Indeed, transhumanism may be beginning with even less invasive amalgamations of human and machine. As we grow more reliant on information technology, we also grow more inclined to carry it around with us in the form of laptops, cellphones, and Palm Pilots, thus making cyborgs of ourselves. According to Brooks, "the devices that are now external to our bodies will soon become internal." Indeed, he foresees a time in the not too distant future when "a direct wireless interface to the Internet, implanted directly in someone's brain, will become very popular":

> Imagine being able to access the world's information resources anywhere, anytime, without having to carry external devices. . . . You will be able to send e-mail while in the middle of a face-to-face meeting, requesting the required follow-up actions. You will be able to Internet chat to a remote colleague about the right negotiating strategy to use with the person to whom you are now talking face-to-face. Such capabilities will be powerful incentives to incorporate this technology into the body.[33]

Brooks anticipates a time when human biology will be so completely enhanced by hardware that it will become meaningless to distinguish between people and robots. Ray Kurzweil, however, predicts that the melding of humanity and computation will occur primarily at the level of software. Extending the vision of a downloaded brain offered by Hans Moravec in *Mind Children,* Kurzweil enthusiastically foresees a time when it will be commonplace to scan the brain, mapping all its neural components and connections, and then to transfer its contents and organization onto a computer. (Since this process will involve scanning and then scraping away layer after layer of brain matter, the original brain will be destroyed in the process.) Well before the end of the twenty-first century, insists Kurzweil, it will be common for people to "port their entire mind file"—in other words, their identity—to a computer:

> Is he—the newly installed mind—conscious? He certainly will claim to be. And being a lot more capable than his old neural self, he'll be persuasive and effective in his position. We'll believe him. He'll get mad if we don't.[34]

The new mind file will, of course, be bodiless, but by then synthetic bodies may be available to house the disembodied subject. And, Kurzweil reminds us, real bodies that can move around the physical world become expendable in the transhuman era. In cyberspace, we can choose whatever body we want: "a more attractive version of ourselves, a hideous beast, or any creature real or imagined."[35] Indeed, Kurzweil confidently predicts that late in the twenty-first century human beings will all have neural implants that will make it possible to tap in to a virtual world anytime, anywhere. (Of course, this forecast is distinctly at odds with his prediction that human beings will, by then, be mere mind files, without physical brains in which to implant devices, but such is the danger of overweening prophecy.)

The concept of "use" clearly has no place in the transhumanist vision. There will be no need to speak of users: since the machine will be within us, or we will be within the machine, humanity and computation will be synonymous. Transhumanists do not regard this amalgamation with technology as dehumanizing but as a means by which we will become superior entities—perhaps no longer precisely human, but superior nevertheless to our frail human selves. Indeed, Kurzweil contends that transhumanism, which essentially involves taking evolution into our own hands, is a necessity for the survival of our species. It is clear to him that, without technological enhancement, the human body cannot compete against the unrelenting efficiency and accuracy of the machine. We can't beat computers; therefore we must, in the most intimate of ways, join them.

Yet at the same time, transhumanist prophecy is uttered in a language that has less to do with human evolution than with the inevitability of progress and the "unfettered technological infiltration of our bodies."[36] According to Kurzweil, "A merger of the technology-inventing species with the computational technology it initiated the creation of" is an "inevitable step . . . in the evolution of intelligence" on our planet.[37] Not of humanity, mind you, but of intelligence. This language of inexorable technological advancement suggests that transhumanism emerges from a thought world in which flesh is not only frail but imminently expendable, and in which the true goal is not the enhancement of *human* capabilities and evolutionary possibilities but the liberation of computation from the limitations of the inanimate world.

Of the three futures which I have discussed, the transhumanist future represents the most direct attempt to rewire human subjectivity—

to tamper not just with devices but with our identities as amalgamations of flesh and machine. Which is perhaps what makes the prophecies particularly chilling, for underlying the visions of a transhumanist future is a fundamental disdain, or at least disregard, for the social contexts of technology use, and, ultimately, for the social agents who use them. The human beings in these visions have no connections to a lifeworld that might prevent them from wishing to port their identities into a computer's hard drive or to dwell entirely within a simulated dimension. In fact, the human beings are virtual non-entities, their brains, to use AI guru Marvin Minsky's famous phrase, mere "meat machines."

Like most visions of the future, transhumanism is represented by its proponents as not only an inevitable but also an entirely apolitical technological development. Nevertheless, we don't need William Gibson's dystopian cyberpunk representations of a posthuman world—a world in which corrupt, grossly wealthy individuals and corporate entities thrive while everyone else lives in a seamy technohuman underworld—to imagine the kinds of struggles that would take place if transhumanism became reality. It is easy, for example, to picture corporations vying for monopolistic power to define the subjectivity of the transhuman entity through the commodification of some new cybernetic body part. And as we picture that possible future, we should also consider this: if we are tyrannized, today, by the ceaseless lure of new and better hardware and software, imagine how difficult it will become to resist the demand to upgrade when upgrading has become commensurate with self-improvement. What intelligent transhuman entity would not eagerly grasp at the opportunity to have a larger memory, a faster processing speed, or access to a more engaging virtual world?

A Final Hope

Each of these prophesied futures—artificial intelligence, ubiquitous computing, and transhumanism—is offered by its proponents as an unavoidable development that will prevail over other versions of the future. The aura of inevitability is a powerful weapon in the struggle to invent the future. But should it really be a matter of concern to us today, as users, which of these three possible futures—or some combination thereof, or an entirely different vision—will prevail? Ultimately,

I think not. What really matters is that we understand that, as John Seely Brown and Paul Duguid point out, these predictions only *seem* inevitable because they include no consideration of social contexts.[38] After all, the real purpose of prophecy is not to predict the future but to marshal social thought, to replace what Max Dublin calls the "ethic of responsibility" with the "ethic of inevitability,"[39] so that we are willing to accept that whatever technological developments the future does bring will be desirable, good, and, in any case, unavoidable. Thus, regardless of whether or not it represents an accurate description of the direction in which computing is headed, all prophecy succeeds the moment we buy into the aura of inevitability. So Turing admitted over half a century ago; and while his prophecy regarding computer intelligence has been enormously influential, that significant admission has remained largely unheeded.

Largely unheeded, too, are the cautionary words of less optimistic prophets, whose gloomy prognostications of a human race increasingly in thrall to its technologies simply do not possess the popular appeal of the future hype. In the Introduction, I suggested that the critiques offered by Jacques Ellul, Neil Postman, and others are as tyrannical as the hype in that they also tend to shut down all avenues of human action. However, that it not entirely true. There is one door which these social critics always leave ajar, if only a crack: the possibility of critical reflection. Life inside the technological system, as Ellul describes it, may be bleak, but we are subject to the forces of that system only so long as we remain unaware of it. The moment we choose, as individuals, to step outside the system and examine it critically, its powers will begin to diminish. If Ellul carefully seals off all other means of escape, it is perhaps because he hopes to compel each of us to take this exit route: to seek, in our own lives, "ways of resisting and transcending technological determinants."[40] Throughout his books, Postman makes the similar assertion that to ask questions about technology "is to break the spell"[41] it has over us. In other words, it is only through critical reflection (what he refers to, in *Teaching as a Subversive Activity*, as "crap detecting")[42] that we can hope to understand how new technologies are shaping our lives and thereby begin to control their effects—disastrous effects which could, without careful stewardship, lead to the demise of culture as we know it.

In a previous book, I spoke highly about what I called the "critical imperative," this intellectual response to technological inevitability which is held out by many social critics as our only hope, a life preserver in an ocean of future hype.[43] And given the extent to which I draw, throughout this book, upon the words of wisdom offered by Postman, Ellul, and other social critics, there can be little doubt about how much I respect and value their insights. At the same time, however, I cannot help but be aware that, over the years, this call for critical reflection has had surprisingly little impact on the ways in which we, as a society, receive technology: most people, it would seem, prefer drowning to rescue. While I am still personally inclined to respect claims regarding the importance of critical reflection as a means of confronting rampant technological development, I also believe that, given its lack of impact and popular appeal, the critical imperative merits reconsideration.

The problem, as I now see it, is that the call for critical reflection comes from a rarefied, privileged realm in which such reflection is possible—a domain of intellectual life and *civilité* (I do not refer to a place, such as academia, so much as to a thought world) which is by nature exclusionary and which is, moreover, being steadily eroded by technoculture. Thus, although the social critics would seem to address the mass of humanity in their call for critical reflection, there is also the unavoidable underlying sense that their pessimism is a form of defense against the pressures of a mass culture in which most of us, with what Postman calls our "dull and even stupid awareness,"[44] are participant.

In fact, the incitement to critical thought is held out as a slender hope in the face of what the critics regard as the real problem: not unchecked technological development, per se, but the unquestioning, mindless way in which most people receive it. According to Langdon Winner, "[I]t seems characteristic of our culture's involvement with technology that we are seldom inclined to examine, discuss, or judge pending innovations with broad, keen awareness of what those changes mean," but instead "willingly sleepwalk through the process of reconstituting the terms of human existence."[45] Similarly, Lewis Mumford points out, "We have multiplied the mechanical demands without multiplying in any degree our human capacity for registering and reacting intelligently to them";[46] Postman protests the "customary mindless inattention" with which we receive culture-transforming technologies such as the television and the computer;[47] and Ellul describes his treatise in *The Technological Society* as "a call to the sleeper to awake."[48] Throughout his books, Marshall McLuhan also bemoans our "docile acceptance"[49] of new media. Indeed, in *Understanding Media,*

McLuhan writes that what is difficult for him to understand is not the impacts of new technologies so much as the unquestioning numbness with which we accept them into our lives: "So extraordinary is this unawareness that *it* is what needs to be explained."[50] Unfortunately, in thus representing the general public as a mindless, lemming-like mass, the social critics actually participate in constructing individual users not as fully participant members of society and agents of cultural change, but as a homogenous entity: the passive, mindless User.

The result, as Raymond Williams astutely observes, is that the members of the privileged minority culture who offer the pessimistic visions in effect lock horns with the social order as a whole.[51] Their "passionate concern for dispassionate objectivity" goes hand in hand with a cool, detached indifference "to a world which [they view] from afar."[52] They have lost their connection with a life world in which objective observation is simply an impossible indulgence, and in which involved coping and purposeful action, not detached reflection, are, as Martin Heidegger emphasizes, the fundamental ways of being and knowing: "The kind of dealing which is closest to us is . . . not a bare perceptual cognition, but rather that kind of concern which manipulates things and puts them to use; and this has its own kind of 'knowledge.'"[53]

For most computer users, then, the critical imperative is an impossible indulgence, for it is only the members of that privileged minority who have the luxury of choosing to distance themselves from digital technologies. Postman's claim that he does not own a computer and writes all of his books and articles by hand[54] is evidence of his integrity as a critic of technology, but there is also an element of elitism in the claim, since the fact is that *somebody* must input all of his handwritten pages into a computer—otherwise we would not be able to read them. Kirkpatrick Sale, author of *Rebels Against the Future*, made precisely this point in a 1997 radio interview: "I can *select* not to have a computer (so far), but I cannot *select* to be apart from the microchip and still be a part of the world in which I want to talk to people (and get books published). I am a prisoner of that world."[55]

It should be said, however, that far from being unique to the social critics, this elitist posture is, in fact, another point of similarity between those who offer optimistic and pessimistic visions of the future. Consider, for instance, Kurzweil's frequent reminders that his own book, *The Age of Spiritual Machines*, was dictated to a computer with superior voice recognition capabilities[56]—reminders which function to place Kurzweil within an inner circle of "digerati" who have access to advanced technologies unavailable to most of us, and who are therefore presumably in a position to decide for the rest of us what social ends those high-tech means should serve. In the end, neither the techno-utopians nor the social critics who counter the hype seem to be speaking about technology in a way which relates to us as social individuals coping with the contingencies and realities of the day-to-day use of computers, cellphones, PDAS, and other high-tech devices.

Recently, I came upon a Toshiba advertisement which inadvertently makes very clear the kinds of limitations within which most of us function when it comes to computer use (see fig. 11). Beneath a picture of a man sitting on a green lawn, using his Toshiba laptop to create a pie chart, are the words, "Life is full of choices. Made yours yet?" The choices to which the ad refers are "where you work," "when you work," and, of course, which computer you will buy—but *not* whether or not you will in fact be a computer user, which is clearly taken as a given. The ad is meant to speak to the ways in which the Toshiba laptop liberates its users, but what it really suggests is that, when it comes to computer use, true choice is rapidly receding before the ephemera of "options" and aesthetic variety. The individual user can customize toolbars, install quirky screen savers, purchase a strawberry-coloured computer, and even, perhaps, work outside instead of in the office, but these "choices" are no more meaningful than the option to press one or two on a touchtone phone. Increasingly, as poet Louis Dudek puts it in his elegant long poem, *Atlantis*, "we can choose / but we cannot choose what we choose."[57] This is not to say that our choices are determined by a self-augmenting technology, but that social, economic, and, indeed, mythical pressures are such that the behaviours and decisions that are considered socially acceptable are increasingly those associated with the use of digital technology, while avoidance of computer use goes hand-in-hand with a self-defeating marginalization. "You can have it *your* way," writes David Brown in *Cybertrends*. Yet, he adds, despite the many options we confront, we are increasingly denied the most basic one: "the option to tune out."[58]

But the fact that choice about whether or not to use computers is no longer socially viable does not mean that we should merely close our eyes and let the merry bandwagon take us where it will. In fact, as I have suggested, there *is* no merry bandwagon, and no out-of-control dynamo—just our own willingness to relinquish responsibility to the

FIGURE 11: *Toshiba advertisement: We cannot choose whether or not to use it.*

claims of others, and thus to allow them the power to construct the User in ways which accord with their own interests and values rather than with the needs of the individual human beings who engage with technology.

What is needed now is neither future hype nor isolated instances of critical reflection, both of which are the province and privilege of exclusive, though oppositional, minorities. Rather, as I have suggested elsewhere in this book, what is needed is the kind of responsible action of which we are all capable. What exactly does this mean? *Responsibility* suggests neither the social critic's aloofness from technology nor the technoprophet's celebration of it, but the average user's day-to-day involvement. Acting responsibly means seeking to direct technological developments in ways which will benefit the people who engage with technology; it means speaking out, on behalf of others, about the local and particular consequences of computer use; and it means making wise decisions, based on human considerations, about when and how to use digital devices. Acceptance of responsibility, when all is said and done, emerges from a rejection of the ethos of inevitability. Where futurists and social critics see a speeding steamroller, responsible computer users see people with whom they are necessarily involved and social forces in which they, as social agents, are fully participant.

Accepting responsibility, moreover, need not entail large, dramatic actions. Quite the opposite, in fact: responsible action has more to do with "small increments and moment-to-moment decisions" than with "loud dramatic struggles."[59] Moreover, since not all computer users have the same power and scope of action, all such acts are equally valued. An office-worker's decision to walk down the hall to speak to a colleague rather than sending an e-mail is as significant a choice as a school administrator's decision not to succumb to pressures to put course offerings on-line when there is no real pedagogical rationale for doing so. And a consumer's decision to make do with an obsolesced but otherwise satisfactory operating system is as significant a choice as an information systems manager's decision to postpone company-wide hardware upgrades for another year or two. And a data entry clerk's decision to inform a software development department of a system's shortcomings and of users' day-to-day workaround strategies is as significant a choice as another computer worker's decision to create a user group which will provide local advocacy for users' interests and needs, rather than merely helping users to cope with and adapt to the status quo.

For me, responsible action has meant, in the past, spending an afternoon in the library rather than trolling for information on-line; it has meant refusing to relegate such day-to-day activities as bill-paying, banking, and shopping to dehumanizing digital transactions; and it has meant designing courses that provoke students to confront the mythology of computer use. Most recently, responsible action has entailed turning my back on the easy grant money available to me should I decide to put my courses on-line and choosing instead to pursue a largely unfundable line of research.

We each must do what we can, and in so doing, we begin to assert ourselves as responsible individuals and active members of the technological community rather than as manifestations of the mindless, unquestioning User. And, as users, we begin to have some say about what the future will bring and who we will become. It is, as I say, not a prophecy but a small hope, with no guarantees.

Notes

Introduction: Do You Compute?

1. Clifford Stoll, *Silicon Snake Oil* (New York: Anchor Books, 1995), p.137.
2. Sherry Turkle, *Life on the Screen: Identity in the Age of the Internet* (New York: Simon & Schuster, 1995), p.30.
3. Bonnie A. Nardi and Vicki L. O'Day, *Information Ecologies: Using Technology with Heart* (Cambridge, MA: The MIT Press, 1999), p.17.
4. Nicholas Negroponte, *Being Digital* (New York: Vintage Books, 1995), p.231.
5. Derrick de Kerckhove, *The Skin of Culture: Investigating the New Electronic Reality* (Toronto: Somerville House, 1995), p.125.
6. Bill Gates, *The Road Ahead* (New York: Viking Penguin, 1995), p.273.
7. Ray Kurzweil, *The Age of Spiritual Machines: When Computers Exceed Human Intelligence* (New York: Penguin Books, 1999), pp.1, 75.
8. Gates, *The Road Ahead*, pp.250–1.
9. Kurzweil, *The Age of Spiritual Machines*, p.202.
10. Raymond Williams, *The Year 2000* (New York: Pantheon Books, 1983), p.133.
11. John Seely Brown and Paul Duguid, "Don't Count Society Out," in *The Invisible Future: The Seamless Integration of Technology into Everyday Life*, ed. Peter J. Denning (New York: McGraw-Hill, 2002), pp.119–20.
12. Jacques Ellul, *The Technological System*, trans. Joachim Neugroschel (1977; reprint, New York: Continuum, 1980), p.161.
13. Ibid., p.325.
14. Ibid., p.235.
15. Michel Foucault, "The Subject and Power," in *Art After Modernism: Rethinking Representation*, ed. Brian Wallis (New York: New Museum of Contemporary Art, 1984), p.420.
16. Erick Heroux, "Community, New Media, Posthumanism: An Interview with Mark Poster," in *The Information Subject* (Amsterdam: G+B Arts, 2001), p.144.
17. Jacques Ellul, *Perspectives on Our Age: Jacques Ellul Speaks on His Life and Work*, ed. William H. Vanderburg; trans. Joachim Neugroschel (Toronto: Canadian Broadcasting Corporation, 1981), p.90.
18. Neil Postman, *Technopoly: The Surrender of Culture to Technology* (New York: Vintage Books, 1992), p.185.
19. Melanie Stewart Millar, *Cracking the Gender Code: Who Rules the Wired World?* (Toronto: Second Story Press, 1998; now available from Sumach Press, Toronto), p.29.
20. Jacques Ellul, *The Technological Society*, trans. John Wilkinson (1954; reprint, New York: Vintage Books, 1964), p.xxxii.

21. Shoshana Zuboff, *In the Age of the Smart Machine: The Future of Work and Power* (New York: BasicBooks, 1988); Heather Menzies, *Whose Brave New World? The Information Highway and the New Economy* (Toronto: Between the Lines, 1996).
22. Bruce Sterling, *The Hacker Crackdown: Law and Disorder on the Electronic Frontier* (New York: Bantam Books, 1992). Retrieved Dec. 7, 2001 from *Hacker Crackdown*. <http://www.lysator.liu.se/etexts/hacker>.

Chapter 1: "We Like to Be Smart"

1. Langdon Winner, *The Whale and the Reactor: A Search for Limits in an Age of High Technology* (Chicago: The University of Chicago Press, 1986), p.114.
2. Sherry Turkle, *The Second Self: Computers and the Human Spirit* (New York: Simon & Schuster, 1984), p.184.
3. Katherine Macklem, "Not All Bad News," *Maclean's*, June 25, 2001, p.39.
4. Showwei Chu, "Tech Workers Fend for Themselves," *The Globe and Mail*, Oct. 15, 2001, p.M1.
5. Heather Menzies, *Whose Brave New World? The Information Highway and the New Economy* (Toronto: Between the Lines, 1996), p.122.
6. Ibid., p.36.
7. Turkle, *The Second Self*, p.20.
8. Thomas K. Landauer, *The Trouble with Computers: Usefulness, Usability, and Productivity* (Cambridge, MA: The MIT Press, 1995), p.191.
9. Harlan Ellison, *The Glass Teat* (1968; reprint, New York: Ace Books, 1983), p.21.
10. Jib Fowles, *Why Viewers Watch: A Reappraisal of Television's Effects* (Newbury Park, CA: Sage Publications, 1992), p.99.
11. Neil Postman, *Amusing Ourselves to Death: Public Discourse in the Age of Show Business* (New York: Viking Penguin, 1985), p.91.
12. Paul Levinson, *The Soft Edge: A Natural History and Future of the Information Revolution* (London: Routledge, 1997), p.164.
13. Ibid., p.165.
14. Theodore Roszak, *The Cult of Information: A Neo-Luddite Treatise on High-Tech, Artificial Intelligence, and the True Art of Thinking* (1986; reprint, Berkeley: University of California Press, 1994), p.186.
15. Jacques Ellul, *The Technological Society*, trans. John Wilkinson (1954; reprint, New York: Vintage Books, 1964), p.366.
16. Jacques Ellul, *The Technological System*, trans. Joachim Neugroschel (1977; reprint, New York: Continuum, 1980), p.30.
17. Ursula Franklin, *The Real World of Technology* (Concord, ON: House of Anansi Press, 1990), p.102.
18. Lewis Mumford, *The Pentagon of Power*, Vol. II: *The Myth of the Machine* (San Diego: Harcourt Brace Jovanovich, 1970), p.127.
19. Lewis Mumford, *Technics and Civilization* (1934; reprint, New York: Harcourt, Brace and World, Inc., 1962), p.283.
20. George Lakoff and Mark Johnson, *Metaphors We Live By* (Chicago: University of Chicago Press, 1980), pp.185–6.
21. *Maclean's*, April 23, 2001.
22. Neil Postman, *Technopoly: The Surrender of Culture to Technology* (New York: Vintage Books, 1992), p.171.
23. Craig Brad, *Technostress: The Human Cost of the Computer Revolution* (Reading, MA: Addison-Wesley, 1984), p.8.

24. Jacob Bigelow, *An Address on the Limits of Education* (Boston: E.P. Dutton and Company, 1865). Retrieved Feb. 25, 2002 from "'An Address on the Limits of Education,' read before the MIT, Nov. 16, 1865, by Jacob Bigelow." *MIT Libraries, Institute Archives and Special Collections: Documents Concerning the Founding of the Early Years of the Institute.* <http://libraries.mit.edu/archives/mithistory/founding.html>.
25. J.B. Bury, *The Idea of Progress* (1932; reprint, New York: Dover Publications Inc., 1960), pp.1–4.
26. Ibid., p.341.
27. Lewis Mumford, *Technics and Human Development*, Vol. I: *The Myth of the Machine* (New York: Harcourt, Brace & World, Inc., 1967), pp.22–4.
28. Jody Berland, "Cultural Technologies and the 'Evolution' of Technological Cultures," in *The World Wide Web and Contemporary Cultural Theory*, ed. Andrew Herman and Thomas Swiss (New York: Routledge, 2000), p.237.
29. Nicholas Negroponte, *Being Digital* (New York: Vintage Books, 1995), p.231.
30. David Noble, *Progress without People: New Technology, Unemployment, and the Message of Resistance* (Toronto: Between the Lines, 1995), p.72.
31. Paulina Borsook, *Cyberselfish: A Critical Romp through the Terribly Libertarian Culture of High Tech* (New York: Public Affairs, 2000), p.54.
32. Bury, *The Idea of Progress*, p.341.
33. Neil Postman, *Building a Bridge to the Eighteenth Century: How the Past Can Improve Our Future* (New York: Alfred A. Knopf, 1999), p.35.
34. Borsook, *Cyberselfish*, p.146.
35. Bill Gates, *The Road Ahead* (New York: Viking Penguin, 1995), p.3.
36. Ibid., p.11.
37. Rob Kling, "Computerization and Social Transformations," *Science, Technology and Human Values* 16,3 (1991), p.342. Available from *Computerization and Social Transformations.* <http://www.slis.indiana.edu/kling/pubs/STHV-92B.htm>.
38. Winner, *The Whale and the Reactor*, p.105.
39. Postman, *Building a Bridge to the Eighteenth Century*, p.5.
40. Mumford, *Technics and Civilization*, pp.3–4.
41. Franklin, *The Real World of Technology*, p.39.
42. Postman, *Technopoly*, pp.13, 63.
43. Melanie Stewart Millar, *Cracking the Gender Code: Who Rules the Wired World?* (Toronto: Second Story Press, 1998; now available from Sumach Press, Toronto), p.51.
44. Mumford, *The Pentagon of Power*, p.21.
45. Ibid., p.91.
46. Max Dublin, *Futurehype: The Tyranny of Prophecy* (London: Penguin Books, 1989), p.37.
47. Borsook, *Cyberselfish*, p.42.
48. Dublin, *Futurehype*, p.51.
49. Franklin, *The Real World of Technology*, p.100.
50. Shoshana Zuboff, *In the Age of the Smart Machine: The Future of Work and Power* (New York: Basic Books, 1988), p.142.
51. Noble, *Progress without People*, p.8.
52. Ibid., p.9; Rudi Volti, *Society and Technological Change* (New York: St. Martin's Press, 1988), p.21.
53. Ellul, *The Technological System*, p.82.

Chapter 2: The Ultimate Hack

1. *The New Hacker's Dictionary*. <http://www.jargon.8hz.com/jargon_toc.html>. Retrieved April 18, 2001.
2. Theodore Roszak, *The Cult of Information: A Neo-Luddite Treatise on High-Tech, Artificial Intelligence, and the True Art of Thinking* (1986; reprint, Berkeley: University of California Press, 1994), p.65.
3. Sherry Turkle, *Life on the Screen: Identity in the Age of the Internet* (New York: Simon & Schuster, 1995), p.32.
4. Sherry Turkle, *The Second Self: Computers and the Human Spirit* (New York: Simon & Schuster, 1984), p.203.
5. Karla Jennings, *The Devouring Fungus: Tales of the Computer Age* (New York: W.W. Norton, 1990), pp.126–7.
6. Ellen Ullman, "Out of Time: Reflections on the Programming Life," in *Resisting the Virtual Life: The Culture and Politics of Information*, ed. James Brook and Iain A. Boal (San Francisco: City Lights Books, 1995), pp.134–5.
7. Bruce Sterling, *The Hacker Crackdown: Law and Disorder on the Electronic Frontier* (New York: Bantam Books, 1992). Retrieved Dec. 7, 2001 from *Hacker Crackdown*. <http://www.lysator.liu.se/etexts/hacker>.
8. Fred Moody, *I Sing the Body Electronic: A Year with Microsoft on the Multimedia Frontier* (New York: Penguin Books, 1995), p.249.
9. John A. Barry, *Technobabble* (Cambridge, MA: The MIT Press, 1993), p.9.
10. Wade Rowland, *The Spirit of the Web: The Age of Information from Telegraph to Internet* (Toronto: Key Porter Books, 1999), p.238.
11. Robert Slater, *Portraits in Silicon* (Cambridge, MA: The MIT Press, 1987), p.242.
12. Daniel Burstein and David Kline, *Road Warriors: Dreams and Nightmares along the Information Highway* (New York: Plume, 1996), p.11.
13. Thierry Bardini and August T. Horvath, "The Social Construction of the Personal Computer User," *Journal of Communication* 45,3 (1995), p.49.
14. Jennings, *The Devouring Fungus*, p.45.
15. Rowland, *The Spirit of the Web*, p.245.
16. Michael Crichton, *Electronic Life: How to Think about Computers* (New York: Ballantine Books, 1983), p.71.
17. Joseph Weizenbaum, *Computer Power and Human Reason: From Judgment to Calculation* (San Francisco: W.H. Freeman, 1976), p.116.
18. Steven Levy, *Hackers: Heroes of the Computer Revolution* (1984; reprint, New York: Penguin Books, 1994), p.7.
19. Ibid., pp.40–1.
20. *The New Hacker's Dictionary*.
21. Levy, *Hackers*, pp.41–5.
22. Howard Rheingold, *The Virtual Community: Homesteading on the Electronic Frontier* (Reading, MA: Addison-Wesley, 1993), pp.67–8.
23. Nicholas Negroponte, *Being Digital* (New York: Vintage Books, 1995), p.225.
24. Turkle, *Life on the Screen*, p.32.
25. Douglas Thomas, "New Ways to Break the Law: Cybercrime and the Politics of Hacking," in *Web Studies: Rewiring Media Studies for the Digital Age*, ed. David Gauntlett (London: Arnold, 2000), p.209.
26. Levy, *Hackers*, p.304.
27. Ibid., p.303.
28. Paulina Borsook, *Cyberselfish: A Critical Romp through the Terribly Libertarian Culture of High Tech* (New York: Public Affairs, 2000), pp.114, 227, 234–5.
29. Ibid., p.235.

30. Barry, *Technobabble*, p.158.
31. Crichton, *Electronic Life*, p.149.
32. Sterling, *The Hacker Crackdown*.
33. Thomas, "New Ways to Break the Law," p.207.
34. Jennings, *The Devouring Fungus*, pp.49–50.
35. Levy, *Hackers*, p.372.
36. John Seabrook, "E-mail from Bill," *The New Yorker*, Jan. 10, 1994, p.52.
37. Rowland, *The Spirit of the Web*, p.285.
38. Moody, *I Sing the Body Electronic*, p.57.
39. Rowland, *The Spirit of the Web*, p.286.
40. Turkle, *The Second Self*, p.37.
41. Steve Woolgar, "Configuring the User: The Case of Usability Trials," in *A Sociology of Monsters: Essays on Power, Technology, and Domination*, ed. John Law (London: Routledge, 1991), p.73.
42. Andrew Ross, "Hacking Away at the Counterculture," in *Technoculture*, ed. Constance Penley and Andrew Ross (Minneapolis: University of Minnesota Press, 1991), p.121.
43. Clifford Stoll, *Silicon Snake Oil* (New York: Anchor Books, 1995), p.9.
44. *The New Hacker's Dictionary*.

Chapter 3: "Problem Exists between Chair and Keyboard"

1. Sherry Turkle, *The Second Self: Computers and the Human Spirit* (New York: Simon & Schuster, 1984), p.21.
2. Gary McCarron, "Pixel Perfect: Towards a Political Economy of Digital Fidelity," *Canadian Journal of Communication* 24 (1999), p.223.
3. Fred Moody, *I Sing the Body Electronic: A Year with Microsoft on the Multimedia Frontier* (New York: Penguin Books, 1995), p.168.
4. Ellen Ullman, *Close to the Machine: Technophilia and Its Discontents* (San Francisco: City Lights Books, 1997), p.2.
5. Joseph Weizenbaum, *Computer Power and Human Reason: From Judgment to Calculation* (San Francisco: W.H. Freeman, 1976), pp.234–5.
6. Heather Menzies, *Whose Brave New World? The Information Highway and the New Economy* (Toronto: Between the Lines, 1996), p.46.
7. Robert R. Johnson, *User-Centered Technology: A Rhetorical Theory for Computers and Other Mundane Artifacts* (Albany: State University of New York Press, 1998), pp.33, 72.
8. Thierry Bardini and August T. Horvath, "The Social Construction of the Personal Computer User," *Canadian Journal of Communication* 45,3 (1995), p.63.
9. Thomas K. Landauer, *The Trouble with Computers: Usefulness, Usability, and Productivity* (Cambridge, MA: The MIT Press, 1995), p.132.
10. Ibid., pp.171–2.
11. Shoshana Zuboff, *In the Age of the Smart Machine: The Future of Work and Power* (New York: BasicBooks, 1988), p.156; David Noble, *Progress without People: New Technology, Unemployment, and the Message of Resistance* (Toronto: Between the Lines, 1995), p.73.
12. Ullman, *Close to the Machine*, pp.11–12.
13. Allucquère Rosanne Stone, *The War of Desire and Technology at the Close of the Mechanical Age* (Cambridge, MA: The MIT Press, 1996), p.167.
14. Donald A. Norman, *The Design of Everyday Things* (New York: Doubleday, 1988), p.200.

15. Edward Yourdan, *The Decline and Fall of the American Programmer* (Englewood Cliffs, NJ: Prentice-Hall, 1993), p.275.
16. Ellen Ullman, "Out of Time: Reflections on the Programming Life," in *Resisting the Virtual Life: The Culture and Politics of Information*, ed. James Brook and Iain A. Boal (San Francisco: City Lights Books, 1995), p.142.
17. Jim Carroll, *Surviving the Information Age* (Scarborough, ON: Prentice Hall Canada, 1997), p.97; Jim Carlton, "Befuddled PC Users Flood Help Lines, and No Question Seems to be Too Basic." *Wall Street Journal*, Mar. 1, 1994. Retrieved Mar. 25, 2002 from *Befuddled PC Users*. <http://www.bears.ece.ucsb.edu/personnel/astornet/humor/humor66.html>.
18. Karla Jennings, *The Devouring Fungus: Tales of the Computer Age* (New York: W.W. Norton, 1990), p.94; Carroll, *Surviving the Information Age*, p.101.
19. Jennings, *The Devouring Fungus*, p.96.
20. Steve Woolgar, "Configuring the User: The Case of Usability Trials," in *A Sociology of Monsters: Essays on Power, Technology, and Domination*, ed. John Law (London: Routledge, 1991), p.89.
21. *Technical Support Nietzsche Style*. <http://www.things.org/~jym/fun/nietzsche-tech-support.html>. Retrieved Sept. 18, 2001.
22. Carroll, *Surviving the Information Age*, p.58.
23. Norman, *The Design of Everyday Things*, p.35.
24. Landauer, *The Trouble with Computers*, p.172.
25. Ursula Franklin, *The Real World of Technology* (Concord, ON: House of Anansi Press, 1990), p.31.
26. Yourdan, *The Decline and Fall of the American Programmer*, p.275.
27. Theodore Roszak, *The Cult of Information: A Neo-Luddite Treatise on High-Tech, Artificial Intelligence, and the True Art of Thinking* (1986; reprint, Berkeley: University of California Press, 1994), p.44.
28. Clayton Lewis and Donald A. Norman, "Designing for Error," in *User Centered System Design: New Perspectives on Human-Computer Interaction*, ed. Donald A. Norman and Stephen W. Draper (Hillsdale, NJ: Lawrence Erlbaum Associates, 1986), p.414.
29. Carroll, *Surviving the Information Age*, p.63.
30. Michael Crichton, *Electronic Life: How to Think about Computers* (New York: Ballantine Books, 1983), p.72.
31. Ibid.
32. Dale K. Carrison, "Is 'User Friendly' Really Possible in Library Automation?" in *What is User Friendly?* ed. F.W. Lancaster (Urbana-Champaign: University of Illinois, 1987), p.45.
33. Christine L. Borgman, "Toward a Definition of User Friendly: A Psychological Perspective," in *What is User Friendly?* ed. Lancaster, p.29.
34. Norman, *The Design of Everyday Things*, p.177.
35. Paulina Borsook, *Cyberselfish: A Critical Romp through the Terribly Libertarian Culture of High Tech* (New York: Public Affairs, 2000), p.236.
36. Johnson, *User-Centered Technology*, pp.28, 119.
37. Norman, *The Design of Everyday Things*, p.172.
38. Landauer, *The Trouble with Computers*, p.127.
39. Roger Shenk, *Data Smog: Surviving the Information Glut* (New York: HarperCollins, 1997), p.80.
40. Donald A. Norman, *The Invisible Computer* (Cambridge, MA: The MIT Press, 1998), pp.80–1.
41. Norman and Draper, *User Centered System Design*, p.496.
42. John A. Barry, *Technobabble* (Cambridge, MA: The MIT Press, 1993), p.158.

43. *The New Hacker's Dictionary*. <http://www.jargon.8hz.com/jargon_toc.html>. Retrieved April 18, 2001.
44. Jaron Lanier, "One-Half of a Manifesto," *Wired* 8,12 (December 2000). Retrieved Jan. 25, 2002 from <http://www.wired.com/wired/archive/8.12/lanier_pr.html>.
45. William Safire, "On Language: Hyper," *New York Times Magazine*, June 10, 2001, p.40.
46. Ullman, "Out of Time," p.141.
47. Noble, *Progress without People*, p.80.
48. Arthur Kroker and Michael A. Weinstein, *Data Trash: The Theory of the Virtual Class* (Montreal: New World Perspectives, 1994), p.23.
49. Johnson, *User-Centered Technology*, p.13.
50. Ibid., p.28.
51. Neil Postman, *Technopoly: The Surrender of Culture to Technology* (New York: Vintage Books, 1992), p.114.
52. Roszak, *The Cult of Information*, p.68.
53. Steve Mann with Hal Niedzviecki, *Cyborg: Digital Destiny and Human Possibility in the Age of the Wearable Computer* (Toronto: Doubleday Canada, 2001), p.36.
54. Ibid., pp.36–7.
55. John Seely Brown, "From Cognitive to Social Ergonomics and Beyond," in *User Centered System Design*, ed. Norman and Draper, pp.464–5, 458.
56. Norman, *The Invisible Computer*, p.75.
57. Andrew Clement and Peter Van den Besselaar, "A Retrospective Look at PD Projects," *Communications of the ACM* 36,6 (1993), p.29.
58. Erran Carmel, Randall D. Whitaker, and Joey F. George, "PD and Joint Application Design: A Transatlantic Comparison," *Communications of the ACM* 36,6 (1993), p.42.
59. Carmel, Whitaker, and George, "PD and Joint Application Design," p.42.
60. Bonnie A. Nardi and Vicki L. O'Day, *Information Ecologies: Using Technology with Heart* (Cambridge, MA: The MIT Press, 1999), p.44.
61. Franklin, *The Real World of Technology*, p.19.
62. Noble, *Progress without People*, pp.80–1.
63. Johnson, *User-Centered Technology*, p.29.
64. Rob Kling, "Computerization and Social Transformations." *Science, Technology and Human Values* 16,3 (Summer 1991), pp.342–68. Retrieved Feb. 25, 2002 from <http://www.slis.indiana.edu/kling/pubs/STHV-92B.htm>.
65. Franklin, *The Real World of Technology*, p.102.
66. Johnson, *User-Centered Technology*, p.45.

Chapter 4: *Caveat Emptor*

1. Thomas K. Landauer, *The Trouble with Computers: Usefulness, Usability, and Productivity* (Cambridge, MA: The MIT Press, 1995), p.7.
2. Clifford Stoll, *Silicon Snake Oil* (New York: Anchor Books, 1995); Alison Armstrong and Charles Casement, *The Child and the Machine: Why Computers May Put Our Children's Education at Risk* (Toronto: Key Porter Books, 1998).
3. Lewis Mumford, *The Pentagon of Power*, Vol. II: *The Myth of the Machine* (San Diego: Harcourt Brace Jovanovich, 1970), p.329.
4. Jean Baudrillard, "The System of Objects," in *Selected Writings*, ed. Mark Poster (Stanford, CA: Stanford University Press, 1988), pp.21–2.

5. Jean Baudrillard, "Mass Media Culture," in *Revenge of the Crystal: Selected Writings on the Modern Object and Its Destiny, 1968–1983*, ed. and trans. Paul Foss and Julian Pefanis (London: Pluto Press, 1990), p.73.
6. John A. Barry, *Technobabble* (Cambridge, MA: The MIT Press, 1993), pp.158–9.
7. Robert H. Anderson and Norman Z. Shapiro, *Beyond User Friendly* (Santa Monica, CA: RAND Corporation, Rand Note #N-2999-RC, December 1989).
8. Paulina Borsook, *Cyberselfish: A Critical Romp through the Terribly Libertarian Culture of High Tech* (New York: Public Affairs, 2000), p.170.
9. Dan Weisberg, "Scalable Hype: Old Persuasions for New Technology," in *Critical Studies in Media Commercialism*, ed. Robin Andersen and Lance Strate (Oxford: Oxford University Press, 2000), p.197.
10. Reproduced in Gillian Dyer, *Advertising as Communication* (London: Routledge, 1982), p.25.
11. Judith Williamson, *Decoding Advertisements: Ideology and Meaning in Advertising* (London: Marion Boyars, 1978), p.13.
12. Heather Menzies, *Whose Brave New World? The Information Highway and the New Economy* (Toronto: Between the Lines, 1996), p.123.
13. Torben Vestergaard and Kim Schroder, *The Language of Advertising* (Oxford: Basil Blackwell, 1985), p.73.
14. Dan Weisberg, "Scalable Hype: Old Persuasions for New Technology," p.188.
15. Williamson, *Decoding Advertisements*, p.50.
16. Marcel O'Gorman, "You Can't Always Get What You Want: Transparency and Deception on the Computer Fashion Scene." *Ctheory* (December 2000). Retrieved Dec. 27, 2001 from <http://www.ctheory.net/text_file.asp?pick=227>.
17. Williamson, *Decoding Advertisements*, p.51.
18. Sherry Turkle, *The Second Self: Computers and the Human Spirit* (New York: Simon & Schuster, 1984), p.185.
19. Dan Gookin and Andy Rathbone, *PCs For Dummies*, 2d ed. San Mateo, CA: IDG Books, 1994), p.304.
20. Gary McCarron, "Pixel Perfect: Towards a Political Economy of Digital Fidelity," *Canadian Journal of Communication* 24 (1999), p.224.
21. Mark Poster, *What's the Matter with the Internet?* (Minneapolis: University of Minnesota Press, 2001), p.51.
22. McCarron, "Pixel Perfect: Towards a Political Economy of Digital Fidelity," p.224.
23. Roger Shenk, *Data Smog: Surviving the Information Glut* (New York: HarperCollins, 1997), p.84.
24. Ibid., p.80.
25. Patrick Brethour, "Worldwide PC Sales Decline for First Time," *The Globe and Mail*, July 21, 2001, p.B1.
26. Lewis Mumford, *Technics and Civilization* (1934; reprint, New York: Harcourt, Brace & World, 1962), p.282.
27. Jacques Ellul, *The Technological Bluff*, trans. Geoffrey W. Bromiley (Grand Rapids, MI: William B. Eerdmans Publishing Company, 1990), p.350.
28. Alvin Toffler, *Powershift: Knowledge, Wealth, and Violence at the Edge of the Twenty-first Century* (New York: Bantam Books, 1990), p.239.
29. Poster, *What's the Matter with the Internet?* pp.47–8.
30. Jan Samoriski, *Issues in Cyberspace: Communication, Technology, Law, and Society on the Internet Frontier* (Boston: Allyn and Bacon, 2002), p.128.
31. Douglas Rushkoff, *Playing the Future: What We Can Learn from Digital Kids* (New York: Riverhead Books, 1999), p.12.

32. Howard Besser, "From Internet to Information Superhighway," in *Resisting the Virtual Life: The Culture and Politics of Information*, ed. James Brook and Iain A. Boal (San Francisco: City Lights Books, 1995), p.62.
33. Bill Gates, *The Road Ahead* (New York: Viking Penguin, 1995), p.165.
34. Raymond Williams, *Keywords: A Vocabulary of Culture and Society* (London: Fontana Press, 1976), p.79.
35. Helene Hanff, *84, Charing Cross Road* (New York: Grossman Publishers, 1970), p.15.
36. Toffler, *Powershift*, p.126.
37. Michael Dawson and John Bellamy Foster, "Virtual Capitalism," in *Capitalism and the Information Age: The Political Economy of the Global Communication Revolution*, ed. Robert W. McChesney, Ellen Meiksins, and John Bellamy Foster (New York: Monthly Review Press, 1998), p.61.
38. Baudrillard, "Mass Media Culture," p.69.
39. Reproduced in John Bear, *Computer Wimp No More: The Intelligent Beginner's Guide to Computers* (Berkeley, CA: Ten Speed Press, 1992), p.184.
40. Williams, *Keywords*, p.79.

Chapter 5: User Documentation

1. Theodore Roszak, *The Cult of Information: A Neo-Luddite Treatise on High-Tech, Artificial Intelligence, and the True Art of Thinking* (1986; reprint, Berkeley: University of California Press, 1994), p.154.
2. Robert R. Johnson, *User-Centered Technology: A Rhetorical Theory for Computers and Other Mundane Artifacts* (Albany: State University of New York Press, 1998), p.124.
3. Dan Gookin and Andy Rathbone, *PCs For Dummies*, 2d ed. (San Mateo, CA: IDG Books, 1994), p.76.
4. *Commodore 64 User's Guide* (Agincourt, ON: Commodore Business Machines, 1982), p.15.
5. John A. Barry, *Technobabble* (Cambridge, MA: The MIT Press, 1993), pp.164–5.
6. Craig Brad, *Technostress: The Human Cost of the Computer Revolution* (Reading, MA: Addison-Wesley, 1984), pp.12, 52.
7. Claire E. O'Malley, "Helping Users Help Themselves," in *User Centered System Design: New Perspectives on Human-Computer Interaction*, ed. Donald A. Norman and Stephen W. Draper (Hillsdale, NJ: Lawrence Erlbaum Associates, 1986), p.379.
8. Gookin and Rathbone, *PCs For Dummies*, p.73.
9. *The New Hacker's Dictionary*. <http://www.jargon.8hz.com/jargon_toc.html>. Retrieved April 18, 2001.
10. *Commodore 64 User's Guide*, p.vii.
11. Johnson, *User-Centered Technology*, p.117.
12. Edmund H. Weiss, *How to Write a Usable User Manual* (Philadelphia: ISI Press, 1985), p.xi.
13. Quoted in John Kirsch, "Trends in the Emerging Profession of Technical Communication," in *The Society of Text: Hypertext, Hypermedia, and the Social Construction of Information*, ed. Edward Barrett (Cambridge, MA: The MIT Press, 1989), p.232.
14. Edward Trapunski, "Technical Writers in New Role," *The Globe and Mail*, Aug. 25, 1992, p.C4.

15. Steve Lohr, "Across the Computer Divide, the Nerds Face the Dummies," *New York Times*, June 6, 1993, p.34.
16. Thomas K. Landauer, *The Trouble with Computers: Usefulness, Usability, and Productivity* (Cambridge, MA: The MIT Press, 1995), p.127.
17. Clifford Stoll, *Silicon Snake Oil* (New York: Anchor Books, 1995), p.66.
18. Randall P. Jenson and Russell T. Osguthorpe, "Better Microcomputer Manuals: A Research-Based Approach," *Educational Technology* 25,9 (1985), p.46.
19. Johnson, *User-Centered Technology*, p.140.
20. Billie Livingston, *Going Down Swinging* (Toronto: Vintage Canada, 1999), p.68.
21. Robert M. Pirsig, *Zen and the Art of Motorcycle Maintenance: An Inquiry into Values* (New York: Bantam Books, 1974), p.147.
22. Ibid., p.24.
23. Johnson, *User-Centered Technology*, p.47.
24. Lohr, "Across the Computer Divide, the Nerds Face the Dummies," p.1.
25. Stoll, *Silicon Snake Oil*, p.66.
26. George Socka, "Books for Dummies," *CMA Magazine* 69,1 (1995), p.33.
27. Lohr, "Across the Computer Divide, the Nerds Face the Dummies," p.1.
28. Gookin and Rathbone, *PCs For Dummies*, p.16.
29. Ibid., p.47.
30. Ibid., p.166.
31. Ibid., pp.53, 58, 110.
32. Ibid., pp.13, 68, 90.
33. Johnson, *User-Centered Technology*, p.146.
34. John Seely Brown and Paul Duguid, *The Social Life of Information* (Boston: Harvard Business School Press, 2000), p.101.
35. Nicholas Negroponte, *Being Digital* (New York: Vintage Books, 1995), p.215.
36. John M. Carroll and Amy P. Aaronson, "Learning by Doing with Simulated Intelligent Help," in *The Society of Text*, ed. Barrett (Cambridge, MA: The MIT Press, 1989), p.434.
37. Michael J. Salvo, "Ethics of Engagement: User-Centered Design and Rhetorical Methodology," *Technical Communication Quarterly* 10,3 (2001), p.280.
38. Michael J. Salvo, "Critical Engagement with Technology in the Computer Classroom," *Technical Communication Quarterly* 11,3 (2002), p.319.
39. Bernadette Longo, "An Approach for Applying Cultural Study Theory to Technical Writing Research," *Technical Communication Quarterly* 7,1 (1998).

Chapter 6: Anxiety Attacks

1. Sanford B. Weinberg and Mark Lawrence Fuerst, *Computer Phobia—How to Slay the Dragon of Computer Fear* (Wayne, PA: Banbury Books, 1984).
2. Gerard George and M.R. Camarata, "Managing Instructor Cyberanxiety: The Role of Self-efficacy in Decreasing Resistance to Change," *Educational Technology* 36,4 (1996), p.49.
3. Mark J. Brosnan, *Technophobia: The Psychological Impact of Information Technology* (London: Routledge, 1998), pp.10–11; Michael W. Gos, "Computer Anxiety and Computer Experience: A New Look at an Old Relationship," *The Clearing House* 69,5 (1996), p.275; Larry D. Rosen, Deborah C. Sears, and Michelle M. Weil, "Treating Technophobia: A Longitudinal Evaluation of the Computerphobia Reduction Program," *Computers in Human Behavior* 9,1 (1993), p.28.

4. Craig Brad, *Technostress: The Human Cost of the Computer Revolution* (Reading, MA: Addison-Wesley, 1984), p.23.
5. See, for example, Paula C. Morrow, Eric R. Prell, and James C. McElroy, "Attitudinal and Behavioral Correlates of Computer Anxiety," *Psychological Reports* 59 (1986), 1199–1204.
6. Geoffrey S. Howard and Robert D. Smith, "Computer Anxiety in Management: Myth or Reality?" *Communications of the ACM* 29 (1986), p.614.
7. Brosnan, *Technophobia*, p.18.
8. Valerie L. Worthington and Yong Zhao, "Existential Computer Anxiety and Changes in Computer Technology: What Past Research on Computer Anxiety Has Missed," *Journal of Educational Computing Research* 20,4 (1999), 300.
9. Gos, "Computer Anxiety and Computer Experience," p.271.
10. Cathy Keen, "New Illness of High-Tech Age." *ScienceDaily Magazine* (July 1998). Retrieved Aug. 15, 2001 from <http://www.sciencedaily.com/releases/1998/07/980731115024l.htm>; Chris Wood, "Dealing with Tech Rage," *Maclean's*, Mar. 19, 2001; Dawn Walton, "Who's Afraid of Their Own Palm Pilot?" *The Globe and Mail*, Feb. 9, 2002.
11. Weinberg and Fuerst, *Computer Phobia*.
12. Lewis Mumford, *Technics and Civilization* (1934; reprint, New York: Harcourt, Brace and World, Inc., 1962), p.327.
13. Heather Menzies, *Whose Brave New World? The Information Highway and the New Economy* (Toronto: Between the Lines, 1996), p.15.
14. Worthington and Zhao, "Existential Computer Anxiety and Changes in Computer Technology," p.310.
15. Gos, "Computer Anxiety and Computer Experience," p.275.
16. Brosnan, *Technophobia*, p.33.
17. Michael Crichton, *Electronic Life: How to Think about Computers* (New York: Ballantine Books, 1983), p.18.
18. For example, George and Camarata, "Managing Instructor Cyberanxiety"; Yixin Zhang and Sue Espinoza, "Relationships among Computer Self-efficacy, Attitudes toward Computers, and Desirability of Learning Computing Skills," *Journal of Research on Computing in Education* 30,4 (1998), pp.420–36; Thomas Hill, Nancy D. Smith, and Millard F. Mann, "Role of Efficacy Expectations in Predicting the Decision to Use Advanced Technologies: The Case of Computers," *Journal of Applied Psychology* 72,2 (1987), pp.307–13; Peggy A. Ertmer et al., "Enhancing Self-efficacy for Computer Technologies through the Use of Positive Classroom Experiences," *Educational Technology Research & Development* 42,3 (1994), pp.45–62.
19. Geoffrey S. Howard, Catherine M. Murphy, and Glenn E. Thomas, "Computer Anxiety Considerations for Design of Introductory Computer Courses," in *Proceedings of the 1986 Annual Meeting of the Decision Sciences Institute* (Atlanta: Decision Sciences Institute, 1986), p.630.
20. Brosnan, *Technophobia*, p.19.
21. George Lakoff and Mark Johnson, *Metaphors We Live By* (Chicago: University of Chicago Press, 1980), p.4.
22. Brosnan, *Technophobia*, pp.147, 10.
23. Nikos Bozionelos, "Computer Anxiety: Relationship with Computer Experience and Prevalence," *Computers in Human Behavior* 17 (2001), p.221.
24. Rosen, Sears, and Weil, "Treating Technophobia," p.48.
25. Brosnan, *Technophobia*, pp.158–68.
26. George and Camarata, "Managing Instructor Cyberanxiety," pp.51, 53.

27. S. Mark Pancer, Margo George, and Robert J. Gebotys, "Understanding and Predicting Attitudes towards Computers," *Computers in Human Behavior* 8,2/3 (1992), p.221.
28. Nina M. Ray and Robert P. Minch, "Computer Anxiety and Alienation: Toward a Definitive and Parsimonious Measure," *Human Factors* 32,4 (1990), p.489.
29. Gos, "Computer Anxiety and Computer Experience," p.273.
30. Bozionelos, "Computer Anxiety," p.215; Rosen, Sears, and Weil, "Treating Technophobia," p.28; Mark J. Brosnan, "The Impact of Psychological, Gender, Gender-Related Perceptions, Significant Others, and the Introducer of Technology upon Computer Anxiety in Students," *Journal of Educational Computing Research* 18,1 (1998), p.63.
31. Brosnan, *Technophobia*, p.173.
32. Ray and Minch, "Computer Anxiety and Alienation," p.478.
33. Wood, "Dealing with Tech Rage," p.41.
34. Michael Apple, *Ideology and Curriculum*, 2d ed. (New York: Routledge, 1990), p.136.
35. Michel Foucault, *Discipline and Punish: The Birth of the Prison*, trans. Alan Sheridan (1975; reprint, New York: Vintage Books, 1979), p.304.
36. Pancer, George, and Gebotys, "Understanding and Predicting Attitudes towards Computers," p.212.
37. Ertmer et al., "Enhancing Self-efficacy for Computer Technologies...," p.45.
38. Michael Snider, "Wired to Another World," *Maclean's*, Mar. 3, 2003, p.24.
39. Bozionelos, "Computer Anxiety," p.214.
40. Ray and Minch, "Computer Anxiety and Alienation," p.479.
41. Wood, "Dealing with Tech Rage," p.40.
42. Keen, "New Illness of High-Tech Age."
43. Worthington and Zhao, "Existential Computer Anxiety and Changes in Computer Technology," pp.301, 303.
44. Sherry Turkle, *The Second Self: Computers and the Human Spirit* (New York: Simon & Schuster, 1984), p.13.
45. For example, Howard and Smith, "Computer Anxiety in Management."
46. Mark Poster, *What's the Matter with the Internet?* (Minneapolis: University of Minnesota Press, 2001), p.109.
47. Wood, "Dealing with Tech Rage," p.41.
48. Brad, *Technostress*, p.48.
49. Andrew R.J. Yeaman, "The Mythical Anxieties of Computerization: A Barthesian Analysis of a Technological Myth," in *Computers in Education: Social, Political, and Historical Perspectives*, ed. Robert Muffoletto and Nancy Nelson Knupfer (Cresskill, NJ: Hampton Press, 1993), p.115.
50. Andrew R.J. Yeaman, "Whose Technology Is It, Anyway?" *Education Digest* 58,5 (1993), p.21.
51. Ray and Minch, "Computer Anxiety and Alienation," p.479.
52. See, for example, Shoshana Zuboff, *In the Age of the Smart Machine: The Future of Work and Power* (New York: BasicBooks, 1988); David Noble, *Progress without People: New Technology, Unemployment, and the Message of Resistance* (Toronto: Between the Lines, 1995).

Chapter 7: Songs of Innocence and Experience

1. Michael Snider, "Hey, Kids! Let's Play Adver-games!" *Maclean's*, Dec. 23, 2002, p.36.
2. Chris Turner, "The Simpsons Generation," *Shift* 10,3 (September/October 2002), p.51.
3. Karla Jennings, *The Devouring Fungus: Tales of the Computer Age* (New York: W.W. Norton, 1990), p.80.
4. Jim Carroll, *Surviving the Information Age* (Scarborough, ON: Prentice Hall Canada, 1997), p.43.
5. Mark Poster, *What's the Matter with the Internet?* (Minneapolis: University of Minnesota Press, 2001), p.107.
6. Keri Facer et al., "Constructing the Child Computer User: From Public Policy to Private Practices," *British Journal of Sociology of Education* 22,1 (2001), p.96.
7. Larry Cuban, *Oversold and Underused: Computers in the Classroom* (Cambridge, MA: Harvard University Press, 2001), p.39.
8. Arnaldo Almeida, Cartoon, *Click Smart Living* (November/December 2002), p.9.
9. Nicholas Negroponte, *Being Digital* (New York: Vintage Books, 1995), p.204.
10. Seymour Papert, *The Children's Machine: Rethinking School in the Age of the Computer* (New York: BasicBooks, 1993), p.ix.
11. Don Tapscott, *Growing Up Digital: The Rise of the Net Generation* (New York: McGraw-Hill, 1998), pp.36–42.
12. Bill Gates, *The Road Ahead* (New York: Viking Penguin, 1995), p.191.
13. See, for example, Alison Armstrong and Charles Casement, *The Child and the Machine: Why Computers May Put Our Children's Education at Risk* (Toronto: Key Porter Books, 1998); Todd Oppenheimer, "The Computer Delusion," *The Atlantic Monthly* (July 1997), pp.45–72; Jane Healy, *Endangered Minds* (New York: Touchstone Books, 1999); Alliance for Childhood, *Fool's Gold: A Critical Look at Computers in Childhood* (College Park, MD: Alliance for Childhood, 2000).
14. Facer et al., "Constructing the Child Computer User: From Public Policy to Private Practices," p.96.
15. Neil Postman, *The Disappearance of Childhood* (1982; reprint, New York: Vintage Books, 1994), p.xi.
16. Ibid., p.xii.
17. Ibid., p.56.
18. Lionel Rose, *The Erosion of Childhood: Child Oppression in Britain 1860–1918* (London: Routledge, 1991), p.3.
19. Ibid.
20. Herbert J. Muller, *The Children of Frankenstein: A Primer on Modern Technology and Human Values* (Bloomington: Indiana University Press, 1970), p.49.
21. Postman, *The Disappearance of Childhood*, p.13.
22. Muller, *The Children of Frankenstein*, pp.72–3.
23. Eulah Croson Laucks, *The Meaning of Children: Attitudes and Opinions of a Selected Group of U.S. University Graduates* (Boulder, CO: Westview Press, 1981), p.13.
24. Lawrence Stone, "Literacy and Education in England, 1640–1900," *Past and Present* 42 (1969), p.92.
25. Philippe Aries, *Centuries of Childhood: A Social History of Family Life*, trans. Robert Baldick (New York: Alfred A. Knopf, 1962), pp.261–2.
26. Michel Foucault, *Discipline and Punish: The Birth of the Prison*, trans. Alan Sheridan (1975; reprint, New York: Vintage Books, 1979).

27. Laucks, *The Meaning of Children,* p.14.
28. Aries, *Centuries of Childhood,* p.119.
29. Postman, *The Disappearance of Childhood,* p.59.
30. Tapscott, *Growing Up Digital,* p.8.
31. Facer et al., "Constructing the Child Computer User," p.91.
32. George B. Leonard, *Education and Ecstasy* (New York: Dell Publishing, 1968), p.141.
33. Ibid., pp.147–8.
34. Tapscott, *Growing Up Digital,* p.8.
35. Ibid., p.136.
36. Heather Menzies, *Computers on the Job: Surviving Canada's Microcomputer Revolution* (Toronto: James Lorimer & Company, 1982), p.128.
37. Facer et al., "Constructing the Child Computer User," p.97.
38. Ellen Rose, *Hyper Texts: The Language and Culture of Educational Computing* (London, ON: The Althouse Press, 2000), p.47.
39. Ursula Franklin, *The Real World of Technology* (Concord, ON: House of Anansi Press, 1990), p.99.
40. Craig Brad, *Technostress: The Human Cost of the Computer Revolution* (Reading, MA: Addison-Wesley, 1984), p.134.
41. David Brown, *Cybertrends: Chaos, Power, and Accountability in the Information Age* (London: Penguin Books, 1997), p.24.
42. Media Awareness Network, *Young Canadians in a Wired World* (2001). Retrieved Dec. 30, 2001 from <http://www.media-awareness.ca/eng/webaware/netsurvey/index.htm>.
43. Facer et al., "Constructing the Child Computer User," p.95.
44. Douglas Rushkoff, *Playing the Future: What We Can Learn from Digital Kids* (1996; reprint, New York: Riverhead Books, 1999), p.12.
45. Sherry Turkle, *Life on the Screen: Identity in the Age of the Internet* (New York: Simon & Schuster, 1995), p.47.
46. Sherry Turkle, *The Second Self: Computers and the Human Spirit* (New York: Simon & Schuster, 1984), p.20.
47. Media Awareness Network, *Young Canadians in a Wired World.*
48. Postman, *The Disappearance of Childhood,* p.63.

Conclusion: The Future User

1. Clifford Stoll, *Silicon Snake Oil* (New York: Anchor Books, 1995), p.133.
2. Max Dublin, *Futurehype: The Tyranny of Prophecy* (London: Penguin Books, 1989), p.32.
3. Alan M. Turing, "Computing Machinery and Intelligence," in *Social Effects of Computer Use and Misuse,* ed. J. Mack Adams and Douglas H. Haden (New York: John Wiley and Sons, 1976), p.190.
4. Hans Morovac, "Rise of the Robots," *Scientific American* (December 1999), pp.124–35. Retrieved Feb. 25, 2002 from <http://www.frc.ri.cmu.edu/~hpm/project.archive/robot.papers/1999/SciAm.scan.html>.
5. Ray Kurzweil, *The Age of Spiritual Machines: When Computers Exceed Human Intelligence* (New York: Penguin Books, 1999), pp.103–5.
6. Sherry Turkle, *Life on the Screen: Identity in the Age of the Internet* (New York: Simon & Schuster, 1995), p.85.
7. Ellen Rose, "Talking Turing: How the Imitation Game Plays Out in the Classroom," *Educational Technology* 38,3 (1998), p.57.

8. Steve Mann with Hal Niedzviecki, *Cyborg: Digital Destiny and Human Possibility in the Age of the Wearable Computer* (Toronto: Doubleday Canada, 2001), pp.29–30.
9. *BotKnowledge*. <http://botknowledge.com>.
10. Nicholas Negroponte, *Being Digital* (New York: Vintage Books, 1995), p.150.
11. Paulina Borsook, *Cyberselfish: A Critical Romp through the Terribly Libertarian Culture of High Tech* (New York: Public Affairs, 2000), pp.236–7.
12. Quoted in Patrick McGee, "Becoming One with your Robot," *Wired* (30 October 2000). Retrieved Jan. 11, 2002 from <http://www.wired.com/news/print/0,1294,39853,00.html>.
13. Turing, "Computing Machinery and Intelligence," p.190.
14. Ray Kurzweil, *The Age of Intelligent Machines* (Cambridge, MA: MIT Press, 1990), p.14.
15. Jaron Lanier, "One-Half of a Manifesto," *Wired* 8,12 (December 2000). Retrieved Jan. 25, 2002 from <http://www.wired.com/wired/archive/8.12/lanier_pr.html>.
16. Rose, "Talking Turing," p.57.
17. Quoted in George Johnson, "This Time, the Future is Closer than You Think," *New York Times*, Dec. 31, 2000, p.1.
18. Ibid., p.4; Kurzweil, *The Age of Spiritual Machines*, p.137.
19. Negroponte, *Being Digital*, p.209.
20. James Gleick, "Theories of Connectivity," *New York Times Magazine*, April 22, 2001, p.65.
21. Jim Krane, "Computing's Next 20 Years: Smaller, Smarter, Wearable," *Telegraph-Journal*, Aug. 7, 2001, p.C2; Chris Wood, "Zap! It's the Future," *Maclean's*, Aug. 20, 2001, pp.25–7.
22. Kurzweil, *The Age of Spiritual Machines*, p.189.
23. Emile Aarts, Rick Harwig, and Martin Schuurmans, "Ambient Intelligence," in *The Invisible Future: The Seamless Integration of Technology into Everyday Life*, ed. Peter J. Denning (New York: McGraw-Hill, 2002), p.237.
24. Negroponte, *Being Digital*, p.213.
25. Quoted in Gleick, "Theories of Connectivity," p.66.
26. Gleick, "Theories of Connectivity," p.112; Matthew Mirapaul, "Designing the Invisible Computer," *New York Times*, Oct. 28, 1999. Retrieved Jan. 11, 2002 from <http://www.nytimes.com/library/tech/99/10/cyber/artsatlarge>.
27. Donald A. Norman, *The Invisible Computer* (Cambridge, MA: The MIT Press, 1998), p.56.
28. Christopher Dewdney, *Last Flesh: Life in the Transhuman Era* (Toronto: HarperCollins, 1998), pp.107–8.
29. Quoted in Mirapaul, "Designing the Invisible Computer."
30. Dewdney, *Last Flesh*, p.2.
31. Mann with Niedzviecki, *Cyborg*, p.15.
32. Rodney A. Brooks, "Flesh and Machines," in *The Invisible Future*, ed. Denning, pp.60–1.
33. Ibid., pp.61–2.
34. Kurzweil, *The Age of Spiritual Machines*, p.126.
35. Ibid., p.144.
36. Brooks, "Flesh and Machines," p.63.
37. Kurzweil, *The Age of Spiritual Machines*, p.255.
38. John Seely Brown and Paul Duguid, "Don't Count Society Out," in *The Invisible Future*, ed. Denning, p.117.
39. Dublin, *Futurehype*, p.14.

40. Jacques Ellul, *The Technological Society*, trans. John Wilkinson (1954; reprint, New York: Vintage Books, 1964), p.xxxii.
41. Neil Postman, *Technopoly: The Surrender of Culture to Technology* (New York: Vintage Books, 1992), p.20.
42. Neil Postman and Charles Weingartner, *Teaching as a Subversive Activity* (New York: Delta, 1969), p.3.
43. Ellen Rose, *Hyper Texts: The Language and Culture of Educational Computing* (London, ON: The Althouse Press, 2000), pp.190–2.
44. Postman, *Technopoly*, p.20.
45. Langdon Winner, *The Whale and the Reactor: A Search for Limits in an Age of High Technology* (Chicago: The University of Chicago Press, 1986), pp.9–10.
46. Lewis Mumford, *Technics and Civilization* (1934; reprint, New York: Harcourt, Brace and World, Inc., 1962), p.273.
47. Neil Postman, *Amusing Ourselves to Death: Public Discourse in the Age of Show Business* (New York: Viking Penguin, 1985), p.161.
48. Ellul, *The Technological Society*, p.xxxiii.
49. Marshall McLuhan, *Understanding Media: The Extensions of Man* (London: Sphere Books Limited, 1964), p.29.
50. Ibid., p.324.
51. Raymond Williams, *The Year 2000* (New York: Pantheon Books, 1983), p.135.
52. Robert D. Romanyshyn, *Technology as Symptom and Dream* (London: Routledge, 1989), p.89.
53. Martin Heidegger, *Being and Time*, trans. John Macquarrie and Edward Robinson (1926; reprint, San Francisco: HarperCollins, 1962), p.95.
54. Neil Postman, *Building a Bridge to the Eighteenth Century: How the Past Can Improve Our Future* (New York: Alfred A. Knopf, 1999), p.55.
55. Quoted in Mark J. Brosnan, *Technophobia: The Psychological Impact of Information Technology* (London: Routledge, 1998), p.156.
56. For example, Kurzweil, *The Age of Spiritual Machines*, p.161.
57. Louis Dudek, *Poems from Atlantis* (Ottawa: The Golden Dog Press, 1980), p.75.
58. David Brown, *Cybertrends: Chaos, Power, and Accountability in the Information Age* (London: Penguin Books, 1997), p.15.
59. Mumford, *Technics and Civilization*, p.6.

Bibliography

Aarts, Emile, Rick Harwig, and Martin Schuurmans. "Ambient Intelligence." In *The Invisible Future: The Seamless Integration of Technology into Everyday Life*, edited by Peter J. Denning, pp.235–50. New York: McGraw-Hill, 2002.

Alliance for Childhood. *Fool's Gold: A Critical Look at Computers in Childhood*. College Park, MD: Alliance for Childhood, 2000.

Anderson, Robert H., and Norman Z. Shapiro. *Beyond User Friendly*. Santa Monica, CA: RAND Corporation, Rand Note #N-2999-RC, Dec. 1989.

Apple, Michael. *Ideology and Curriculum*, 2d ed. New York: Routledge, 1990.

Aries, Philippe. *Centuries of Childhood: A Social History of Family Life*. Translated by Robert Baldick. New York: Alfred A. Knopf, 1962.

Armstrong, Alison, and Charles Casement. *The Child and the Machine: Why Computers May Put Our Children's Education at Risk*. Toronto: Key Porter Books, 1998.

Bardini, Thierry, and August T. Horvath. "The Social Construction of the Personal Computer User." *Journal of Communication* 45,3 (1995), pp.40–65.

Baudrillard, Jean. "The System of Objects." In *Selected Writings*, edited by Mark Poster, pp.10–28. Stanford, CA: Stanford University Press, 1988.

—. "Mass Media Culture." In *Revenge of the Crystal: Selected Writings on the Modern Object and Its Destiny, 1968–1983*, edited and translated by Paul Foss and Julian Pefanis, pp.63–97. London: Pluto Press, 1990.

Barry, John A. *Technobabble*. Cambridge, MA: The MIT Press, 1993.

Bear, John. *Computer Wimp No More: The Intelligent Beginner's Guide to Computers*. Berkeley, CA: Ten Speed Press, 1992.

Berland, Jody. "Cultural Technologies and the 'Evolution' of Technological Cultures." In *The World Wide Web and Contemporary Cultural Theory*, edited by Andrew Herman and Thomas Swiss, pp.235–58. New York: Routledge, 2000.

Besser, Howard. "From Internet to Information Superhighway." In *Resisting the Virtual Life: The Culture and Politics of Information*, edited by James Brook and Iain A. Boal, pp.59–70. San Francisco: City Lights Books, 1995.

Bigelow, Jacob. *An Address on the Limits of Education*. Boston: E.P. Dutton & Company,1865. [On-line.] MIT Libraries. <http://libraries.mit.edu/archives/mithistory/founding.html>. Feb. 25, 2002.

Borgman, Christine L. "Toward a Definition of User Friendly: A Psychological Perspective." In *What Is User Friendly?* edited by F.W. Lancaster, pp.29–44. Urbana-Champaign: University of Illinois Press, 1987.

Borsook, Paulina. *Cyberselfish: A Critical Romp through the Terribly Libertarian Culture of High Tech*. New York: Public Affairs, 2000.

Bozionelos, Nikos. "Computer Anxiety: Relationship with Computer Experience and Prevalence." *Computers in Human Behavior* 17 (2001), pp.213–24.

Brad, Craig. *Technostress: The Human Cost of the Computer Revolution*. Reading, MA: Addison-Wesley, 1984.

Brethour, Patrick. "Worldwide PC Sales Decline for First Time." *The Globe and Mail*, July 21, 2001, pp.B1, B4.

Brooks, Rodney A. "Flesh and Machines." In *The Invisible Future: The Seamless Integration of Technology into Everyday Life*, edited by Peter J. Denning, pp.57–63. New York: McGraw-Hill, 2002.

Brosnan, Mark J. "The Impact of Psychological, Gender, Gender-Related Perceptions, Significant Others, and the Introducer of Technology upon Computer Anxiety in Students." *Journal of Educational Computing Research* 18,1 (1998), pp.63–78.

—. *Technophobia: The Psychological Impact of Information Technology*. London: Routledge, 1998.

Brown, David. *Cybertrends: Chaos, Power, and Accountability in the Information Age*. London: Penguin Books, 1997.

Brown, John Seely. "From Cognitive to Social Ergonomics and Beyond." In *User Centered System Design: New Perspectives on Human-Computer Interaction*, edited by Donald A. Norman and Stephen W. Draper, pp.457–86. Hillsdale, NJ: Lawrence Erlbaum Associates, 1986.

Brown, John Seely, and Paul Duguid. *The Social Life of Information*. Boston: Harvard Business School Press, 2000.

—. "Don't Count Society Out." In *The Invisible Future: The Seamless Integration of Technology into Everyday Life*, edited by Peter J. Denning, pp.117–44. New York: McGraw-Hill, 2002.

Burstein, Daniel, and David Kline. *Road Warriors: Dreams and Nightmares along the Information Highway*. New York: Plume, 1996.

Bury, J.B. *The Idea of Progress: An Inquiry into Its Growth and Origins*. 1932. Reprint, New York: Dover Publications Inc., 1960.

Carlton, Jim. "Befuddled PC Users Flood Help Lines, and No Question Seems to Be Too Basic." *Wall Street Journal*, Mar. 1, 1994. [On-line.] <http://www.bears.ece.ucsb.edu/personnel/astronet/humor/humor66.html>. Mar. 25, 2002.

Carmel, Erran, Randall D. Whitaker, and Joey F. George. "PD and Joint Application Design: A Transatlantic Comparison." *Communications of the ACM* 36,6 (June 1993), pp.40–8.

Carrison, Dale K. "Is 'User Friendly' Really Possible in Library Automation? In *What Is User Friendly?* edited by F.W. Lancaster, pp.45–51. Urbana-Champaign: University of Illinois Press, 1987.

Carroll, Jim. *Surviving the Information Age*. Scarborough, ON: Prentice Hall Canada, 1997.

Carroll, John M., and Amy P. Aaronson. "Learning by Doing with Simulated Intelligent Help." In *The Society of Text: Hypertext, Hypermedia, and the Social Construction of Information*, edited by Edward Barrett, pp.423–52. Cambridge, MA: The MIT Press, 1989.

Chu, Showwei. "Tech Workers Fend for Themselves." *The Globe and Mail*, Oct. 15, 2001, p.M1.

Clement, Andrew, and Peter Van den Besselaar. "A Retrospective Look at PD projects." *Communications of the ACM* 36,6 (June 1993), pp.29–37.

Commodore 64 User's Guide. Agincourt, ON: Commodore Business Machines, Ltd., 1982.

Crichton, Michael. *Electronic Life: How to Think about Computers*. New York: Ballantine Books, 1983.

Cuban, Larry. *Oversold and Underused: Computers in the Classroom*. Cambridge, MA: Harvard University Press, 2001.

Dawson, Michael, and John Bellamy Foster. "Virtual Capitalism." In *Capitalism and the Information Age: The Political Economy of the Global Communication Revolution*, edited by Robert W. McChesney, Ellen Meiksins, and John Bellamy Foster, pp.51–67. New York: Monthly Review Press, 1998.

de Kerckhove, Derrick. *The Skin of Culture: Investigating the New Electronic Reality*. Toronto: Somerville House Publishing, 1995.

Dewdney, Christopher. *Last Flesh: Life in the Transhuman Era*. Toronto: HarperCollins, 1998.

Dublin, Max. *Futurehype: The Tyranny of Prophecy*. London: Penguin Books, 1989.

Dudek, Louis. *Poems from Atlantis*. Ottawa: The Golden Dog Press, 1980.

Dyer, Gillian. *Advertising as Communication*. London: Routledge, 1982.

Ellison, Harlan. *The Glass Teat*. 1968. Reprint, New York: Ace Books, 1983.

Ellul, Jacques. *The Technological Society*. Translated by John Wilkinson. 1954. Reprint, New York: Vintage Books, 1964.

—. The *Technological System*. Translated by Joachim Neugroschel. 1977. Reprint, New York: Continuum Publishing Company, 1980.

—. *Perspectives on Our Age: Jacques Ellul Speaks on His Life and Work*. Edited by William H. Vanderburg. Translated by Joachim Neugroschel. Toronto: Canadian Broadcasting Corporation, 1981.

—. *The Technological Bluff*. Translated by Geoffrey W. Bromiley. Grand Rapids, MI: William B. Eerdmans Publishing Company, 1990.

Ertmer, Peggy A., Elizabeth Everbeck, Katherine S. Cennamo, and James D. Lehman. "Enhancing Self-efficacy for Computer Technologies through the Use of Positive Classroom Experiences." *Educational Technology Research and Development* 42,3 (1994), pp.45–62.

Facer, Keri, John Furlong, Ruth Furlong, and Rosamund Sutherland. "Constructing the Child Computer User: From Public Policy to Private Practices." *British Journal of Sociology of Education* 22,1 (2001), pp.91–108.

Foucault, Michel. *Discipline and Punish: The Birth of the Prison*. Translated by Alan Sheridan. 1975. Reprint, New York: Vintage Books, 1979.

—. "The Subject and Power." In *Art After Modernism: Rethinking Representation*, edited by Brian Wallis, pp.417–32. New York: New Museum of Contemporary Art, 1984.

Fowles, Jib. *Why Viewers Watch: A Reappraisal of Television's Effects*. Newbury Park, CA: Sage Publications, 1992.

Franklin, Ursula. *The Real World of Technology*. Concord, ON: House of Anansi Press, 1990.

Gates, Bill. *The Road Ahead*. New York: Viking Penguin, 1995.

George, Gerard, and M.R. Camarata. "Managing Instructor Cyberanxiety: The Role of Self-efficacy in Decreasing Resistance to Change." *Educational Technology* 36,4 (1996), pp.49–54.

Gleick, James. "Theories of Connectivity." *New York Times Magazine*, Apr. 22, 2001, pp.62–7, 101, 108, 112.

Gookin, Dan, and Andy Rathbone. *PCs For Dummies*. 2d ed. San Mateo, CA: IDG Books, 1994.

Gos, Michael W. "Computer Anxiety and Computer Experience: A New Look at an Old Relationship." *The Clearing House* 69,5 (1996), pp.271–6.

Hanff, Helene. *84, Charing Cross Road*. New York: Grossman Publishers, 1970.

Healy, Jane M. *Endangered Minds*. New York: Touchstone Books, 1999.

Heidegger, Martin. *Being and Time*. Translated by John Macquarrie and Edward Robinson. 1926. Reprint, San Francisco: HarperCollins, 1962.

Heroux, Erick. "Community, New Media, Posthumanism: An Interview with Mark Poster." In *The Information Subject*, pp.139–46. Amsterdam: G+B Arts, 2001.

Hill, Thomas, Nancy D. Smith, and Millard F. Mann. "Role of Efficacy Expectations in Predicting the Decision to Use Advanced Technologies: The Case of Computers." *Journal of Applied Psychology* 72,2 (1987), pp.307–13.

Howard, Geoffrey S., Catherine M. Murphy, and Glenn E. Thomas. "Computer Anxiety Considerations for Design of Introductory Computer Courses." In *Proceedings of the 1986 Annual Meeting of the Decision Sciences Institute*, pp.630–2. Atlanta: Decision Sciences Institute, 1986.

Howard, Geoffrey S., and Robert D. Smith. "Computer Anxiety in Management: Myth or Reality?" *Communications of the ACM* 29 (1986), pp.611–15.

Jennings, Karla. *The Devouring Fungus: Tales of the Computer Age*. New York: W.W. Norton and Company, 1990.

Jenson, Randall P., and Russell T. Osguthorpe. "Better Microcomputer Manuals: A Research-Based Approach." *Educational Technology* 25,9 (1985), pp.42–7.

Johnson, George. "This Time, the Future is Closer than You Think." *New York Times*, Dec. 13, 2000, pp.1, 4.

Johnson, Robert R. *User-Centered Technology: A Rhetorical Theory for Computers and Other Mundane Artifacts*. Albany: State University of New York Press, 1998.

Keen, Cathy. "New Illness of High-Tech Age." *ScienceDaily Magazine* (July 1998). [On-line]. *ScienceDaily*. <http://www.sciencedaily.com/releases/1998/07/9807311150241.htm>. Aug. 15, 2001.

Kirsch, John. "Trends in the Emerging Profession of Technical Communication." In *The Society of Text: Hypertext, Hypermedia, and the Social Construction of Information*, edited by Edward Barrett, pp.209–34. Cambridge, MA: The MIT Press, 1989.

Kling, Rob. "Computerization and Social Transformations." *Science, Technology and Human Values* 16, 3 (Summer 1991), pp.342–68. [On-line.] Indiana University School of Library and Information Science. <http://www.slis.indiana.edu/kling/pubs/STHV-92B.htm>. Feb. 25, 2002.

Krane, Jim. "Computing's Next 20 Years: Smaller, Smarter, Wearable." *Telegraph-Journal* (Saint John), Aug. 7, 2001, p.C2.

Kroker, Arthur, and Michael A. Weinstein. *Data Trash: The Theory of the Virtual Class*. Montreal: New World Perspectives, 1994.

Kurzweil, Ray. *The Age of Intelligent Machines*. Cambridge, MA: MIT Press, 1990.

—. *The Age of Spiritual Machines: When Computers Exceed Human Intelligence*. New York: Penguin Books, 1999.

Lakoff, George, and Mark Johnson. *Metaphors We Live By*. Chicago: University of Chicago Press, 1980.

Landauer, Thomas K. *The Trouble with Computers: Usefulness, Usability, and Productivity*. Cambridge, MA: The MIT Press, 1995.

Lanier, Jaron. "One-Half of a Manifesto." *Wired* 8,12 (December 2000). [On-line]. *Wired Magazine*. <http://www.wired.com/wired/archive/8.12/lanier_pr.html>. Jan. 25, 2002.

Laucks, Eulah Croson. *The Meaning of Children: Attitudes and Opinions of a Selected Group of U.S. University Graduates*. Boulder, CO: Westview Press, 1981.

Leonard, George B. *Education and Ecstasy*. New York: Dell Publishing Co., 1968.

Levinson, Paul. *The Soft Edge: A Natural History and Future of the Information Revolution*. London: Routledge, 1997.

Levy, Steven. *Hackers: Heroes of the Computer Revolution*. 1984. Reprint, New York: Penguin Books, 1994.

Lewis, Clayton, and Donald A. Norman. "Designing for Error." In *User Centered System Design: New Perspectives on Human-Computer Interaction*, edited by Donald A. Norman and Stephen W. Draper, pp.411–32. Hillsdale, NJ: Lawrence Erlbaum Associates, 1986.

Livingston, Billie. *Going Down Swinging*. Toronto: Vintage Canada, 1999.

Lohr, Steve. "Across the Computer Divide, the Nerds Face the Dummies." *New York Times*, June 6, 1993, pp.1, 34.

Longo, Bernadette. "An Approach for Applying Cultural Study Theory to Technical Writing Research." *Technical Communication Quarterly* 7,1 (1998), pp.53–73.

Macklem, Katherine. "Not All Bad News." *Maclean's*, June 25, 2001, pp.38–9.

Mann, Steve, with Hal Niedzviecki. *Cyborg: Digital Destiny and Human Possibility in the Age of the Wearable Computer*. Toronto: Doubleday Canada, 2001.

McCarron, Gary. "Pixel Perfect: Towards a Political Economy of Digital Fidelity." *Canadian Journal of Communication* 24 (1999), pp.221–41.

McGee, Patrick. "Becoming One with Your Robot." *Wired* (October 30, 2000). [On-line]. *Wired Magazine*. <http://www.wired.com/news/print/0,1294,39853,00.html>. Jan. 11, 2002.

McLuhan, Marshall. *Understanding Media: The Extensions of Man*. London: Sphere Books Limited, 1964.

Media Awareness Network. *Young Canadians in a Wired World* (2001). [On-line.] Media Awareness Network. <http://www.media-awareness.ca/eng/webaware/netsurvey/index.htm>. Dec. 30, 2001.

Menzies, Heather. *Computers on the Job: Surviving Canada's Microcomputer Revolution*. Toronto: James Lorimer & Company, 1982.

—. *Whose Brave New World? The Information Highway and the New Economy*. Toronto: Between the Lines, 1996.

Mirapaul, Matthew. "Designing the Invisible Computer." *New York Times* (Oct 28, 1999). [On-line]. *New York Times*. <http://www.nytimes.com/library/tech/99/10/cyber/artsatlarge>. Jan. 11, 2002.

Moody, Fred. *I Sing the Body Electronic: A Year with Microsoft on the Multimedia Frontier*. New York: Penguin Books, 1995.

Morovac, Hans. "Rise of the Robots." *Scientific American* (December 1999). [On-line.] *Scientific American*. <http://www.frc.ri.cmu.edu/~hpm/project.archive/robot.papers/1999/SciAm.scan.html>. Feb. 25, 2002.

Morrow, Paula C., Eric R. Prell, and James C. McElroy. "Attitudinal and Behavioral Correlates of Computer Anxiety." *Psychological Reports* 59 (1986), pp.1199–1204.

Muller, Herbert J. *The Children of Frankenstein: A Primer on Modern Technology and Human Values*. Bloomington: Indiana University Press, 1970.

Mumford, Lewis. *Technics and Civilization*. 1934. Reprint, New York: Harcourt, Brace & World, Inc., 1962.

—. *Technics and Human Development*. Volume I: *The Myth of the Machine*. New York: Harcourt, Brace & World, Inc., 1967.

—. *The Pentagon of Power*. Volume II: *The Myth of the Machine*. San Diego: Harcourt Brace Jovanovich, 1970.

Nardi, Bonnie A., and Vicki L. O'Day. *Information Ecologies: Using Technology with Heart*. Cambridge, MA: The MIT Press, 1999.

Negroponte, Nicholas. *Being Digital*. New York: Vintage Books, 1995.

Noble, David. *Progress without People: New Technology, Unemployment, and the Message of Resistance*. Toronto: Between the Lines, 1995.

Norman, Donald A. *The Design of Everyday Things*. New York: Doubleday, 1988.

—. *The Invisible Computer*. Cambridge, MA: The MIT Press, 1998.

Norman, Donald A., and Clayton Lewis. "Designing for Error." In *User Centered System Design: New Perspectives on Human-Computer Interaction*, edited by Donald A. Norman and Stephen W. Draper, pp.411–32. Hillsdale, NJ: Lawrence Erlbaum Associates, 1986.

O'Gorman, Marcel. "You Can't Always Get What You Want: Transparency and Deception on the Computer Fashion Scene." *Ctheory* (December 2000). [Online.] Ctheory. <http://www.ctheory.net/text_file.asp?pick=227>. Dec. 27, 2001.

O'Malley, Claire E. "Helping Users Help Themselves." In *User Centered System Design: New Perspectives on Human-Computer Interaction*, edited by Donald A. Norman and Stephen W. Draper, pp.377–98. Hillsdale, NJ: Lawrence Erlbaum Associates, 1986.

Oppenheimer, Todd. "The Computer Delusion." *The Atlantic Monthly* (July 1997), pp.45–62.

Pancer, S. Mark, Margo George, and Robert J. Gebotys. "Understanding and Predicting Attitudes towards Computers." *Computers in Human Behavior* 8,2/3 (1992), pp.211–22.

Papert, Seymour. *The Children's Machine: Rethinking School in the Age of the Computer*. New York: BasicBooks, 1993.

Pirsig, Robert M. *Zen and the Art of Motorcycle Maintenance: An Inquiry into Values*. New York: Bantam Books, 1974.

Poster, Mark. *What's the Matter with the Internet?* Minneapolis: University of Minnesota Press, 2001.

Postman, Neil. *Amusing Ourselves to Death: Public Discourse in the Age of Show Business*. New York: Viking Penguin, 1985.

—. *Technopoly: The Surrender of Culture to Technology*. New York: Vintage Books, 1992.

—. *The Disappearance of Childhood*. 1982. Reprint, New York: Vintage Books, 1994.

—. *Building a Bridge to the Eighteenth Century: How the Past Can Improve Our Future*. New York: Alfred A. Knopf, 1999.

Postman, Neil, and Charles Weingartner. *Teaching as a Subversive Activity*. New York: Delta, 1969.

Ray, Nina M., and Robert P. Minch. "Computer Anxiety and Alienation: Toward a Definitive and Parsimonious Measure." *Human Factors* 32,4 (1990), pp.477–91.

Rheingold, Howard. *The Virtual Community: Homesteading on the Electronic Frontier*. Reading, MA: Addison-Wesley, 1993.

Romanyshyn, Robert D. *Technology as Symptom and Dream*. London: Routledge, 1989.

Rose, Ellen. "Talking Turing: How the Imitation Game Plays Out in the Classroom." *Educational Technology* 38,3 (1998), pp.56–61.

—. *Hyper Texts: The Language and Culture of Educational Computing*. London, ON: The Althouse Press, 2000.

Rose, Lionel. *The Erosion of Childhood: Child Oppression in Britain 1860–1918*. London: Routledge, 1991.

Rosen, Larry D., Deborah C. Sears, and Michelle M. Weil. "Treating Technophobia: A Longitudinal Evaluation of the Computerphobia Reduction Program." *Computers in Human Behavior* 9,1 (1993), pp.27–50.

Ross, Andrew. "Hacking Away at the Counterculture." In *Technoculture*, edited by Constance Penley and Andrew Ross, pp.107–34. Minneapolis: University of Minnesota Press, 1991.

Roszak, Theodore. *The Cult of Information: A Neo-Luddite Treatise on High-Tech, Artificial Intelligence, and the True Art of Thinking*. 1986. Reprint, Berkeley: University of California Press, 1994.

Rowland, Wade. *The Spirit of the Web: The Age of Information from Telegraph to Internet*. Toronto: Key Porter Books, 1999.

Rushkoff, Douglas. *Playing the Future: What We Can Learn from Digital Kids*. 1996. Reprint, New York: Riverhead Books, 1999.

Safire, William. "On Language: Hyper." *New York Times Magazine*, June 10, 2001, pp.40, 42.

Salvo, Michael J. "Ethics of Engagement: User-Centered Design and Rhetorical Methodology." *Technical Communication Quarterly* 10,3 (2001), pp.273–90.

—. "Critical Engagement with Technology in the Computer Classroom." *Technical Communication Quarterly* 11,3 (2002), pp.317–37.

Samoriski, Jan. *Issues in Cyberspace: Communication, Technology, Law, and Society on the Internet Frontier*. Boston: Allyn and Bacon, 2002.

Seabrook, John. "E-mail from Bill." *The New Yorker*, Jan. 10, 1994, pp.48–61.

Shenk, Roger. *Data Smog: Surviving the Information Glut*. New York: HarperCollins, 1997.

Slater, Robert. *Portraits in Silicon*. Cambridge, MA: The MIT Press, 1987.

Snider, Michael. "Hey, Kids! Let's Play Adver-games!" *Maclean's*, Dec. 23, 2002, pp.36–7.

—. "Wired to Another World." *Maclean's*, Mar. 3, 2003, pp.23–4.

Socka, George. "Books for Dummies." *CMA Magazine* 69,1 (1995), p.33.

Sterling, Bruce. *The Hacker Crackdown: Law and Disorder on the Electronic Frontier*. New York: Bantam Books, 1992. [On-line.] Lysator at Linköping University. <http://www.lysator.liu.se/etexts/hacker>. Dec. 7, 2001.

Stewart Millar, Melanie. *Cracking the Gender Code: Who Rules the Wired World?* Toronto: Second Story Press, 1998; now available from Sumach Press, Toronto.

Stoll, Clifford. *Silicon Snake Oil: Second Thoughts on the Information Highway*. New York: Anchor Books, 1995.

Stone, Allucquère Rosanne. *The War of Desire and Technology at the Close of the Mechanical Age*. Cambridge, MA: The MIT Press, 1996.

Stone, Lawrence. "Literacy and Education in England, 1640–1900." *Past and Present* 42 (1969), pp.69–139.

Tapscott, Don. *Growing Up Digital: The Rise of the Net Generation*. New York: McGraw-Hill, 1998.

Technical Support Nietzsche Style. [On-line.] <http://www.things.org/~jym/fun/nietzsche-tech-support.html>. Sept. 18, 2001.

Thomas, Douglas. "New Ways to Break the Law: Cybercrime and the Politics of Hacking." In *Web Studies: Rewiring Media Studies for the Digital Age*, edited by David Gauntlett, pp.202–11. London: Arnold, 2000.

Toffler, Alvin. *Powershift: Knowledge, Wealth, and Violence at the Edge of the Twenty-first Century*. New York: Bantam Books, 1990.

Trapunski, Edward. "Technical Writers in New Role." *The Globe and Mail*, Aug. 25, 1992, p.C4.

Turing, Alan M. "Computing Machinery and Intelligence." In *Social Effects of Computer Use and Misuse*, edited by J. Mack Adams and Douglas H. Haden, pp.184–202. New York: John Wiley and Sons, 1976. Originally published in *Mind* 59,236 (1950), pp.434–60.

Turkle, Sherry. *The Second Self: Computers and the Human Spirit*. New York: Simon & Schuster, 1984.

—. *Life on the Screen: Identity in the Age of the Internet*. New York: Simon & Schuster, 1995.

Turner, Chris. "The Simpsons Generation." *Shift* 10,3 (September/October 2002), pp.44–61.

Ullman, Ellen. "Out of Time: Reflections on the Programming Life." In *Resisting the Virtual Life: The Culture and Politics of Information*, edited by James Brook and Iain A. Boal, pp.131–43. San Francisco: City Lights Books, 1995.

—. *Close to the Machine: Technophilia and Its Discontents*. San Francisco: City Lights Books, 1997.

Vestergaard, Torben, and Kim Schroder. *The Language of Advertising*. Oxford: Basil Blackwell, 1985.

Volti, Rudi. *Society and Technological Change*. New York: St. Martin's Press, 1988.

Walton, Dawn. "Who's Afraid of Their Own Palm Pilot?" *The Globe and Mail*, Feb. 9, 2002, p.F6.

Weinberg, Sanford B., and Mark Lawrence Fuerst. *Computer Phobia—How to Slay the Dragon of Computer Fear*. Wayne, PA: Banbury Books, 1984.

Weisberg, Dan. "Scalable Hype: Old Persuasions for New Technology." In *Critical Studies in Media Commercialism*, edited by Robin Andersen and Lance Strate, pp.186–98. Oxford: Oxford University Press, 2000.

Weiss, Edmund H. *How to Write a Usable User Manual*. Philadelphia: ISI Press, 1985.

Weizenbaum, Joseph. *Computer Power and Human Reason: From Judgment to Calculation*. San Francisco: W.H. Freeman and Company, 1976.

Williams, Raymond. *Keywords: A Vocabulary of Culture and Society*. London: Fontana Press, 1976.

—. *The Year 2000*. New York: Pantheon Books, 1983.

Williamson, Judith. *Decoding Advertisements: Ideology and Meaning in Advertising*. London: Marion Boyars, 1978.

Winner, Langdon. *The Whale and the Reactor: A Search for Limits in an Age of High Technology*. Chicago: The University of Chicago Press, 1986.

Wood, Chris. "Zap! It's the Future." *Maclean's*, Aug. 20, 2001, pp.25–30.

—. "Dealing with Tech Rage." *Maclean's*, Mar. 19, 2002, pp.40–1.

Woolgar, Steve. "Configuring the User: The Case of Usability Trials." In *A Sociology of Monsters: Essays on Power, Technology, and Domination*, edited by John Law, pp.57–99. London: Routledge, 1991.

Worthington, Valerie L., and Yong Zhao. "Existential Computer Anxiety and Changes in Computer Technology: What Past Research on Computer Anxiety Has Missed." *Journal of Educational Computing Research* 20,4 (1999), pp.299–315.

Yeaman, Andrew R.J. "The Mythical Anxieties of Computerization: A Barthesian Analysis of a Technological Myth." In *Computers in Education: Social, Political, and Historical Perspectives*, edited by Robert Muffoletto and Nancy Nelson Knupfer, pp.105–28. Cresskill, NJ: Hampton Press, 1993.

—. "Whose Technology Is It, Anyway?" *Education Digest* 58,5 (1993), pp.19–23.

Yourdan, Edward. *The Decline and Fall of the American Programmer*. Englewood Cliffs, NJ: Prentice-Hall, 1993.

Zhang, Yixin, and Sue Espinoza. "Relationships among Computer Self-efficacy, Attitudes toward Computers, and Desirability of Learning Computing Skills." *Journal of Research on Computing in Education* 30,4 (1998), pp.420–36.

Zuboff, Shoshana. *In the Age of the Smart Machine: The Future of Work and Power*. New York: BasicBooks, 1988.

Index